Securing Lifelong Retirement Income

Securing Lifelong Retirement Income: Global Annuity Markets and Policy

EDITED BY

Olivia S. Mitchell, John Piggott, and Noriyuki Takayama

OXFORD
UNIVERSITY PRESS

OXFORD

UNIVERSITY PRESS

Great Clarendon Street, Oxford ox2 6DP

Oxford University Press is a department of the University of Oxford.
It furthers the University's objective of excellence in research, scholarship,
and education by publishing worldwide in

Oxford New York

Auckland Cape Town Dar es Salaam Hong Kong Karachi
Kuala Lumpur Madrid Melbourne Mexico City Nairobi
New Delhi Shanghai Taipei Toronto

With offices in

Argentina Austria Brazil Chile Czech Republic France Greece
Guatemala Hungary Italy Japan Poland Portugal Singapore
South Korea Switzerland Thailand Turkey Ukraine Vietnam

Oxford is a registered trade mark of Oxford University Press
in the UK and in certain other countries

Published in the United States
by Oxford University Press Inc., New York

© Pension Research Council, The Wharton School, University of Pennsylvania, 2011

British Library Cataloguing in Publication Data

Data available

Library of Congress Cataloging in Publication Data

Data available

Typeset by SPI Publisher Services, Pondicherry, India
Printed in Great Britain
on acid-free paper by
MPG Books Group, Bodmin and King's Lynn

ISBN 978–0–19–959484–9

1 3 5 7 9 10 8 6 4 2

Preface

As the world ages, millions of savers and investors are beginning to wake up to the fact that they face longevity risk. This refers to the possibility that an individual, or indeed, an entire cohort of people, might live much longer than expected and hence become exposed to the chance of running out of retirement money. This volume focuses on how insurers and other financial market players can help protect against this critical and increasingly important financial and demographic challenge, taking an international focus.

As this book points out, there are three main ways to protect against longevity. Traditional societies relied on large, multigenerational families, but reliance on one's children is a less attractive option than it was in the past. State provision was mainly a twentieth-century phenomenon and, as we note, faces substantial challenges in many nations. Last is the insurance industry which can cover the long lives of some retirees by pooling survival risk across the population, including those who live less long. The particular question this volume addresses is whether and how more general and formalized private longevity insurance provision can be provided, and is being offered, through annuity products. We are delighted to represent the vigorous debate currently underway by academics, financial experts, regulators, and plan sponsors, all seeking to define a new future for mechanisms to help protect against outliving one's wealth.

Previous research studies published by the Pension Research Council and the Boettner Center of the Wharton School of the University of Pennsylvania have focused on pensions and retirement adequacy around the world. In this volume, as in our many others, we have relied on many fine contributors, coeditors, and commentators. In the present instance, John Piggott and Noriyuki Takayama provided the impetus to turn a rich set of conversations and ideas into a high-quality research volume worthy of the Pension Research Council series. The Senior Partners and Institutional Members of the Pension Research Council are also very much appreciated for their intellectual and financial support. The Institute of Economic Research at Hitotsubashi University in Tokyo hosted an early meeting for the researchers, under the direction of Professor Takayama. Additional support was provided by the Pension Research Council, the Boettner Center for Pensions and Retirement Research, and the Ralph H. Blanchard Memorial Endowment at the Wharton School of the University of Pennsylvania. The manuscript was expertly prepared and carefully edited by Andrew Gallagher and Matt Rosen, with help from Irene Shaffer.

On behalf of these institutions and individuals, we thank all of our fine collaborators and supporters for their help and intellectual guidance in these times of financial turmoil.

Olivia S. Mitchell

Pension Research Council
Boettner Center for Pensions and Retirement Research
The Wharton School

Contents

List of Figures

x List of Figures

List of Tables

Notes on Contributors

Mukul G. Asher is Professor of Public Policy at the Lee Kuan Yew School of Public Policy of the National University of Singapore. He specializes in public finance, social security reforms, and India's external economic relations. He has been a consultant to many governments and multilateral institutions including the World Bank and the International Labor Organization. He received the Ph.D. in Economics from Washington State University.

Hazel Bateman is Associate Professor of Economics and the Director of the Centre for Pensions and Superannuation at the University of New South Wales in Sydney, Australia. Her research interests include public and private provision for retirement, pension finance, and behavioral aspects of retirement saving. She received the Ph.D. from the University of New South Wales.

Monika Bütler is Professor of Economics and Public Policy at St. Gallen University, Switzerland, and Managing Director of the Swiss Institute for Empirical Economic Research SEW-HSG. Her field of research is aging and pensions, family economics, and political economics. She received the Ph.D. in Economics from the University of St. Gallen.

Edmund Cannon is Professor of Economics, Finance, and Management at the University of Bristol. His research interests include macroeconomics, long-run economic development, productivity, regional growth rates, the role of financial markets, agricultural history, and the effect of demographic change and pensions on the macroeconomy. He received the D.Phil. in Economics from the University of Oxford.

Barbara Kaschützke is researcher in the Finance Department of the Goethe University Frankfurt, at the Chair of Investment, Portfolio Management, and Pension Finance. Her fields of specialization include pension regulation, institutional investors, and payout phase of funded pensions. Previously, she worked in mergers and acquisitions with Rothschild GmbH in Frankfurt and London. She received the Doctorate in Business Administration in Finance at the Goethe University Frankfurt.

Bo Larsson is an Analyst at the Swedish Pensions Agency and Assistant Professor at Dalarna University College. His research focuses on finance, risk, taxation, and public finance. He received the Ph.D. in Economics from Stockholm University.

Raimond Maurer holds the endowed Chair of Investment, Portfolio Management, and Pension Finance in the Finance Department at the Goethe University Frankfurt. His research concentrates on asset management, lifetime portfolio choice, and pension finance. He advises the German Society of Actuaries and the Association of Certified International Investment Analysts, and he serves on the Advisory Board for the Pension Research Council at Wharton. He received his habilitation and Ph.D. in Business from Mannheim University.

Moshe A. Milevsky is Professor of Finance at the Schulich School of Business at York University in Toronto and the Executive Director of The IFID Centre. His research focuses on insurance, investments, pensions, retirement, and annuities. He received the Ph.D. in Business Finance from York University.

Olivia S. Mitchell is the International Foundation of Employee Benefit Plans Professor and the Chair of the Department of Insurance and Risk Management, Executive Director of the Pension Research Council, and Director of the Boettner Center on Pensions and Retirement Research at the Wharton School. Her areas of research and teaching are private and public insurance, risk management, public finance and labor markets, and compensation and pensions, with a US and an international focus. She received the Ph.D. degree in Economics from the University of Wisconsin-Madison.

Edward Palmer is Professor of Social Insurance Economics at Uppsala University, Sweden, and is Senior Adviser to the Swedish Social Insurance Agency. His research focuses on social security and pensions; previously, he worked on the Swedish pension reform, and he is a Consultant for the World Bank and other international institutions. He received the Ph.D. in Economics from Stockholm University.

John Piggott is Professor of Economics in the Australian School of Business, University of New South Wales, where he also heads up the Australian Institute for Population Ageing Research. His research examines economic and financial aspects of population aging. He received the Ph.D. in Economics from the University of London.

Jose Ruiz is Professor of Finance in the Business School at the University of Chile. His interests include pension economics, risk management, and capital markets. He received the Ph.D. in Applied Economics from the Wharton School at the University of Pennsylvania.

Junichi Sakamoto is Chief Adviser to the Pension Management Research Group of the Nomura Research Institute and Lecturer at the University of Tokyo, Nihon University, and Sophia University. Previously, he was the Director of the Japanese Government's Actuarial Affairs Division of the

Pension Bureau of the Ministry of Health, Labor, and Welfare. He received the MS in Mathematics from the University of Tokyo, Japan.

Ling-wu Shao is a doctoral student in Finance at the Schulich School of Business, York University. His Ph.D. research is investigating the money's worth of annuity products in Canada.

Stefan Staubli is Research Associate at the Swiss Institute for Empirical Economic Research at the University of St. Gallen. His research focuses on labor supply effects of government expenditure programs and the role of annuities in financing retirement. He received the Ph.D. from the University of St. Gallen.

Noriyuki Takayama is the JRI Pension Research Chair Professor at the Institute of Economic Research with Hitotsubashi University in Tokyo and is a Distinguished Scholar at the Research Institute for Policies on Pension and Aging. His research interests include intergenerational economic issues, public and private pensions, and household saving and wealth formation. He received the Ph.D. from the University of Tokyo.

Ian Tonks is Professor of Finance in the School of Management at the University of Bath. His research focuses on pension economics, fund manager performance, market microstructure, and the new issue market. He has also consulted with the Bank of England and the Financial Services Authority.

Deepa Vasudevan is a researcher who focuses on pension systems and reforms, macroeconomic policy, the monetary sector, and financial markets. She received the Ph.D. in Financial Studies from the University of Delhi, India.

Anthony Webb is Associate Director of Research at the Center for Retirement Research at Boston College. His work examines the role of annuities in retirement asset decumulation, as well as the impact of pensions and Social Security on retirement. He received the Ph.D. in Economics from the University of California, San Diego.

Abbreviations

ABS	Australian Bureau of Statistics
AEW	Annuity equivalent wealth
AFTS	Australia's Future Tax System
ALDA	Advanced life deferred annuity
APRA	Australian Prudential Regulatory Authority
ATO	Australian Taxation Office
AVS	First-pillar welfare scheme
BLS	Bureau of Labor Statistics
CLHIA	Canadian Life and Health Insurance Association
CMI	Central Mortality Investigation Bureau
CPI	Consumer price index
CREF	College Retirement Equities Fund
CRRA	Constant relative risk aversion
DA	Deferred annuity
DAV	Deutsche Aktuarvereinigung
DB	Defined benefit
DC	Defined contribution
DCA	Dollar cost averaging
EPF	Employees' Pension Fund
EPI	Employees' Pension Insurance
ER	Early retirement
ETF	Exchange traded fund
FaHCSIA	Department of Family, Housing, Community Services and Indigenous Affairs
FDC	Funded defined contribution
FPF	Farmers' Pension Fund
FRBM	Fiscal Responsibility and Budget Management
FSA	Financial Services Authority
GDV	Gesamtverband der Deutschen Versicherungswirtschaft
GLWB	Guaranteed Lifetime Withdrawal Benefit

GSA	Group Self Annuitization
IA	Immediate annuity
IAI	Institute of Actuaries of India
ILO	International Labor Organization
INE	Instituto Nacional de Estadísticas
IRA	Individual Retirement Account
IRDA	Insurance Regulatory and Development Authority
IRS	Individual retirement saving
LIC	Life Insurance Corporation of India
LIF	Life Income Funds
LPiA	Lifetime payout income annuity
LPP	Federal Law on Occupational Retirement, Survivors and Disability Pension Plans
LRIF	Locked-In Retirement Fund
LSRB	Lump-Sum Retirement Benefit Plans
LTC	Long-term care
MAA	Mutual Aid Association
MPG	Minimum pension guarantee
MWR	Money's worth ratio
NDC	Notional defined contribution
NP	National Pension
NPF	National Pension Fund
NPS	New Pension Scheme
NR	Normal retirement
OECD	Organisation for Economic Co-operation and Development
PASIS	*pension asistencial*
PAYGO	Pay-as-you-go
PFRDA	Pension Fund Regulatory and Development Authority
PW	Phased withdrawal
PWER	PW at the early retirement age
PWNR	PW at the normal age
RBL	Reasonable Benefit Limits
RCLA	Ruin Contingent Life Annuity
RCV	Residual capital value

RMLA	Reverse mortgage loan annuity
RRIF	Registered Retirement Income Fund
RRSP	Registered Retirement Saving Plan
SAFP	Superintendencia de Administradoras de Fondos de Pensiones
SCOMP	*sistema de consultas y ofertas de montos de pensión*
SEK	Swedish kronor
SG	Superannuation Guarantee
SPIA	Single premium immediate annuity
SSA	Social Security Administration
S2P	State Second Pension
SWiP	Systematic withdrawal plan
TAP	Term allocated pension
TFR	Total fertility rate
TIAA	Teachers Insurance and Annuity Association
TIPS	Treasury inflation-protected securities
TQPP	Tax-Qualified Pension Plans
TW	Temporary withdrawal
UF	Unidad de Fomento
VA	Variable annuity
WRAMAF	Workers' Retirement Allowance Mutual Aid Fund

Chapter 1

Turning Wealth into Lifetime Income: The Challenge Ahead

Olivia S. Mitchell and John Piggott

In the last century, governments have shouldered a growing share of financial provision for the elderly. This trend was sustainable as long as populations were kept young by above-replacement fertility rates, so that growing labor forces provided a ready source for financing the retired. But as the twentieth century ended and the twenty-first began, the reality of population aging has made it clear that such promises are exerting a burdensome fiscal strain. While government payouts will likely continue to increase for many decades, it is now evident that future retirees will not be as well off as they had thought. Indeed, several countries have already reduced government-financed retirement promises by raising the retirement age, changing benefit indexation, and reducing retiree and dependent benefits. This process has been exacerbated by the steady decline in defined benefit occupational pensions which formerly paid lifetime benefits. Today, however, workers are more likely to receive defined contribution plans (if any pension at all), which provide retirees with lump sums or phased withdrawals.

This trend presents a substantial social challenge, especially when seen in the context of a globally aging population. The United Nations (2008) has estimated that the number of people in the world over the age of 60 totaled a little over three-quarters of a billion in 2008; by 2050, over 2 billion people are expected to be over age 60, or a 250 percent increase. Those over 80 are expected to increase from about 105 million today to nearly 400 million by mid-century. In the same period, total population will increase from 6.9 to 9.1 billion – a rise of about 31 percent. The retreat of the public sector and the burgeoning of an ageing world are clearly related, but their combined impact compounds the magnitude of the issue.

In the international context, there are only three major sources of longevity insurance. First is large families, which played a central role in old-age support in the past. Second is state provision, which was primarily a twentieth-century phenomenon and faces challenges in the future. Third is the insurance industry, which is able to pay for some long-lived retirees by pooling survival risk across others who do not live long. A question we take up in this volume is whether the twenty-first century is likely to be an era of more general and formalized private longevity insurance provision through annuities. We have gathered a global group of experts to examine current practice in both developed and emerging economies, to provide guidance to address several questions including: What do annuity markets look like today? What is the potential to transform this product type into a familiar and widely used financial instrument like a mortgage or life insurance? What is the appropriate regulatory structure for lifetime payout annuities?

To answer these questions, we analyze a variety of countries. Some have mandatory annuitization (the United Kingdom, Sweden); others have mandatory accumulation plans without requiring annuitization (Australia, Chile, Switzerland); and still others remain heavily dependent on traditional social security with private annuities representing what might best be described as a residual market (Germany, Japan). Also in some nations, innovations in longevity insurance products have been embraced, apparently rather successfully (e.g., in Canada and the United States; Milevsky and Shao 2011). And in others – notably among emerging economies – India stands out as a country of nearly 1 billion people without a significant annuity market. Not included in this study is China, as it has only just started down this track with its incipient Enterprise Annuity program.

The demographic context

As we have argued earlier, the global demographic transition underpins a renewed interest in annuity markets. Accordingly, it is instructive to summarize the demographic profiles of the countries represented in the volume, outlined in Table 1.1. We include some 'old' economies, such as Germany and Japan, some younger developed countries such as the United Kingdom, Australia, Canada, and the United States, and still other nations that are exporting their young workers such as India. In every case, however, all are aging. Thus, across developed countries, fertility rates are now below the 2.1 rate required to sustain a steady state population, and in some countries the figures are low indeed. As a result, the aged dependency ratio is set to increase, most notably in Japan where the 2050 projection of 0.74 means there will be only 1.37 workers to support each retiree.

TABLE 1.1 Demographic profiles of selected countries (current and projected)

Country	Population (millions)	Total fertility rate	Life expectancy at birth	Aged dependency ratio	2050 aged dependency ratio
Australia	21.5	1.85	82.2	0.21	0.40
Canada	33.9	1.62	81.4	0.20	0.43
Chile	17.1	1.89	79.1	0.13	0.36
Germany	82.1	1.34	80.5	0.31	0.59
India	1214.5	2.52	65.2	0.08	0.20
Japan	127.0	1.27	83.7	0.35	0.74
Sweden	9.3	1.85	81.6	0.28	0.41
Switzerland	7.6	1.49	82.5	0.26	0.45
The United Kingdom	61.9	1.85	80.1	0.25	0.38
The United States	317.6	2.02	79.9	0.19	0.35

Source: United Nations (2008).

The demand for annuities

One theme that emerges from the studies in this volume is that voluntary life annuity markets are generally thin. This is not a surprise, since annuity markets are characterized by asymmetric information; accordingly, in the absence of appropriate regulatory support, they tend not to be efficient. In general, low demand for annuities is explained by several factors, including retiree bequest motives, their reluctance to lose discretionary control over their capital, the crowding-out of private annuities by public pensions, and adverse selection, where price is increased and value reduced for those with normal life expectancies.

Nevertheless, two countries studied in this volume, Chile and Switzerland, do host substantial voluntary markets for annuities. What is interesting about these two nations is that both rely heavily on mandatory accumulation policies for retirement. Thus, Ruiz and Mitchell (2011) show that in Chile, a combination of policy settings and market features combine to generate high annuity demand. There, annuities represent good value with a relatively high money's worth ratio (MWR). Also of particular interest is the establishment of an online bidding mechanism in which all providers participate, making market information much more accessible. Access to accumulations is available to early retirees, if they have substantial balances taken as an annuity. Additionally, pension payouts have been limited to those having twenty years of contributions, leading risk-averse retirees with relatively modest accumulations to nevertheless choose annuitization.[1]

Switzerland also stands out as a nation with a strong voluntary annuity market. Bütler and Staubli (2011) suggest several explanations for the penetration of the Swiss market. First, good money's worth values are important, and in many cases, these exceed unity. But second, behavioral factors are also influential. For instance, information provided to pension fund members emphasizes what Brown et al. (2008) refer to as a 'consumption' frame, as opposed to an accumulation or returns frame, and much political debate is conducted in terms of consumption outcomes. And third, defaults matter. While MWRs for the mandatory accumulations are very high, super-mandatory conversions lead to lower MWRs for that portion of annuitization. Yet, most retirees make polar choices, and most annuitize both the mandatory and super-mandatory components of their retirement benefits. Indeed, the Swiss case shows that lower income individuals with access to means-tested government benefits are less likely to annuitize. This is consistent with the view that crowding-out is important.

Chile and Switzerland both rely on a mandatory accumulation policy as a mainstay of earnings-related retirement provision. They share this characteristic with Australia, as analyzed in this volume by Bateman and Piggott (2011). The surprising fact, however, is that while Chile and Switzerland have strong voluntary annuity markets, in Australia they are almost nonexistent. Thus, in the nine months to September 2009, only seventeen life annuities were sold in the entire nation. One reason is that Australia lacks the traditional defined benefit social security system, and instead it has a means-tested pension that is quite generous as a poverty alleviation instrument. For instance, for a single individual, it delivers about 28 percent of average fulltime earnings, wage indexed, and this is available to all eligible residents at age 65 regardless of labor force participation history. Couples receive about 41 percent of average earnings. Over half the eligible retired population today receives the full age pension and over three-quarters receive some means-tested benefit. As a result, there seems to be little residual demand for private annuities.

Over the last decade, the Australian annuities market has ebbed and flowed in response to policy decisions which have affected the way in which annuity purchase impacts upon the means-tested first-pillar, tax rules, and the impact of decisions taken by the national prudential (regulatory) authority. Framing would appear to provide part of the explanation, since Australia's pension industry emphasizes accumulations and returns, while downplaying the level of consumption an accumulation might deliver. In addition, the authors suggest that policy coordination might be a possible explanation, a theme to which we return later.

In several other countries described in this volume, the conventional wisdom also seems to apply, namely that voluntary annuities are often a hard sell. Interestingly, this remains true even when MWRs are high, in part because publicly provided social security can crowd out private provision as in the United Kingdom. Thus, Cannon and Tonks (2011) report that, while the UK compulsory annuity market is very active, the voluntary market is very small. The same applies to Sweden, as noted by Palmer and Larsson (2011). In Germany, as reported by Kaschützke and Maurer (2011), annuities also have high MWRs, yet market volume remains small. And Sakamoto (2011) likewise reports very low take-ups of voluntary annuities in Japan.

Progress and obstacles in insuring the risk

Innovations in the annuity market are also of interest, despite obstacles to efficient supply raised in several of the chapters. As Asher and Vasudevan (2011) point out, it is essential to have disaggregated morbidity and mortality databases in order for the market to work efficiently, and for investors to learn how to match assets and long-term liabilities. At the same time, greater financial literacy and more robust regulation are also greatly needed. While Asher and Vasudevan write about the Indian context, these points are also relevant in most other countries as well. To illustrate our points, we offer a brief and selective discussion focusing on longevity projections and risks, product innovation, and policy coordination to support longevity insurance markets.

Longevity projections and risks

Many approaches have been used and proposed to project mortality. Mortality improvements have been estimated from medical scenarios, but this has consistently underestimated mortality. Analysts have often claimed biological limits for humankind only for mortality improvements to overtake their projections, sometimes within a few years (Oeppen and Vaupel 2002).

Demographers rely more heavily on extrapolation of past trends. Lee and Carter (1992) both formalized and popularized extrapolative methods, which give better estimates of life expectancy but often imply an implausible degree of accuracy (Alho 1992). Their approach also has limitations. Some analysts argue that future mortality improvements will now have to come at older ages, thus reducing the impact on life expectancy at birth. Others suggest that developments such as the increased incidence of obesity will inhibit future increases in life expectancy in developed countries (Olshansky et al. 2005).

Current actuarial approaches, including those used by the Society of Actuaries and the UK Institute of Actuaries, are based on actuarial life tables. Here, mortality projections are, at best, crude and based on high-, medium-, and low-projected deterministic tables (or sometimes they assume deterministic improvement trends). These tables therefore offer limited guidance on the risk arising from longevity changes and hence have major limitations for pricing or capital assessment for insurers.

Increasingly, in the international sphere, attention is being placed on alternative and more sophisticated models better-suited to risk management and pricing. Active life expectancy, which is the period of life free from disability, is important for financial products and longevity risks. Modern stochastic modeling incorporating disability-specific mortality indicates higher active life expectancies than cruder models and provides a basis for assessing morbidity risks and their financial impact (Manton and Land 2000).

What is still lacking, however, is an integrated approach based on modern statistical models that captures the essential characteristics of mortality and morbidity data across different populations, takes into account mortality and morbidity risk factors, produces estimates of risk for longevity products, and recognizes the need for professional and commercial application and acceptance. Developing this framework could greatly enhance the development of more robust annuity markets, since it would provide the basis for risk spreading through reinsurance. Reinsurance is occurring, but it is limited in its reach.

Product innovation

The life payout annuity has been around for a long time, and until recently, there has been remarkably little innovation in its basic form. In this volume, however, several authors discuss product innovations that may make annuities more attractive. For instance, Webb (2011) emphasizes the importance of the mortality multiplier, pointing out that annuities are most effective when used to finance consumption at advanced old age. The advanced life deferred annuity (ALDA), so named by Milevsky (2005), could be purchased at retirement or earlier, and it would provide an inflation-indexed income stream starting at some advanced age, and conditional on survival to that age. Such products can be very reasonably priced because of the size of the survival credit embedded within them; a related product was also discussed by Bateman et al. (2001).

While the ALDA gains leverage from increasing mortality rates at later ages, a more sophisticated product analyzed by Milevsky and Shao (2011) is the Guaranteed Lifetime Withdrawal Benefit (GLWB). This is an investment product which has attached to it a provision for a life annuity payment contingent on the invested portfolio falling below some wealth threshold (or some other sort of index of declining market performance). It can potentially be a very efficient instrument since it delivers insurance when the consumer needs it, that is, when the market declines. The authors report that this product has become popular in Canada; whether this represents a step toward more widespread sales of industry-based longevity insurance remains to be seen.

Policy coordination to promote longevity insurance

The longevity insurance market faces a key difficulty: information is not symmetric between buyer and seller, resulting in adverse selection. This problem, combined with the other challenges documented earlier, means that such regulatory support may be needed to have annuities develop and function efficiently. The discussion by Asher and Vasudevan (2011) takes up the key challenges to be met by coordinated government policy.

In the real world, of course, policy surrounding longevity insurance products and associated market regulation tends to be divided across several agencies. For instance, in Australia, a product provider requires approvals and agreements from the Australian Prudential Regulator Authority (APRA), the Taxation Office, and the Department of Family and Community Services, which administers the age pension (Bateman and Piggott 2011). Not only do these agencies approach their regulatory responsibilities in isolation from one another but also none has a mandate to support the longevity insurance market. As a result, it becomes difficult to devise and market an innovative product. Furthermore, incentives to purchase life annuities rather than take lump sums have been entirely removed. Accordingly, a plausible reason for the success of the annuity markets in Chile and Switzerland is that coordinated regulation supports these markets. Where this is absent, the market struggles.

Unfortunately, it appears that coordinated policy is the exception rather than the rule. In Japan, for example, Sakamoto (2011) points to a taxation anomaly making life annuities an unattractive purchase, and in India, Asher and Vasudevan (2011) suggest that policy on life annuities is sorely underdeveloped.

Conclusion

In the old days, longevity risk management was first and foremost a family obligation. When development, migration, and the scattering of families became more common, government and employers became the mainstays of longevity insurance in the twentieth century. In the twenty-first century, demographic shift and government overspending has put all three of these sources under stress. Smaller families mean fewer children, so many are becoming increasingly vulnerable to an old age without substantial family support. The public sector, with its growing number of retirees to support, is backing away from promises which were, perhaps, unrealistic from the start.

What remains, then, is self-provision, mediated by the financial and insurance sector. The developed world may be just at the beginning of large-scale reliance on the private sector to deliver this insurance. Yet, as this volume shows, much new knowledge will be needed to make the private sector efficient. Knowledge about increasing longevity, and the distributions of outcomes around such projections, is at an early stage. Knowledge to inform regulatory specification, such as risk-based solvency requirements required to effectively price annuities, is also sparse and undeveloped. The role of asset–liability matching, and the possibility that governments may be able to structure debt issues to allow matching to be better achieved, remains largely unexplored. In sum, much remains to be done to deal with the demands of a robust privately based longevity insurance regime. The next decade will determine how well we can meet this challenge.

Note

[1] Recent changes to minimum benefit requirements will make these much easier to obtain, and this may impact annuity demand.

References

Alho, J.M. (1992). 'Comment on "Modelling and Forecasting U.S. Mortality,"' *Journal of the American Statistical Association*, 87: 673–74.

Asher, Mukul G. and Deepa Vasudevan (2011). 'Market Structure and Challenges for Annuities in India,' in O.S. Mitchell and J. Piggott, eds., *Revisiting Retirement Payouts: Market Developments and Policy Issues*. Oxford, UK: Oxford University Press.

Bateman, Hazel and John Piggott (2011). 'Too Much Risk to Insure? The Australian (non-) Market for Annuities,' in O.S. Mitchell and J. Piggott, eds., *Revisiting Retirement Payouts: Market Developments and Policy Issues*. Oxford, UK: Oxford University Press.

—— G. Kingston, and J. Piggott (2001). *Forced Saving: Mandating Private Retirement Incomes*. Cambridge: Cambridge University Press.

Brown, Jeffery R., Jeffrey R. Kling, Sendhil Mullainathan, and Marian V. Wrobel (2008). 'Why Don't People Insure Late Life Consumption? A Framing Explanation of the Under-Annuitization Puzzle,' *American Economic Review: Papers and Proceedings*, 98: 304–9.

Bütler, Monika and Stefan Staubli (2011). 'Payouts in Switzerland: Explaining Developments in Annuitization,' in O.S. Mitchell and J. Piggott, eds., *Revisiting Retirement Payouts: Market Developments and Policy Issues*. Oxford, UK: Oxford University Press.

Cannon, Edmund and Ian Tonks (2011). 'Compulsory and Voluntary Annuity Markets in the United Kingdom,' in O.S. Mitchell and J. Piggott, eds., *Revisiting Retirement Payouts: Market Developments and Policy Issues*. Oxford, UK: Oxford University Press.

Kaschützke, Barbara and Raimond Maurer (2011). 'The Private Life Annuity Market in Germany: Products and Money's Worth Ratios,' in O.S. Mitchell and J. Piggott, eds., *Revisiting Retirement Payouts: Market Developments and Policy Issues*. Oxford, UK: Oxford University Press.

Lee, R.D. and L.R. Carter (1992). 'Modelling and Forecasting U.S. Mortality,' *Journal of the American Statistical Association*, 87: 659–71.

Manton, K.G. and K.C. Land (2000). 'Active Life Expectancy Estimates for the U.S. Elderly Population: A Multi-dimensional Continuous-Mixture Model of Functional Change Applied to Completed Cohorts 1992–1996,' *Demography*, 37(3): 253–65.

Milevsky, Moshe A. (2005). 'Real Longevity Insurance with a Deductible: Introduction to Advanced-Life Delayed Annuities (ALDA),' *North American Actuarial Journal*, 9(4): 109–22.

—— Ling-wu Shao (2011). 'Annuities and Their Derivatives: The Recent Canadian Experience,' in O.S. Mitchell and J. Piggott, eds., *Revisiting Retirement Payouts: Market Developments and Policy Issues*. Oxford, UK: Oxford University Press.

Oeppen, J. and J.W. Vaupel (2002). 'Enhanced: Broken Limits to Life Expectancy,' *Science*, 296: 1029–31.

Olshansky, S.J., Douglas J. Passaro, Ronald C. Hershow, Jennifer Layden, Bruce Carnes, Jacob Brody, Leonard Hayflick, Robert N. Butler, David B. Allison, and David S. Ludwig (2005). 'A Possible Decline in Life Expectancy in the United States in the 21st Century,' *New England Journal of Medicine*, 352: 1103–10.

Palmer, Edward and Bo Larsson (2011). 'The Swedish Annuity Market: Where It Is and Where It's Headed,' in O.S. Mitchell and J. Piggott, eds., *Revisiting Retirement Payouts: Market Developments and Policy Issues*. Oxford, UK: Oxford University Press.

Ruiz, Jose and Olivia S. Mitchell (2011). 'Pension Payouts in Chile: Past, Present, and Future Prospects,' in O.S. Mitchell and J. Piggott, eds., *Revisiting Retirement Payouts: Market Developments and Policy Issues*. Oxford, UK: Oxford University Press.

Sakamoto, Junichi (2011). 'Annuity Markets in Japan,' in O.S. Mitchell and J. Piggott, eds., *Revisiting Retirement Payouts: Market Developments and Policy Issues*. Oxford, UK: Oxford University Press.

United Nations (2008). *World Population Prospects: The 2008 Revision, Population Database*. New York, NY: United Nations. http://esa.un.org/unpp

Webb, Anthony (2011). 'The United States Longevity Insurance Market,' in O.S. Mitchell and J. Piggott, eds., *Revisiting Retirement Payouts: Market Developments and Policy Issues*. Oxford, UK: Oxford University Press.

Annuity Markets Around the World

Chapter 2

The Swedish Annuity Market: Where it is and Where it's Headed

Edward Palmer and Bo Larsson

Economic theory predicts that rational individuals should demand annuities during the dissaving phase of the life cycle (Yaari 1965), but annuity markets in many countries are small and Sweden is no exception (Palmer 2008). Indeed, the voluntary demand for annuities in Sweden is quite low, as in other high-income countries (Impavido et al. 2003). While public, occupational, and private retirement schemes all provide lifelong benefits, until recently, the scope for choice within the institutional framework of the public and occupational schemes was limited by the dominance of defined benefit (DB) arrangements. This changed dramatically in 1994, as first the public pension scheme and then the major occupational schemes began a transition to a defined contribution (DC) model. This move from DB to DC personal accounts in both the public and occupational schemes has paved the way for further change, making it possible for individuals to increasingly combine public, occupational, and private accounts to acquire various forms of privately provided annuity products at – and after – retirement. For this to happen, however, legislation will have to be adopted that enables individuals to combine personal financial accounts from public, occupational, and private FDC (funded defined contribution) schemes, and to choose freely from a range of annuity products tailored to suit people exiting the labor market with varying situations and preferences.

While financial innovations in Sweden have become prevalent for private saving efforts during the working and accumulation phase of the life cycle, the Swedish retirement products' marketplace looks pretty much as it did in the 1950s. Still absent are products designed to accommodate the varying needs associated with income support and care of the older elderly population. The extensive Swedish safety net for the elderly is likely to remain in place in the future, but it is unlikely that the benefits provided by the public sector will be sufficient in scope and design to provide more than a basic universal safety net. Given this perspective, there is room for product innovation in the financial market to cater to the needs of the older population in the near future.

In what follows, we begin with an overview of the Swedish pension landscape, followed by an analysis of the current state of demand for annuities using a unique microeconomic database constructed for the purposes of this study. We continue with an analysis of what is likely to drive future demand, and we end with concluding remarks.

The Swedish pension landscape

Beginning with legislation in 1994, Sweden transformed the earnings-related component of its public pension commitment from a DB to a DC model. The earnings-related public benefit was transformed into a notional defined contribution (NDC) system with a contribution rate of 16 percent, and a funded mandatory component with a contribution rate of 2.5 percent. The wage-indexed ceiling on contributory earnings for both of these together is about twice the average wage. About 90 percent of the working population is also covered by an occupational scheme that provides a small supplement to the public benefit under the ceiling, and the entire benefit above the ceiling. The move to DC in the public system spearheaded a similar move within all four major occupational schemes. As a consequence of these reforms, all public and practically all occupational earnings-related benefits have now been transformed from DB to DC.

Shortly after the passage of the 1994 public system reform, the occupational scheme for blue-collar workers which covers over 40 percent of all employees was also converted to an FDC plan. Subsequently, the same evaluation was followed by two major public employee schemes, the local government employee plan in 1998, and state employees in 2003 (for coverage below the ceiling). Finally, the system covering private-sector white-collar workers converted to the FDC system in 2007. As a result, all occupational supplements to the public schemes are transitioning to FDC personal account schemes.

The typical Swedish worker now contributes a total of 7 percent of earnings to mandatory and occupational FDC schemes (2.5 and 4.5 percent, respectively). In both the public and occupational schemes, the participant's retirement account balance is converted into an annuity. In many cases, there is a choice between a traditional and a unit-linked annuity. The Swedish traditional approach would pay a life annuity including a profit-sharing arrangement, to be discussed below in more detail. A unit-linked annuity gives a variable annuity rate based on the annual performance of the participant's investment portfolio, and the benefit is recalculated annually based on the participant's account value at the time of recalculation, normally using a cohort life expectancy estimate fixed at the age of retirement.

As a result, the typical Swedish worker has considerable income protection in old age through the combined mandatory public and occupational benefits. A career worker who entered the labor force at age 20 and worked to age 65 can expect a gross replacement rate of around 65 percent, assuming real wage growth of 2 percent and a real annual financial return of 3.5 percent (The World Bank 2007). More generous assumptions about the financial return, of course, yield a higher replacement rate (Palmer 2002a).

Looking ahead, it would appear that Swedes have a substantial annuity base in the form of the mandatory public NDC scheme, plus the mandatory and occupational FDC schemes. Accordingly, substantial financial saving is likely to be transformed into annuities in the future, implying a large potential for this market. In addition, there is still room at the top for private voluntary insurance.

Demand for annuities in Sweden

Next, we analyze the present demand and market for annuities, and we identify factors likely to determine future demand and the capacity of the market to develop to meet this demand. As in other high-income countries, the development of demand for voluntary annuities in Sweden has been held back by comprehensive mandatory public and quasi-mandatory occupational pensions.[1] Prior to the pension reforms described above, the prevailing belief was that the public pension replaced 65 percent of income at age 65, and occupational pensions added an additional 10 percent. Yet this was only true in a world with no real wage growth, since benefits in pre-NDC Sweden were based on the average of the participant's best fifteen years of earnings; for most workers, this would be the final fifteen years prior to claiming a benefit, and, with real earnings growth, this average would be considerably below pre-retirement pay. For instance, with 2 percent real growth, the actual replacement rate would be 56 percent rather than 65 percent. With the expectation of such high income replacement rates, the perceived need for personal saving for retirement was (and still is) not strong.[2] Furthermore, the public sector provides all medical care and medicine in kind with only a small co-payment, along with substantial basic home help; it also provides, if necessary, institutional care for the disabled elderly.

Financial market events in the mid-1980s set the stage for growth in demand for private insurance. Until that point, the Swedish financial market was highly regulated and the return on financial saving was repressed by the regulatory structure, a fact reflected in households' financial portfolios. In 1980, household financial assets were comprised of currency, deposits, and bonds (78 percent), and only 11 percent of voluntary saving went to private pension insurance and another 9 percent to equities and mutual funds.[3] Almost thirty years later, private pension saving constituted 25 percent of total household financial assets, and equities and mutual funds about 28 percent (in 2009). This is in part due to deregulation of the Swedish financial market in the mid-1980s. Private companies turned to public stock offerings to finance investments, derivatives developed, and share prices became buoyant. At the same time, mutual funds became an option for personal saving. Then in 1993, unit-linked insurance was introduced and individual retirement saving (IRS) accounts came into being in 1994.

These developments were important for the development of the financial market and the disposition of personal saving. In addition, three specific events occurring around 1990 were especially important for the growth of private voluntary insurance. The first was the beginning of the public pension reform: the publicly provided widow's benefit was abolished in 1990, beginning with the cohort of women born in 1945. The effect of this change on the insurance market was dramatic: in 1980, only about 5 percent of men and 2 percent of women aged 20–64 utilized a tax deduction for premium payments for private voluntary pension insurance. The percentage increased gradually during the 1980s, still with a slightly larger percentage of men than women purchasing insurance (Palmer 2002*b*). With the abolition of the widow's benefit in the public scheme, by 2008, 43 percent of women aged 20–64 claimed a deduction for premium payments for private insurance, compared with 36 percent of men (Table 2.1).

TABLE 2.1 Distribution of tax-deductible pension saving (2008)

Age (year)	Percent of population utilizing a deduction		Average amount of deduction (1000 kronor)	
	Men	Women	Men	Women
20–24	11.2	10.5	2.3	1.9
25–34	33.8	38.3	3.8	3.2
35–44	42.4	50.2	5.7	4.6
45–54	39.1	51.3	8.2	6.4
55–64	34.3	45.3	11.3	8.9
65+	3.4	2.3	14.4	9.4
20–64	35.0	43.0	7.1	5.8

Source. Authors' calculations based on Statistics Sweden (2009).

The second important event was the introduction of unit-linked insurance in 1993. Only seven years after its introduction, by the year 2000, unit-linked insurance had grown so rapidly that the proportion of assets held by individuals in private voluntary insurance was about equally divided between traditional and unit-linked insurance (Palmer 2002*b*). A third event believed to have affected the demand for voluntary pension insurance occurred in 1995, when the amount of the allowable tax deduction was cut from the equivalent of $9,000 to $4,500 (US, using an exchange rate of 7.5 SEK per USD). With the change in the tax deduction, the average nominal amount of the yearly deduction decreased from the equivalent of $1,250 (US) in 1980 to $850 (US) in 2008 (or 6,400 SEK in Table 2.1 at an exchange rate of 7.5 SEK per USD; Palmer 2002*b*).

In sum, in spite of a dramatic reduction in the allowable personal income tax deduction for premium payments for private insurance, the share of individual voluntary insurance in total financial assets of households was 25 percent in 2009 versus 11 percent in 1980. The demand for private insurance has therefore increased substantially in the past three decades, and the demand for annuities will follow in the not-so-distant future.

The current distribution of pension benefits is also an indicator of the demand for private annuities, especially the market for voluntary pension insurance for today's pensioners. Table 2.2 presents data for payments of benefits from mandatory public, quasi-mandatory occupational (contractual), and voluntary insurance purchases by age group, for the year 2008. Generally, the data suggest that public, contractual/occupational, and voluntary individual benefits fulfill different needs.

The first set of pensioners is a group of beneficiaries aged 55–60. Age 55 is the minimum age at which an occupational or private voluntary benefit can be claimed in Sweden, and 61 is the minimum age to claim a public benefit. In 2008, benefit recipients aged 55–60 constituted 6 percent of all beneficiaries. The information on the total number of pensioners in this age group, together with the number of persons with an occupational or voluntary benefit, indicates that about half of those claiming a voluntary insurance benefit are also recipients of an occupational benefit. The average occupational benefit is 53,000 SEK and the average private voluntary benefit is 32,000 SEK. An individual with both would have about 85,000 SEK per year or 7,000 SEK per month, close to the social assistance minimum. Hence, it is not likely that this benefit normally is the sole source of income for the recipient.

A second subset is the group aged 61–64 with a relatively large occupational benefit, on average. In this age interval, people tend to have either an occupational or a voluntary individual benefit, but seldom both. Note also that the average public benefit among claimants in this age group is very small, indicating that most wait until age 65 to claim a full public

TABLE 2.2 Number of pensions and type of benefit received (2008)

Age (year)	Number of recipients (with at least one type of benefit)	Average benefit (1000 SEK)	Type of benefit					
			Public		Occupational		Private	
			Number of recipents	Average benefit (1000 SEK)	Number of recipents	Average benefit (1000 SEK)	Number of recipients	Average benefit (1000 SEK)
55–60	126,517	52	0	0	98,494	53	42,411	32
61–64	234,725	110	86,425	65	167,420	103	67,282	42
65–69	473,264	190	460,329	126	429,962	56	214,323	37
70–74	362,199	181	362,095	139	316,422	37	92,549	38
75–79	303,161	160	303,148	131	250,280	30	32,728	40
80–84	247,458	147	247,454	122	190,560	29	16,617	41
85–89	165,910	136	165,907	112	119,364	29	9,969	43
90+	77,532	124	77,529	101	49,547	33	4,905	41
55+	1,990,766	153	1,702,893	123	1,622,049	47	480,784	38
65+	1,629,524	167	1,616,462	126	1,356,135	40	371,091	38

Note: SEK refers to the Swedish krona.
Source: Authors' calculations based on Statistics Sweden (2009).

benefit. Age 65 is important in the Swedish context because, until 2001 when the right to work until age 67 was legislated, most employees were prevented from working longer by contracts entered into by central management and labor organizations. From age 65 onward, continued employment required an agreement between the employee and the employer. Although early retirement with a public benefit can be claimed from age 61 and workers can also continue past the age of 65, most still view age 65 as being the 'normal' pension age.

Occupational benefits are used to cover early retirement from the labor force (*a*) for those few occupations where early retirement is specified in the employment contract (e.g., firemen), and (*b*) for persons who either upon the initiative of the employer or by their own initiative voluntarily choose to leave the labor force in their early 60s deferring their claim on their public benefit until later, usually at the age of 65 (although this is in the process of changing as more people have begun to work until 67 within the framework of the new public system). For those who take out occupational benefits prior to the age of 65, occupational pensions are normally actuarially adjusted from age 65 to compensate for the early retirement payments.

The data in Table 2.2 show that the age group 65–70 constitutes a third significant group with regard to payments from occupational and individual voluntary schemes (note that the minimum pension age for the public pension is 61, but that the normal age at which people claim a public pension is 65, a custom established when 65 was the 'full-benefit' pension age in the old system). The data suggest a clear tendency to claim both occupational and voluntary benefits for the statutory minimum five-year period, where permitted by the conditions of the contract.

Finally, the data in Table 2.2 also show that the percentage of benefit recipients with a private voluntary pension declines relatively rapidly with age. This pattern reflects two market characteristics. The first is an increasing tendency for younger cohorts to purchase individual voluntary insurance, which in part explains the significantly higher incidence of payments from voluntary schemes to younger cohorts of pensioners. Secondly, however, the data can reflect preferences for five- or ten-year withdrawals to enhance consumption during the initial period of retirement. A third possibility is that voluntary insurance is particularly pervasive among persons with short lives. This implies the possibility of adverse selection, due to the knowledge that one will have a shorter life than normal. Nevertheless, there is little evidence toward this: of those that had either or both of private voluntary pension saving or occupational pension and withdrew it at the earliest possible time (at 55 years of age), the vast majority waited until age 65 or older to withdraw their public pensions. There were 805 people who had an opportunity to draw benefits at age 55 in 1992 and actually did it, but only 123 of those persons started to withdraw a public pension at the earliest possible age of 61. Far more (491 persons) waited until their 65th year to withdraw the public pension. Finally, although available data are insufficient to draw a firm conclusion, the overall picture of the distribution of claims among the age groups leads us to the tentative conclusion that life annuities are not much more prevalent than the approximate 7 percent figure for persons 75 and older indicates.

What about the future demand for private voluntary annuities? The age, income, and gender distribution of tax deductions for premiums paid for private voluntary pensions provides an indication of the trend (see Table 2.1). Whereas about 20 percent of present pensioners aged 65 or older receive a payment from voluntary insurance, about 40 percent of the population aged 20–64 claimed a deduction in 2008 for premiums paid to a private voluntary plan. Whether this will lead to five- or ten-year withdrawals or life annuities is impossible to say because Sweden presently has no national data on the types of contracts.

The underlying data from Statistics Sweden behind Table 2.1, while not provided here, show several dominant characteristics of persons aged 20–64 presently claiming a tax deduction for voluntary private pension or life insurance. The first is that, for both men and women, the percentage claiming a deduction increases with income. Second, the log increase in the size of deduction is slower than the log increase in income, with an estimated elasticity of 0.71. Thirdly, more women than men claim a deduction at all ages from 25 to 64. Fourthly, the average deduction of women was greater than that of men for all income classes above the average, up to the highest income class.

The main conclusion is that 40 percent of current workers claim a deduction for private insurance, indicating that the demand for annuities will be higher in the future than it presently is. A second conclusion is that the legislation abolishing the publicly provided widow's benefit for persons born in 1945 and later affected women's demand for private insurance. Indirectly, it may also have affected men's demand for insurance including a survivor benefit, although we have no data to verify this likely outcome.

Finally, it is important to note that the conversion from DB to DC has probably itself influenced the demand for private individual insurance. To the extent that the DB schemes contained some degree of implicit redistribution from long- to short-career contributors, which was certainly true of the public scheme, the general message of the transition is that for a given contribution rate, the transition is to the advantage of persons with longer contribution periods. A result of this change both within the public and occupational schemes can be increased demand for private insurance from persons with shorter earnings careers.

In many countries, the conversion to DC would be a disadvantage for women. Generally speaking, in Sweden this is not the case. This is because in the public NDC and FDC schemes, periods of up to four years per child in conjunction with the birth of a child are covered with non-contributory rights financed externally from the state-budget. This transfer is generally sufficient to compensate for time spent away from the labor force in conjunction with childbirth.

For all of these reasons, in the not-so-distant future, around 40 percent of new retirees will be in the market for privately provided retirement products. In theory, individuals should be especially interested in insuring against the risk of a long life, but as we have seen, the current evidence from Sweden is that this is not the case. Instead, voluntary insurance has been availed, first, to enhance consumption during early retirement (for those aged 55–64) prior to claiming a public (and supplementary occupational) benefit at age 65 or later, and, second, to supplement public and occupational benefits primarily in the first decade of retirement, in the age group 65–74. Only a small percentage of retirees aged 80 or older presently have a voluntary benefit.

Determinants of the demand for voluntary and occupational annuities

To analyze the demand for pension products, we are interested first in the kinds of products people choose, that is, life annuities or phased withdrawals of five or ten years (standard products in Sweden), and who makes these withdrawals. In the absence of such straightforward information, we have to approach the question through the back door and deduce what people have done by using a longitudinal income database. That is what we do in this section: we analyze the behavior of pension savers by examining actual withdrawal patterns.

Overview of individual data

The data used come from the LISA database from Statistics Sweden which reports comprehensive information on individuals' income and various individual characteristics. An overview of the withdrawal patterns for non-public, that is, private voluntary and occupational pensions appears in Figure 2.1. Here, it is clear that the first type of pension claimed at the earliest possible age to claim a pension (age 55) is a pension from individuals' own private pension saving. Since this saving is tax-deductible, this behavior would be logical if people have a lower tax rate when they claimed this benefit than when they paid their premiums and claimed their deduction earlier. It would also be logical for individuals who had saved some money this way but not enough to matter in the long run to claim a short

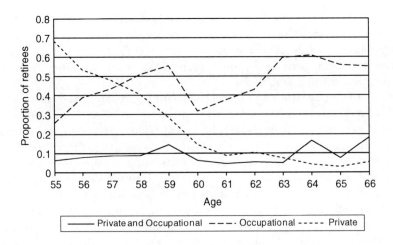

Figure 2.1 Share of private and occupational pension for those retired in 1992. *Source:* Authors' calculations based on Statistics Sweden (2009).

payout period as soon as they can. In general, this enhances consumption at a relatively early age, but is hardly consistent with the idea that people purchase insurance to provide for inactive years in old age.

The older the retirees, the larger the fraction that first starts drawing the occupational pension or takes a combination of both the occupational and private pension saving. This is due to the fact that occupational benefits provide a means to leave the labor force partially or wholly for persons who for one or another reason desire to do this, but are healthy and do not qualify for disability. In a very limited number of occupations, occupational benefits provide the normal means of exit for persons whose contractual labor agreements *require* that they leave the labor force prior to age 65, which until 1999 was the full-benefit retirement age in both the public and occupational schemes. For persons desiring to retire prior to age 65, an occupational benefit was – and still is – the major benefit workers claimed, leaving a claim of the larger public benefit until age 65 or later. This behavior leads to an actuarial reduction in the occupational benefit when it is converted to a supplement to the public benefit, when the latter is claimed.

Figure 2.2 shows how the private pension is actually withdrawn by pension savers. To construct the figure, we classify the withdrawals into four distinct categories: withdrawals of the minimum allowed duration of five years (23.4 percent of total observations), those we can deduce have a life annuity (21.7 percent of total observations), withdrawals that terminated before the final year of our dataset (2007) but longer than five years (44.9 percent of total observations), and finally those that have either several

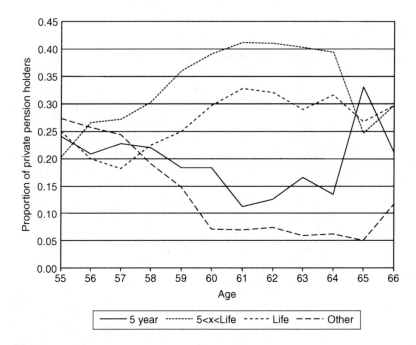

Figure 2.2 Form of private pension withdrawal (1992). *Source:* Authors' calculations based on Statistics Sweden (2009).

insurances or individual pension saving accounts for at least five years, but who stop and later start up payments, which we call 'other' (9.9 percent of all persons). For example, this group may start with a private pension, stop this pension then start later another private pension perhaps together with an occupational benefit and/or a public benefit; often this latest started private pension is not terminated before 2007, the end of our observation period (70 percent of other are not terminated by 2007). The outcome of this pension career would be a life annuity.

Older retirees tend to have a longer withdrawal duration, suggesting that the aim of early withdrawals is to liquidate funds that might have been deposited for the sole purpose of utilizing the tax-deduction. The fraction of those withdrawing private pension saving for the minimum five years is constant at around 20 percent, with a temporary peak at age 65.

Analysis of data

In the remainder of this section, we analyze what characterizes the choice of withdrawal period for private pension saving. To do this, we use a multinomial Logit model (Greene 1997). In 1992, just over 103,000 people who did not receive any payments in 1991 started drawing a private voluntary, occupational, or public pension (or some combination of these). About a quarter of these (25,942 persons) with a first-time benefit in 1992 had a private voluntary pension sometime between 1992 and 2007, and were still alive in 2007 or died after the private pension payments were terminated. This is the dependent variable in our analysis. With the help of the multinominal Logit model, we examine the relative odds that an individual who had a private voluntary benefit claimed it as a life annuity, which is the basis for comparison, claimed it for at least five years but less than life ($5 < x <$ life), five years (5), or other (described earlier).

The independent variables depicted in Table 2.3 include the worker's level of occupational pension (*occ*), level of income after starting drawing pension (*inc*), level of education (*edu*), sex (female is coded as 1), and age in 1992 (*age*) when first drawing a benefit. Dummies are used to denote white-collar private employees (*itp*), municipal and county council employees (*mun*), blue-collar private employees (*stp*), and central government employees (*gov*). Income variables are measured in tens of thousands of SEK (Swedish kronor). The highest level of education attained is coded from 1 through 6, where 1 is pre-high-school shorter than nine years, 2 is pre-high-school equivalent to nine years, 3 refers to high-school, 4 to post high-school education of fewer than two years, 5 is post-high-school education longer than two years, and 6 is post-graduate education (enrolled in a Ph.D. program).

From Table 2.3, it is evident that all variables matter for at least one of the types of withdrawals, in terms of being significant. Judging by McFadden's R^2, the age and age-squared terms are especially important for the model's overall explanatory power. We have also experimented with dropping the dummies for four occupational pension categories, which does not have a big effect on the model's explanatory power, indicating that category is much less important than age. We obtain the same outcome when we delete the occupational benefit level. By examining alternative models, we see that the parameter estimates are stable, as most parameters are in the same range for all specifications with one exception (which is insignificant); parameter estimates do not change signs in the alternative specifications. The magnitude of correlation is also below 0.33 for all the included variables and most correlations are in the range $+/-0.1$.

To interpret Table 2.3, the coefficients show the log of the relative probabilities with the 'Life annuity' as the benchmark. For example, if the level of income provided by the occupational pension rose by SEK 10,000, this reduces the probability that an individual will choose a five-year withdrawal period for his or her private voluntary benefit. This suggests that either these two sorts of pension options are substitutes or that they are

TABLE 2.3 Estimated multinomial model for persons of age 55–67 drawing private voluntary benefit during some years during 1992–2007

Model:

$$\ln(P_{i,j}/P_{i,Life}) = \beta_{j,0} + \beta_{j,Occ}\cdot occ + \beta_{j,inc}\cdot inc + \beta_{j,edu}\cdot edu + \beta_{j,sex}\cdot sex + \beta_{j,age}\cdot age$$
$$+ \beta_{j,age^2}\cdot age^2 + \beta_{j,itp}\cdot itp + \beta_{j,mun}\cdot mun + \beta_{j,stp}\cdot stp + \beta_{j,gov}\cdot gov,$$
$$j = \{5 < x < Life, 5, Other\}$$

Duration in years (intercept)				
5 < x < Life	−66.21***	0.66***	−67.66***	−70.27***
5	102.36***	0.40***	102.09***	107.89***
Other	81.03***	−1.43***	77.90***	81.43***
Level of occupational pension in tens of thousands SEK				
5 < x < Life	0.01***	0.01***	0.01***	
5	−0.02***	−0.03***	−0.02***	
Other	−0.0021	−0.01**	−0.0009	
Level of income year after first drawing benefit				
5 < x < Life	−0.01***	−0.01***	−0.01***	−0.01***
5	−0.02***	−0.03***	−0.02***	−0.02***
Other	0.0046**	0.01***	0.0049**	0.0047**
Level of education, 6 levels coded, 1 for low and 6 for highest (9 for undefined)				
5 < x < Life	−0.08***	−0.08***	−0.04***	−0.07***
5	−0.10***	−0.09***	−0.10***	−0.12***
Other	0.03ˆ	0.05**	0.06***	0.03
Female (0 for men, 1 for women)				
5 < x < Life	0.17***	0.17***	0.23***	0.14***
5	0.16***	0.14***	0.20***	0.20***
Other	0.10ˆ	0.15**	0.14**	0.11*
Age in 1992				
5 < x < Life	2.21***		2.27***	2.34***
5	−3.39***		−3.36***	−3.57***
Other	−2.55***		−2.44***	−2.57***
Age in 1992 squared				
5 < x < Life	−0.02***		−0.02***	−0.02***
5	0.03***		0.03***	0.03***
Other	0.02***		0.02***	0.02***
Private white-collar occupational pension (dummy)				
5 < x < Life	0.10**	0.12**		0.12**
5	0.02	−0.01		−0.01
Other	0.23***	0.31***		0.23***
Municipal and county council employee occupational pension (dummy)				
5 < x < Life	0.29***	0.32***		0.30***
5	0.27***	0.23***		0.25***

(continued)

TABLE 2.3 *(Continued)*

Model:

$$\ln(P_{i,j}/P_{i,Life}) = \beta_{j,0} + \beta_{j,Occ}\cdot occ + \beta_{j,inc}\cdot inc + \beta_{j,edu}\cdot edu + \beta_{j,sex}\cdot sex + \beta_{j,age}\cdot age$$
$$+\beta_{j,age^2}\cdot age^2 + \beta_{j,itp}\cdot itp + \beta_{j,mun}\cdot mun + \beta_{j,stp}\cdot stp + \beta_{j,gov}\cdot gov,$$
$$j = \{5 < x < \text{Life}, 5, \text{Other}\}$$

Other	0.32***	0.31***		0.31***
Private blue-collar occupational pension (dummy)				
5 < x < Life	0.19***	0.19***		0.17**
5	0.47***	0.45***		0.49***
Other	0.12	0.38***		0.13^
Central government employee occupational pension (dummy)				
5 < x < Life	0.59***	0.60***		0.61***
5	0.37***	0.36***		0.33***
Other	0.21**	0.28***		0.20**
Log-likelihood	−31224	−31990	−31357	−31288
McFadden R^2	0.05	0.02	0.04	0.04
LR-test (chi-square)	2942.6***	1410.1***	2677***	2814.9***

Notes: Number of observations: 25,942. Significance levels: 0***, 0.001**, 0.01*, 0.05^. SEK refers to the Swedish krona.
Source: Authors' calculations based on Statistics Sweden (2009).

largely entirely different products, purchased with different intentions. The analysis also shows that blue-collar, municipal, county council, and central government workers are likely to choose a minimum withdrawal period of five years for the private voluntary benefit, whereas this variable is insignificant for private white-collar workers. There is a similar significant tendency for these categories of workers to take a benefit for more than five years but less than for life, and a significant – but relatively weaker – tendency for white-collar workers to do the same. Even if they go in the same direction, the results are weakest for white-collar workers which suggests a greater relative proclivity for life annuities for this group. We also see that having higher income is associated with a smaller probability of drawing a non-life benefit, suggesting that those who choose shorter payouts use the money to supplement – or replace – income during the younger years of withdrawal. In addition, the more educated are less likely to elect both short- and intermediate-term payout schemes.

We find it surprising that women have a higher probability of selecting non-life annuities than men, since several studies suggest that women tend to adopt more prudent investment strategies than men in other countries (Hinz et al. 1997; Sundén and Surette 1998; Agnew et al. 2003). Yet, other studies on Swedish data have shown that women are more likely to make active investment choices in the Swedish DC scheme (Engström and Wersterberg 2003), and that the gender effect appears in the context of high-risk but not low-risk choices (Säve-Söderberg 2009). Additionally, the youngest cohort studied here is eligible for widow's benefits, which could also explain why this group of women is less likely not to elect the life annuity. There is also evidence that less risk averse individuals are more likely to have voluntary pension saving, indicating that it could be that the women with voluntary pension saving value the longevity risk less (Larsson and Säve-Söderberg 2010).

To sum up, most of the evidence offered here supports a view that many individuals opt in favor of shorter rather than full-life annuities.

The future demand for life annuities in Sweden

A recurring theme in the literature on the demand for annuities is that most consumers tend not to purchase lifetime payout annuities, and thus far the Swedish data concur: those aged 55–70 years tend not to buy life annuities, perhaps because the mandatory pension system provides a consumption-smoothing device that individuals consider sufficient. It also seems that those who do purchase private insurance are not mainly considering bequests, since they use the assets to finance their own consumption when relatively young. It may be, though we cannot verify it, that people may not be informed about or understand the benefits of annuitization, or may not recognize the need to save for the contingency of disability when very old. Or maybe individuals are constrained from trading across states because financial markets are incomplete, preventing them from creating an optimum insurance portfolio (Impavido et al. 2003).

The literature has also emphasized that, when a choice is possible in annuities, the price tax may be too high (e.g., Warshawsky 1998; Mitchell et al. 2006; Brown 2007). Demand is nipped in the bud if potential annuitants cannot expect to get their money's worth in the marketplace. And conversely, we must also acknowledge that large insurance companies might not find it profitable to provide custom-tailored individual annuities. In the Swedish setting, seven large companies receive around 95 percent of individual premium payments and have command over 95 percent of all the assets of life insurance companies (Palmer 2008). Largely, the same companies also manage the occupational pension schemes. The question is, to what extent will these companies seek to develop new voluntary products without receiving an impetus in the form of new legislation?

A dilemma confronting potential annuitants is that the 'normal' pension age is too young to move all one's money from active equity investments into a 'risk free' investment policy associated with the purchase of a market annuity. More generally, it is often reasonable to defer annuitization until after a decade or so from age 65; Milevsky (2001) shows that utility-max-imizing individuals would be best off deferring the decision to annuitize until the age of 75–80, given that they can benefit from the returns on the alternative strategy of investing in the equity market until this age. Seen in this perspective, it is likely rational for Swedes to contract five to ten withdrawal plans, within the private voluntary and occupational insurance supplements to the public mandatory scheme. This is especially true if these withdrawal plans offer a unit-link alternative where retirees retain command over the investment strategy. Of course, this alternative also requires a certain degree of sophistication to steer around the backside of market bubbles.

One might argue that the Swedish proclivity to transform saving into consumption during the younger years of retirement is the result of a poor understanding of what the future has in store. This is because both the older public pay-as-you-go DB scheme and the new NDC schemes provide price-indexed annuities; as workers experience real wage growth, the ratio of a pension to an average wage will fall. This decline in the relative living standard vis á vis contemporaneous workers becomes more marked with increasing age. Yet, few Swedes transform financial saving into annuities purchased at a more advanced age, 75–80, to provide for older, old age. Statistics Sweden data indicate that only around 2 percent of persons aged 65 or older claim a deduction for premium payments for private pension or life insurance. Instead, this population relies almost exclusively on pay-ments from the mandatory public scheme for income support. Indirectly, the evidence that most utilize their private insurance before reaching the age of 75 suggests a reliance on the public sector to provide sufficient health and home care in the terminal years of life.

There are two reasons to believe that future coverage will not be consid-ered sufficient, despite the public sector pension in Sweden. The first reason is that coverage is already less than what many people would desire. Public assistance in home care is more or less at a minimum guarantee level for the elderly who want to remain at home, and it is likely to be even less in the future. For those who need it, institutional care is provided but even this care has a basic minimum guarantee character, with little room for individual choice. Second, there is a clear trend toward increasing relative affluence among a large segment of the pensioner population (Gustafsson et al. 2009). This suggests that there is a growing segment of the elderly that could afford long-term care (LTC) insurance if it were to be provided. Indeed, individuals could save on their own to meet 'extra' LTC needs, but in principle, it would be most efficient to purchase insurance.

For Swedes, one of the uncertainties is the extent to which the public commitment will develop in the future. Other more general unknowns, as outlined for example in Mitchell et al. (2006), are both future developments in health and service technology, and the length of time people can expect to be frail. As these authors point out, one of the deterrents to providing LTC insurance is the possibility of adverse selection. Of course, if prudent actuaries suspect adverse selection, they may price an insurance of this kind unfavorably, further reducing demand. This is a frequently cited reason for mandating insurance. A mandate would, however, also have to have a ceiling, which given the sheer scope of aging must be low. For a market to develop, it is important that the extent of the public commitment be made clear. This seems to be the present challenge for policy.

It would also seem reasonable to create legislation that enables individuals to freely combine their balances from the three separate sources of pension saving they presently have – their mandatory FDC account, the 'quasi-mandatory' occupational account, and their private voluntary account – to purchase one or more insurance products with potentially different features. These features could be as simple as a life annuity, combining two or three of these balances, a deferred annuity, or a combination. Our evidence indicates a potential demand for such products in the not-too-distant future. Ultimately, whether demand does emerge must depend on the ability of the market to offer saleable products on the scale necessary to create viable risk pools (Mitchell and McCarthy 2004).

Conclusion

This chapter has analyzed the structure of demand for retirement products in Sweden. While there is no good database with information on products chosen by whom, we rely on a longitudinal income database from Statistics Sweden for about 103,000 persons who claimed their benefits first in 1992. Choosing this early date made it possible to follow individuals for fifteen years, through 2007, the last year for which data were available. Our multinomial Logit model helps identify which individuals elected shorter or longer withdrawals of their private voluntary pension accounts, focusing on the five-year benefit (the minimum possible withdrawal time in Sweden), a withdrawal of more than five years but less than life, and a life annuity. We find that most workers, except for white-collar workers, are more likely to choose the five-year withdrawal, as are women and the least-educated.

Nevertheless, the pattern of usage of private insurance could already be in the process of changing, since deductions for premium payments to private insurance have been high for two decades leading up to 2010. This sets the stage for a structural change, though there is no indication yet that this has occurred. It is also important to recognize that the future ability of the public sector to pay for LTC is unknown. Currently, the average individual tends not to buy insurance to cover this risk, without knowing more about the future limit of public coverage and how the coverage will be financed. In fact, if future coverage were to be based on ability to pay, as it is today, it might be inefficient for people to save to cover this contingency. Accordingly, the present state of uncertainty is unlikely to drive a large demand for and accommodating supply of annuity products for the oldest old phase of the life cycle.

Notes

[1] Individuals working at places of employment covered by one of the major employer–labor agreements are automatically covered by the agreement, regardless of whether they are affiliated to the union covering their specific occupation.

[2] In fact, studies of the effect of the introduction of the universal earnings-related public scheme in 1960 indicated that the personal saving rate during the period 1960–80 would have been four percentage points higher on average in the absence of this public scheme (Markowski and Palmer 1979; Palmer 1981; Berg 1983). This is evidence that the promise of a public pension in the future contributed significantly to crowding out private saving for some time.

[3] Financial assets exclude individuals' assets in occupational plans and the mandatory premium pension scheme, as well as shares in the value of apartments owned by individuals, all of which are counted as household financial assets in the national accounts. The source for this data is Statistics Sweden (2009).

References

Agnew, John, Pierluigi Balduzzi, and Annika Sundén (2003). 'Portfolio Choice, Trading and Returns in a Large 401(k) Plan,' *American Economic Review*, 93: 193–215.

Berg, Lennart (1983). Consumption and Saving – A Study of Household Behavior (Konsumtion och sparande – en studie av hushållens beteende). Ph.D. dissertation, Uppsala University, Uppsala, Sweden.

Brown, Jeffrey (2007). *Rational and Behavioral Perspectives on the Role of Annuities in Retirement Planning.* NBER Working Paper No. 13537. Cambridge, MA: National Bureau of Economic Research.

Engström, Stefan and Anna Wersterberg (2003). 'Which Individuals Make Active Investment Decisions in the New Swedish Pension System?,' *Journal of Pension Economics and Finance*, 2: 225–45.

Greene, William H. (1997). *Econometric Analysis*, 3rd edition. Upper Saddle River, NJ: Prentice-Hall.

Gustafsson, Björn, Mats Johansson, and Edward Palmer (2009). 'The Welfare of Sweden's Old Age Pensioners in Times of Bust and Boom from 1990,' *Ageing & Society*, 29: 539–61.

Hinz, Richard P., David D. McCarthy, and John A. Turner (1997). 'Are Women Conservative Investors? Gender Differences in Participant-Directed Pension Investments,' in Michael Gordon, Olivia S. Mitchell and Marc Twinney, eds., *Positioning Pensions for the Twenty-First Century*. Philadelphia, PA: University Pennsylvania Press, pp. 91–106.

Impavido, Gregorio, Craig Thorburn, and Mike Wadsworth (2003). *A Conceptual Framework for Retirement Products: Risk Sharing Arrangements between Providers and Retirees*. London, UK: Watson Wyatt.

Larsson, Bo and Jenny Säve-Söderberg (2010). *Targeting Risk Lovers? Incentives for Voluntary Pension Savings with Heterogeneous Risk Preferences*. Working Paper. Stockholm, Sweden: Stockholm University.

Markowski, Aleksander and Edward Palmer (1979). 'Social Insurance and Saving in Sweden,' in George M. Von Furstenberg, ed., *Social Security versus Private Saving*. Cambridge, MA: Ballinger Publishing Co., pp. 167–90.

Milevsky, Moshe A. (2001). 'Optimal Annuitization Policies: Analysis and Options,' *North American Actuarial Journal*, 5(1): 57–69.

Mitchell, Olivia S. and David McCarthy (2004). 'Annuities for an Ageing World,' in Elsa Fornero and E. Luciano, eds., *Developing an Annuity Market in Europe*. Cheltenham, UK: Edward Elgar Publishing, pp. 19–68.

—— John Piggott, Michael Sherris, and Shaun Yow (2006). 'Financial Innovations for an Aging World,' in C. Kent, A. Park, and D. Rees, eds., *Demography and Financial Markets*. Frenchs Forrest, Australia: Pegasus Press, pp. 299–336.

Palmer, Edward (1981). *Determination of Personal Consumption – Theoretical Foundations and Empirical Evidence from Sweden*. Stockholm, Sweden: Almqvist and Wicksell International.

—— (2002a). 'Swedish Pension Reform – How Did It Evolve and What Does It Mean for the Future?,' in M. Feldstein and H. Siebert, eds., *Coping with the Pension Crisis: Where Does Europe Stand?* Chicago, IL: University of Chicago Press, pp. 171–205.

—— (2002b). 'The Evolution of Public and Private Insurance in Sweden in the 1990's,' in *Regulating Private Pension Schemes – Trends and Challenges*. Paris, France: OECD, pp. 37–50.

—— (2008). *The Market for Retirement Products in Sweden*. Washington, DC: World Bank.

Säve-Söderberg, Jenny (2009). *Self-Directed Pensions: Gender, Risk and Portfolio Choices*. Working Paper. Stockholm, Sweden: Stockholm University.

Statistics Sweden (2009). *Electronic Statistical Database*. Stockholm, Sweden: Statistics Sweden. http://www.scb.se/Statistik/FM/FM0105/2009K03/Hushallens_stallning_1980_2009kv3.pdf

Sundén, Annika and Brian J. Surette (1998). 'Gender Differences in the Allocation of Assets in Retirement Savings Plans,' *American Economic Review*, 88: 207–11.

The World Bank (2007). *Pensions Panorama – Retirement-Income Systems in 53 Countries*. Washington, DC: The World Bank.

Warshawsky, Mark J. (1998). 'Private Annuity Markets in the United States,' *Journal of Risk and Insurance*, 55(3): 518–28.

Yaari, Menahem E. (1965). 'Uncertain Lifetime, Life Insurance and the Theory of the Consumer,' *Review of Economic Studies*, 32(2): 137–50.

Chapter 3

Market Structure and Challenges for Annuities in India

Mukul G. Asher and Deepa Vasudevan

Pension systems address longevity and inflation risks in various ways. For the most part, the richer OECD countries tend to rely on social insurance programs to address longevity risk, and to address the inflation risk, some countries apply price or wage indexation to pensions, while others rely on ad hoc increases in nominal pension benefits. In India, most people do not benefit from nor are they covered by pension (and healthcare) benefits on a universal basis. Typically, only the armed forces, civil servants, and some private sector employees have access to pensions. As a result, longevity and inflation risks are mitigated only for a small proportion of the labor force. This chapter discusses the need for robust annuity markets in India, along with an overview of annuity products and providers. We also outline challenges facing the development of the industry in India along with reform directions.

The rationale for robust annuity markets in India

In India, the insurance industry has divided deferred annuities into two phases from the risk management perspective, focusing on the accumulation phase and the payout phase, and there are often different providers of these two phases. Here, we understand the annuity to be an insurance product involving periodic payments during retirement that addresses longevity risk (some annuity products also address inflation risk and survivor risk). Annuities may be immediate at the time of retirement, deferred so purchase takes place during the working years, or within a specified time after retirement. Many types of annuities are normally priced on the basis of product features as well as interest rates and other economic variables. Terms and conditions of annuity products, particularly the level and duration of income stream, provided from a given capital sum, have equity and adequacy implications.

TABLE 3.1 Labor force and demographic indicators in India

Demographic indicator	Time period	Value
Life expectancy at birth (years)	2009[a]	69.89
Male	2009[a]	67.46
Female	2009[a]	72.61
Male life expectancy at age 60 (years)	2000–5	17
Female life expectancy at age 60 (years)	2000–5	19
Total fertility rate (number of children)[b]	2007	2.68
Population (million)	2001	1,028
Females (million)	2001	496
Males (million)	2001	532
Sex ratio (females per thousand males)	2001	933
Population above age 60 (million)	2005	79.4
Population above age 60 (million)	2050	315.6
Total workforce (million)	2001	424.6
Urban workforce (million)	2001	97.7
Rural workforce (million)	2001	326.9

[a] Estimate.
[b] Total fertility rate is defined as the average number of live childbirths over a woman's lifetime.
Source: Central Intelligence Agency (2009), United Nations Population Fund (2008, 2009), Office of the Registrar General (2001).

In our view, there are several reasons why India would benefit from developing a robust annuity market. First, India is experiencing a demographic transition characterized by declining fertility rate and increasing life expectancy. People are having fewer children but live much longer than before, so the population is aging rapidly. Projections indicate that the proportion of population aged 65 or older that may be classified as retired will rise to 8 percent in 2031, and it will rise to over 13 percent by 2051. In absolute terms, the number of persons aged 65 or older will grow from 62.5 million in 2011, to 121.8 million in 2031, and to about 229.4 million in 2051.[1] There is however significant interstate variations in fertility rate; states such as Kerala and Tamil Nadu, which have below-average fertility rates, are expected to age earlier than other states (Table 3.1).[2]

Both the level and the pace of aging are likely to provide significant challenges. Life expectancy at 60 years was anticipated at 17.5 years in 2001; by 2006, it was revised upward to 19 years.[3] Longevity will rise further, particularly for the salaried middle and upper class with access to superior education and health facilities. Uncertainty in longevity trends is, however, complicating the task of pricing annuities in India. This is in part because the combination of lower fertility and higher life expectancy creates longevity risk, or the risk that retirees will outlive their savings. Traditional family structures addressed the problem by providing for the financial needs of dependents through the income of earning members of the family. Frequent mobility of labor and migration from rural to urban jobs has broken down traditional extended families, and created nuclear family units in which the degree of self-reliance by nuclear families in providing for their retirement needs is expected to increase.

Another factor is that in the future, India will find it increasingly unsustainable to maintain and expand its existing defined benefit (DB) pensions. With fewer workers expected to experience lifetime (or even long-term) employment with a single employer and pension plan sponsor, the portable defined contribution (DC) model offering greater flexibility has become more attractive. While precise data are unavailable, it appears that the share of contract workers who receive lower or no pension and healthcare benefits is rising, in both public and private sectors in India. As a result, these workers will need to rely on their own savings to a greater extent in financing retirement, boosting the demand for annuities. Furthermore, the civil servant DB pension schemes are economically unsustainable. Central and state government budgets are already burdened with large fiscal deficits, and the resources needed to address the retirement needs of vast numbers of elderly people are likely to be too enormous to be fiscally sustainable. The need to refocus on the goals of the Fiscal Responsibility and Budget Management (FRBM) Acts by the Centre and several states may result in further expenditure contraction and debt curtailment. As a result, state-financed income support will be curtailed in the future, yet elderly retired persons will need income support for longer periods of time.

Another consideration is that India has been projected to need to create 140 million jobs between 2005 and 2020, nearly 30 percent of the world's total, and most of the new jobs will be in the informal sector (ILO 2008). Many of the informal sector workers will have some ability to save for their retirement, thus generating a demand for annuities.[4] These workers require avenues for retirement saving which generate reasonable market-based returns and in which they have confidence.

The effectiveness of the New Pension Scheme (NPS) launched in 2004 will also require the existence of well-developed and fairly priced annuities. NPS is a DC system of individual pension accounts jointly funded by the employer and employee, each of whom contributes 10 percent of gross salary. Members can select a pension fund manager and allocate funds to an investment scheme of their choice. A key feature of the NPS is that withdrawals are not normally permitted until the age of 60. At retirement, accumulated balances are divided into two components: at least 40 percent of the account balance must be mandatorily used for purchasing annuities;

and the remainder may be withdrawn as a lump sum. Investors have the flexibility to leave the scheme before attaining the age of 60, but in that case they are required to annuitize 80 percent of their accumulated balance. Thus, it is expected that there should be a variety of competitively priced annuity options to suit the retirement needs of different members. The NPS is mandatory only for central government workers, but twenty-three state governments have already adopted it for their employees. Moreover, since May 2009 the NPS has been made available to any Indian citizen who wants to subscribe to it on a voluntary basis. Therefore, the reach of NPS is potentially very large. As membership of NPS grows, the number of persons with requirements for annuitizing is likely to increase substantially.[5]

Annuities are also relevant even for those who do not participate in the NPS. Many self-employed professionals and small business owners would find annuity products useful in managing retirement risks. In addition, micro-pension schemes are expected to have a limited but important function in providing retirement income, and these also need to address payout options including annuities (Asher and Shankar 2007).

Annuity markets in India: an overview

As noted earlier, the potential demand for annuities in India is large. Next, we show that the market for annuities is not well developed and it lacks the depth and volume that will be necessary to efficiently administer annuities for future retirees.

Annuities may be classified on the basis of the type and periodicity of payouts, as well as by the additional benefits related to the annuity stream. So in the case of an immediate annuity, payouts commence at once on purchase; in the case of a deferred annuity, payouts start at some prescribed future date. The payout may be made as a single lump sum, or fixed periodic amounts, or variable amounts linked to an underlying index of assets or prices. Payouts may also cease after a specified period, continue for the duration of the annuitant's life, or pass on to nominated survivors at a reduced rate (see Figure 3.1).

The basic annuity product is also enhanced by adding other benefits. For instance, inflation-indexed benefits address inflation risk by maintaining, partially or fully, the real value of future payouts. Variable annuities offer investors flexibility to exercise some choice over the underlying assets, in return for riskier and non-fixed income streams. A relatively new class of annuities has recently developed in the United States, the United Kingdom, and Australia, to cater to those with reduced life spans. Termed 'enhanced' annuities, they provide additional payouts to high-risk lives;

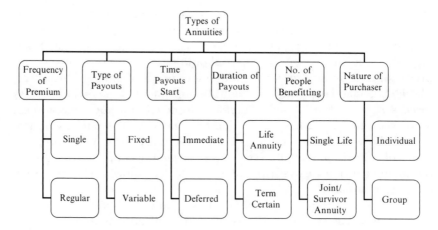

Figure 3.1 Types of annuities.
Source: Authors' adaptation of data from Swiss RE(2007).

also available are 'impaired' annuities which pay substantially higher amounts to individuals with proven serious medical conditions.[6] In this way, annuities can be created across the risk spectrum, ranging from fairly simple structures with relatively low risk to structures that expose retirees to higher risk and provide higher incomes. Some annuity products also combine survivor and other benefits. An annuity is thus like any other product where design features impact on the annuity benefits which can be purchased from a given capital sum. Therefore, price discovery for different annuity products reflecting fair actuarial value is important.

In India, there are currently twenty-three life insurance companies, of which twenty-two are in the private sector. The Life Insurance Corporation of India (LIC) is the sole annuity provider in the public sector, and is the market leader. According to the Insurance Regulatory and Development Authority (IRDA 2010), of the 3.2 million general annuity and pension plans in force in March 2007, about 2.9 million, or 91 percent, were written by LIC.[7] It appears that annuities constitute a relatively small segment of the insurance sector.[8] Life insurance products are likely the most important in terms of volume as well as premiums generated, but there has been a sharp rise in the purchase of pension policies of late. These policies are separately classified and are not included in annuities. A disaggregation of first-year premiums underwritten during 2007–8 suggests that annuity products contributed only 2.75 percent of the total premium underwritten, whereas life insurance and pension products contributed 59.5 and 37.6 percent respectively (IRDA 2008). Pension products are relevant during the accumulation phase, when they facilitate regular saving for the purpose of providing for retirement. At retirement or the vesting stage, the holder of a pension plan has the option to purchase one of the several annuity options.[9] The rising demand for pension products therefore can potentially translate into higher demand for annuities in the future (Table 3A.1).

The supply side of the market has witnessed some product innovation. For instance, almost all insurers now offer joint life annuities which provide survivors' benefits,[10] and increasing annuities, which are designed to at least partially mitigate the impact of inflation on annuity streams. Deferred plans are available to allow individuals to choose the age from which they wish to receive annuity streams; such plans may be viewed as saving with annuity products. Annuities that return the initial capital on the death of the purchaser within a specified period are widely available. Each product innovation, however, impacts on the premium for the investor; it permits a variety of risk-management preferences to be addressed from the perspective of the consumer.[11] Typically, Indian insurance companies offer an 'open market option' that permits investors in pension accumulation plans to shop for the best annuity provider at the time of vesting. This practice promotes competition and transparency in the market.

Annuity demand is typically low even in markets such as the United Kingdom where compulsory annuitization norms have resulted in better understanding of the benefits of annuitization.[12] The observed 'annuity demand puzzle' reflects a clear preference to retain some or all pension wealth in non-annuity forms. Several reasons have been advanced in the literature for this phenomenon. First is that annuities markets often suffer from adverse selection, created by the tendency of those who do not expect to live long to avoid buying annuities, thus limiting the pool to customers with substantial longevity risk. Since individuals have private information about their life expectancies that may not be available to the insurance company, there is a tendency for those with higher expected life expectancies to be more motivated to purchase annuities. On the supply side, the prevalence of asymmetric information in the annuity market makes its pricing more complex (Akerlof 1970). The outcome is that buyers often perceive annuities as being overpriced.

Additionally, annuities are usually illiquid so annuitants forfeit the option to liquidate and exit in case of unforeseen expenditures. This inherent inflexibility may deter retirees who desire greater control over their consumption decisions. Further, unlike traditional fixed income assets, most annuities do not return the initial principal used to purchase an annuity so that the products do not enable individuals to leave a bequest.[13] If annuities are not mandatory, retirees tend to opt for higher return instruments such as bank deposits and small saving instruments. However, if annuity returns are made relatively attractive and its benefits are better understood, demand may increase.

TABLE 3A.1 Annuity products offered in India

Annuity options	LIC	SBI LIFE – Immediate Annuity	ICICI Prudential – Immediate Annuity	Max New York Life	Bajaj Allianz Life – Pension Guarantee Scheme	Met Life India
Annuity for life	Yes	Yes	Yes	Yes	Yes	Yes
Life annuity with return of purchase price on death of annuitant	Yes	Yes	Yes	Yes	Yes	Yes
Life annuity guaranteed for a term, and then payable for life	Annuity certain for 5/10/15/20 years and after that payable for life	Annuity certain for 5/10/15 years and after that payable for life	Annuity certain for 5/10/15 years and after that payable for life	Annuity certain for 5/10/15/20 years and after that payable for life	Annuity certain for 5/10/15/20 years and after that payable for life	Annuity certain for 5/10/15 years and after that payable for life
Increasing annuity	Annuity increases by 3% every year	Annuity increases by 1%, 2%, or 3% every year	NA	NA	NA	Annuity increases by 3% every year
Joint-Survivor Annuity 1	100% of annuity payable to spouse on death of annuitant	100% of annuity payable to spouse on death of annuitant	100% of annuity payable to spouse on death of annuitant	NA	NA	100% of annuity payable to spouse on death of annuitant
Joint-Survivor Annuity 2	50% of annuity payable to spouse on death of annuitant	50% of annuity payable to spouse on death of annuitant	100% of annuity payable to spouse on death of annuitant, with purchase price returned to nominee after death of spouse	NA	NA	NA

Source: Authors' calculations from several industry sites.

Key challenges for India

India faces several formidable challenges in developing deep and broad annuity markets which can address longevity and related risks in an efficient, equitable, and affordable manner.

Actuarial issues

India is experiencing sustained improvement in longevity, though its speed and extent remains uncertain.[14] Given India's heterogeneity of ethnic and occupational groups, annuity providers face considerable challenges in pricing different annuity products.

One problem is that life insurance companies, the only ones authorized to provide annuities, rely on standardized mortality tables to estimate this variable. The common industry standard is LIC's computation of Ultimate Mortality Rates of Annuitants (1996–8), which has increasingly become unsuitable for the following reasons (see Table 3A.2). Yet the mortality rates used for longevity prediction were calculated nearly a decade ago, and hence they are not up to date. Since then, advances in health facilities, nutrition, and overall income levels have changed, and these are certain to have improved life expectancy at retirement. Furthermore, official mortality statistics are based on mortality patterns of occupational pensioners, who are relatively better-off salaried individuals. They are therefore likely to have higher life expectancies as compared to those not eligible for occupational pensions. Since annuity providers realize that price calculations based on underestimated life expectancies would result in underpriced annuities, they have an incentive to mark up their prices to cover the probability that the annuitant would live considerably longer than predicted.

It is also important to note that the official life tables do not adjust for variations in mortality across population groups such as urban and rural dwellers, unskilled versus highly educated labor, and by sex. For instance, women tend to live longer than men: on attaining 60 years, women have a life expectancy of over 17 years, whereas men are expected to live for only another 15.7 years. Applying uniform rates across persons with different longevity risks distorts the demand for annuities. Workers with low expected longevity will be priced out of the market, thus reducing the number of retirees who voluntarily opt for annuities. And if purchase of annuities is mandatory, there will be a perverse transfer of resources from low-risk (short-lived) to high-risk (long-lived) investors.

Miscalculation of longevity trends can seriously impair profits of life insurance companies if they underestimate longevity, or provide lower than actuarially fair annuity benefits to customers if longevity is overesti-

TABLE 3A.2 Mortality tables and life expectancy calculations for India

Age (years)	Mortality rate	Age (years)	Mortality rate	Age (years)	Mortality rate
20	0.000919	53	0.006058	86	0.115136
21	0.000961	54	0.00673	87	0.123723
22	0.000999	55	0.007401	88	0.132652
23	0.001033	56	0.008069	89	0.141924
24	0.001063	57	0.00871	90	0.151539
25	0.00109	58	0.009397	91	0.161495
26	0.001113	59	0.01013	92	0.171794
27	0.001132	60	0.010907	93	0.182436
28	0.001147	61	0.011721	94	0.193419
29	0.001159	62	0.01175	95	0.204746
30	0.001166	63	0.01212	96	0.216414
31	0.00117	64	0.012833	97	0.228425
32	0.00117	65	0.013889	98	0.240778
33	0.001171	66	0.015286	99	0.253473
34	0.001201	67	0.017026	100	0.266511
35	0.001246	68	0.019109	101	0.279892
36	0.001308	69	0.021534	102	0.293614
37	0.001387	70	0.024301	103	0.307679
38	0.001482	71	0.02741	104	0.322087
39	0.001593	72	0.030862	105	0.336836
40	0.001721	73	0.034656	106	0.351928
41	0.001865	74	0.038793	107	0.367363
42	0.002053	75	0.043272	108	0.383139
43	0.002247	76	0.048093	109	0.399258
44	0.002418	77	0.053257	110	0.41572
45	0.002602	78	0.058763	111	0.432524
46	0.002832	79	0.064611	112	0.44967
47	0.00311	80	0.070802	113	0.467159
48	0.003438	81	0.077335	114	0.484989
49	0.003816	82	0.08421	115	0.503163
50	0.004243	83	0.091428	116	0.521678
51	0.004719	84	0.098988	117	0.540536
52	0.005386	85	0.106891	118	0.559737

Source: Institute of Actuaries of India (2010).

mated. James and Sane (2003) provide empirical evidence on annuity pricing policies by the (then monopoly provider) LIC which used inappropriate mortality tables and did not sufficiently anticipate the interest rate declines of 2001–2. They estimate that the money's worth ratio (MWR), defined as the ratio of the expected discounted flow of annuity benefits divided by initial capital invested, fell from over 1 to between 0.8 and 0.9 for new annuity purchasers in 2002–3.

More robust and disaggregated mortality and morbidity data would enable better price discovery in the annuities market, particularly based on the mortality and claim experiences of LIC as well as private insurers over a recent time period.[15] Such tables, regarded in other countries as a public good, could be made widely and easily accessible to all stakeholders, including researchers. In such an event, MWR analysis could be regularly conducted and publicized.

Distribution channels for annuities

The marketing and distribution of annuities, like all insurance products, depends heavily on insurance agents. Individual agents in India procured 72 percent of the total new life business premiums in 2007–8; corporate agents (such as banks) distributed about 11 percent; and brokers and direct selling accounted for the remaining (IRDA 2008). Individual agents are a critical customer interface point for the insurance industry, and they play a key role in influencing the final purchase decision, especially for individual life and pension policies. Therefore, they need to be trained to disseminate knowledge about the benefits of annuities.

The present incentive structure for agents is often skewed in favor of non-annuity insurance products. A life insurance agent earns a commission of 2 percent of the initial amount on a single premium annuity product. On annuities with periodic premium payments, the commissions allowed are 7.5 percent of premiums paid in the first year and 5 percent of premiums paid in subsequent years. By contrast, a typical whole life endowment policy enables an agent to earn a premium of 25 percent of the first year's premium; 7.5 percent of the second and third year's premiums paid; and 5 percent thereafter until maturity. The large differential in commissions earned increases the insurance agent's incentive to promote non-annuity products.

A solution to this anomaly need not lie in increasing commissions; indeed, this would ultimately increase costs to the annuitant. Instead what would be more efficient is the development of low-cost, technology-intensive distribution channels. For instance, an initiative to restructure India Post, which has a countrywide presence, would help it act as an efficient distribution channel for a wide variety of financial products including annuities. Of course, this would also require the organizational restructuring and technological upgrading of the management information systems of this enterprise.

Establishment of other distribution channels will further develop the market. For instance, multilevel marketing processes or internet-based sales could be developed as additional distribution models (Pejawar 2008). The concept of 'telcassurance,' or selling insurance through telecom distribution channels, can also be adopted for the annuity product space. In this setting, the range of possible annuity sellers would include high-end company-owned exclusive telecom franchises, smaller telecom stores, and neighborhood shops in rural and semi-urban areas.[16] The development of several distribution channels could help enhance annuity penetration, improve awareness of retirement-financing instruments, and facilitate competition.

As annuity markets grow, it may also be useful to set up a national electronic system for comparing standardized annuity rate quotations from different providers. India's experience with nationwide electronic platforms for the National Stock Exchange of India resulted in enhanced transparency and lowering of trading costs, and this may provide a good precedent for annuity markets. For instance, an electronic bidding system for annuity quotes operates successfully in Chile, and it allows individuals to make more informed choices.[17]

Phased or programmed withdrawals

Annuity-like products such as phased withdrawals could also be developed by the industry. A typical phased withdrawal product involves accumulated sums invested in an individual retirement account that are withdrawn periodically over a number of years (typically 15–20). Unlike annuities, under a programmed withdrawal arrangement, the funds are not transferred into a common risk pool. This option is particularly attractive to those with relatively small balances (in the Indian context, less than INR 5 lakh capital sum in 2007 prices) and for those who do not anticipate a long life in retirement. Phased withdrawal products could be a possible investment option for the lump sum portion of saving accumulated under the NPS. Phased withdrawal arrangements could also be incorporated into the design of small saving schemes.[18] Allowing phased withdrawals is feasible in Chile, where at retirement, individuals must opt either for an annuity or a programmed (phased) withdrawal. In that case, about two-thirds of workers chose to annuitize, and phased withdrawals are more prevalent among workers with lower incomes and saving.[19] Nevertheless, such a phased withdrawal scheme requires careful design to ensure that the purchasers do not outlive their retirement savings. The design would also need to address concerns of the tax authority that consumers do not excessively defer withdrawal to avoid taxes.[20]

A multipler social security system could assist in addressing the possibility that phased withdrawals may end even while the person requires retirement support. India could strengthen social pensions and social assistance schemes accessed by the elderly poor to address this issue. India may also consider developing annuity products which could be repriced with different risk-sharing mechanisms between the annuity purchasers, providers, and the government. Additionally, reverse mortgage products that permit retirees to access the equity in their housing may also merit consideration. A commercial bank in India has introduced a reverse mortgage loan annuity (RMLA) product, which combines annuity with simple reverse mortgage and thereby addresses longevity risk. To date, however, the response in India has been relatively limited.

Inflation risk

Annuity payouts may continue for twenty years or more after retirement, and if they are fixed in nominal terms, inflation may lead to a steady erosion of value. Increasing longevity compounds the cumulative impact of even low inflation rates.[21] Inflation losses are particularly damaging for retirees because they may not be able to make up by increasing their earnings or saving power.

Current annuity options in India only partially address such inflation risks. For instance, SBI Life offers payouts with annual increments of 1, 2, or 3 percent, but since inflation is usually much higher, these do not fully hedge this risk. To date, annuity suppliers have been averse to issuing inflation-indexed annuities because of the absence of inflation hedges in the market. The complete absence of indexed instruments may create incentives for annuity providers to hedge against inflation by investing in riskier assets such as real estate, equity, or high-return derivatives; or charge higher rates for taking on inflation risk. To develop better inflation-linked products, it would be helpful for indexed bonds to be issued by the Reserve Bank of India. Such bonds do, however, shift the risk of unanticipated inflation to society at large which then manifests as contingent fiscal liability.

Market risks

This refers to the possibility of earning lower-than-expected returns due to adverse changes in asset prices (interest rates, exchange rates, equity prices, real estate prices) than expected, during the term of the products. Annuities are long-term financial instruments and are consequently subject to higher market risk than short duration products. In our view, the most challenging issue for annuity underwriters is to match annuity-related liabilities with an appropriate pool of long-term investments. In India, however, most annuity payouts tend to be fixed and guaranteed at purchase, so annuity providers invest predominantly in long-term corporate bonds and government securities.

An adequate supply of bonds, both government and corporate, with longer term maturities (at least fifteen years) would be necessary to address asset–liability mismatches of annuity issuers in India.[22] As the long-term debt market is limited to infrequent issues of long-term government debt, insurance companies that sell life annuities are substantially invested in assets with maturities lower than their future annuity liabilities. As a result, annuity providers are exposed to reinvestment risk, and are likely to safeguard their position by assigning a higher pricing to annuities.

The mandatory annuitization regulation of NPS will result in a steep growth in demand for annuities in the future as the present cohort of members reach retirement. As a result, disproportionate proportions of liabilities of the life insurance companies in India would be in the form of annuity products. To avoid asset–liability mismatch, asset portfolios would need to be adjusted accordingly. Thus, the creation of a large pool of long-term assets, at least partly indexed to inflation, would be critical to sustain the growth of annuities.

It is also worth noting that the global economic crisis has increased the market risk of annuities. In particular, the steep decline in Indian equity markets[23] has emphasized the need for insurance companies to find alternative investment avenues that can provide sustained returns commensurate with those historically obtained from equities.

Annuitization age

Annuity returns are a function of prevailing interest rates at the time of annuity purchase, which in turn depend on the macroeconomy. Thus, two persons retiring at different times with the same accumulated savings may earn different returns from the same annuity scheme interest rates. If the purchase of annuities at the time of retirement is to be made mandatory, then annuitants will forfeit the option to defer the purchase of annuities until rates are favorable. This provision may significantly reduce the incomes available to those who retire during periods of economic downturns and low interest rates.

So as to mitigate this risk, retirees could be permitted to hold the annuity portion in their retirement accounts until market conditions are favorable; and compulsorily annuitize by, say, the age of 70.[24] However, retirees are likely to need professional advice on timing the market; the Pension Fund

Regulatory and Development Authority (PFRDA) will have to play an important role in educating and guiding investors particularly in the early stages of development of the annuities market.

Financial education and literacy

The need for financial education and retirement planning information for investors as well as pension advisors, distributors, and employers is critical.[25] PFRDA and IRDA, in association with employers and insurance companies, must ensure that annuity purchasers have access to information about the benefits and costs of different schemes and providers. Improved financial literacy has been observed to lead to greater participation as well as higher average saving in other countries.[26]

Conclusion

In this chapter, we have argued that India will need to develop wider and deeper annuity markets to more satisfactorily address longevity and other risks during the retirement period. Rapid population aging and rising life expectancies will lead to potentially huge demand for conventional annuity and annuity-like products such as programmed withdrawal and conversion of housing equity into retirement income. As the formal sector grows, where long-term employer–employee relationships are prevalent, pension formation will increase. Mandatory annuitization under the NPS Scheme could boost demand for annuities. Consequently, while India's annuity market is currently small, it is expected to grow rapidly.

Nevertheless, there are several key challenges that must be tackled to enhance the market's functioning. More mortality and morbidity data on a disaggregated basis are required to price annuity type products more accurately and flexibly for different groups. Greater innovation in both products and distribution channels would reduce transaction costs and accommodate different risk preferences. If annuities are to be mandated, it would be useful to make the age for annuitization flexible, so as to mitigate the impact of macroeconomic cycles. And last, but surely not least, there is a great need for better financial education and literacy so people better understand how to save for retirement and decumulate their assets in old age. India will be better able to address these challenges if the number and variety of players specializing in different segments of the insurance industry grows substantially. Further, insurance regulation would benefit by becoming more robust and transparent, benchmarked to best-practice international standards.

Notes

[1] The population projections cited herein were made for two different assumptions of the future total fertility rate (TFR). Scenario A assumes that states with higher current TFRs would decline to the 'replacement level' of 2.1 children, and Scenario B assumes that the TFR will decline to 1.85 children, close to the levels observed in states such as Kerala. Both scenarios are consistent with the goal of India's National Population Policy 2000, that fertility will decline to the point where, on an average, there are two children per family. Our chapter relies on data for Scenario B and hence projections are more optimistic (Population Reference Bureau 2008).

[2] The Population Reference Bureau (2008) projects that the proportion of population aged 65 or older will exceed the proportion of population under age 15 by 2041 in Kerala and by 2051 in Tamil Nadu.

[3] This is based on an extrapolation of Census data.

[4] A significant minority of these workers will, however, be lifetime poor and hence will need to rely on social assistance programs whose effectiveness and viability will depend on fiscal position as well as the efficient delivery of government services.

[5] The issue of whether NPS should contain mandatory annuitization provision is discussed later in the chapter.

[6] A detailed explanation of types of annuities and the benefits of each, as well as factors affecting annuities, is available from the Pension Annuity Advisory Service at http://www.pension-annuity.co.uk/

[7] This data has to be interpreted carefully. When a consumer buys a pension product, he buys an accumulation product and it is counted as 'pension'. When this pension product vests, there being no guarantees and with the possibility of the annuity provider being different, it is counted as annuity.

[8] Data on the number of annuities outstanding is currently not available in India.

[9] Most pension plans do not require participants to annuitize the entire corpus; instead, upon vesting, the participant has the option to withdraw part of the proceeds as a lump sum.

[10] These are vital as women as a group live longer but have lower exposure (and remuneration) from labor market activities.

[11] Table 3A.1 highlights some of the annuity products offered by a sample of insurance companies in India.

[12] The compulsory annuities market is estimated to be ten times the size of the voluntary annuities market. The profile of a typical annuitant in the two markets is vastly different: a purchaser of a voluntary annuity is likely to be female and around 70 years of age whereas the average compulsory market annuity purchaser would be male and around 65 years (Cannon and Tonks 2006).

[13] The bequest motive has been addressed by annuities that offer that option of returning the initial principal to a nominee. For instance, ICICI Prudential offers an annuity plan in which the initial purchase price, or the value of the investment corpus at the end of the accumulation phase with which the annuity

was purchased, is returned to the annuitant's nominee on the death of the annuitant.

[14] This tends to make life insurers price annuities conservatively. For example, calculations based on LIC's mortality table show that the implied life expectancy at age 60 is about 20 years, but Census extrapolations indicate that it is 19 years (Table 3A.2).

[15] Recent reports indicate that The Mortality and Morbidity Investigating Centre, an affiliate of the Institute of Actuaries of India (IAI) and the Life Insurance Council, is in the process of generating new and improved mortality and morbidity tables (Hindu Business Line 2009).

[16] Asthana (2009) points out that telecom dealers tend to be entrepreneurs with sound selling skills and have a fairly large prospect base of customers. In small towns, their influence may be significant.

[17] The concept of using electronic platforms to disseminate information about annuity rates has already been adopted successfully in Chile. The *sistema de consultas y ofertas de montos de pensión* or 'SCOMP' system allows prospective annuity buyers to send a quote into the system through the pension fund, insurance company, or agent. The system transmits the quote to annuity suppliers, and their response is sent back to the purchaser, who can choose an annuity offer, make a new quote, opt out of annuitization, or ask for an external quote (see Mitchell and Ruiz 2011).

[18] For instance, some senior citizens' saving schemes could be designed with phased withdrawals at the payout stage (Asher and Vasudevan [2008] discuss reforms for small savers).

[19] Some fear that a disproportionate share of liabilities of life insurance companies in Chile is in the form of annuities; this would mean that their asset–liability matching would differ considerably from that of an average life insurance company.

[20] A typical phased withdrawal design suggested by industry veterans is:

1. Divide the purchase price by the then expectation of life. This is the maximum withdrawal that can be allowed. The minimum would be around 30 percent of the maximum. The annuitant can withdraw within these limits.
2. In Year 2, divide the balance amount by the then expectation of life and repeat the process outlined in Step 1.
3. This continues till the annuitant is 80/65, when conventional annuity is purchased with balance amount.

[21] Barr and Diamond (2008) point out that even with 2 percent annual inflation, the real value of a nominal benefit after ten years is only 82 percent of its original value, and only two-thirds after twenty years.

[22] In 2008–9, the maturity profile of Central Government debt securities was skewed toward shorter term debt. Of the total outstanding stock of government securities, 26 percent had less than five years to maturity, 40 percent had between five and ten years, and only 34 percent of securities had more than ten years left

to maturity as at end-March 2009 (Reserve Bank of India 2009). This suggests that reinvestment risk is currently significant for annuity providers.

[23] The BSE Sensex lost about 55 percent of its value between January 2008 and January 2009.

[24] This is the practice in the United Kingdom where the purchase of annuities is no longer mandated, though retirees have strong tax incentives to annuitize their pension fund by the age of 75 years.

[25] In the course of research for this chapter, it was observed that some private insurance companies in India have well-designed websites that provide very useful information, and knowledge available extends beyond details of schemes on offer. Topics such as the need for and benefits of retirement planning and features of different types of annuities are discussed, and online tools for simulation of life insurance premiums and payouts are provided. Other insurance companies might consider upgrading their web pages to facilitate consumer knowledge in a similar manner.

[26] In the United States, for instance, company-sponsored education has been found to improve participation as well as saving.

References

Akerlof, George (1970). 'The Market for Lemons: Qualitative Uncertainty and the Market Mechanism,' *Quarterly Journal of Economics*, 84(3): 488–500.

Asher, Mukul G. and Deepa Vasudevan (2008). 'Lessons for Asian Countries from Pension Reforms in Chile.' PIE Discussion Paper No.381. Tokyo, Japan: Hitotsubashi University.

—— Savita Shankar (2007). 'Time to Mainstream Micro-Pensions in India,' *Pravartak*, 2(3): 95–102.

Asthana, Nitish (2009). 'The Next Frontier,' *IRDA Journal*, 7(5): 14–17.

Barr, Nicholas and Peter Diamond (2008). *Reforming Pensions: Principles and Policy Choices*. London, UK: Oxford University Press.

Cannon, Edmund and Ian Tonks (2006). 'Survey of Annuity Pricing.' Research Report No. 318. Norwich, UK: Department of Work and Pensions.

Central Intelligence Agency (2009). *World Factbook*. Washington, DC: Central Intelligence Agency. https://www.cia.gov/library/publications/the-world-factbook/geos/in.html

Hindu Business Line (2009). 'New Table for Mortality Rates to be Finalized Soon,' *The Hindu Business Line*, June 13, 2009.

Institute of Actuaries of India (IAI) (2010). *Published Mortality Tables*. Mumbai, India: Institute of Actuaries of India. http://www.actuariesindia.org/Publication%20and%20Library%20Facility/Publication/mort_annuity_04.html

Insurance Regulatory and Development Authority (IRDA) (2008). *Annual Report 2007–08*. New Delhi, India: Insurance Regulatory and Development Authority.

——(2010). *Indian Insurance Industry*. New Delhi, India: Insurance Regulatory and Development Authority.

International Labor Organization (ILO) (2008). *Global Employment Trends*. Geneva, Switzerland: International Labor Organization.

James, Estelle and Renuka Sane (2003). 'Annuity Markets In India: What are the Key Public Policy Issues?' *Economic and Political Weekly*, 38(8): 729–39.

Mitchell, Olivia S. and Jose Ruiz (2011). 'Pension Payouts in Chile: Past, Present, and Future Prospects,' in O.S. Mitchell and J. Piggott, eds., *Revisiting Retirement Payouts: Market Developments and Policy Issues*. Oxford: Oxford University Press.

Office of the Registrar General (2001). *Census of India 2001*. New Delhi, India: Office of the Registrar General. http://www.censusindia.net/

Pejawar, A. (2008). 'Distribution Channels.' Paper presented at 2008 Insurance Summit. Pune, India: National Insurance Academy.

Population Reference Bureau (2008). *The Future Population of India: A Long Range Demographic View*. New Delhi, India: Population Reference Bureau. http://www.popfound.org/Population%20Projection%20PFI_PRB.pdf

Reserve Bank of India (2009). *Annual Report*. New Delhi, India: Reserve Bank of India. http://rbi.org.in/scripts/AnnualReportPublications.aspx?year = 2009

Swiss RE (2007). *Annuities: A Private Solution to Longevity Risk*. Zurich, Switzerland: Swiss RE. http://media.swissre.com/documents/sigma3_2007_en.pdf

United Nations Population Fund (2008). *World Population Prospects: The 2008 Revision Population Database*. New York, NY: United Nations Population Fund. http://esa.un.org/unpp/

——(2009). *State of World Population 2009*. New York, NY: United Nations Population Fund. http://www.unfpa.org/webdav/site/global/shared/swp/englishswop09.pdf

Chapter 4

Annuities and their Derivatives: The Recent Canadian Experience

Moshe A. Milevsky and Ling-wu Shao

This chapter examines the market for income annuities, broadly defined, in the Canadian marketplace. We begin with a survey of the Canadian single premium immediate annuity (SPIA) marketplace and describe the types of SPIA products available, who sells them, and the size of the market. Next, we briefly discuss the tax motivation for buying SPIA products and how the tax treatment differs from that in the United States, a nontrivial distinction. Subsequently, we discuss the money's worth ratios (MWRs) of Canadian SPIA products, and specifically how their quoted prices reacted during the 2007/8 financial and credit crisis. We also describe the Guaranteed Lifetime Withdrawal Benefit (GLWB) product recently introduced in Canada. The product was imported from the US market (where they are known as variable annuities) and grew to a billion-dollar market within a few months. We also offer some suggestions on the optimal allocation to these products and some concluding thoughts.

The Canadian single premium immediate annuity marketplace

The Canadian SPIA market consists of up to twenty active insurance companies, most of whom operate as both life insurance and annuities providers in Canada;[1] they are a subset of the 100 or so life and health insurers licensed to operate within Canada. At any one time, only around a dozen or so of these companies tend to offer quotes on a broad range of SPIAs. Some of these companies have dropped in and out of the market over time as well as in and out of offering certain SPIA products over time. The overall size of the Canadian annuity market is sizeable, accounting for over 30 billion dollars of total premiums received in 2007 by the Canadian Life and Health insurance industry; only a fraction of these are SPIAs, that is, the income version of annuities (CLHIA 2009).

Standard Canadian SPIA prices (as reported by CANNEX Financial Exchanges, the source of our database) are quoted in the form of a nominal monthly payment for the length of the annuity purchaser's life that is exchanged for an upfront premium payment of $100,000. For example, on July 19, 2000, the SPIA quote by Canada Life for a 55-year-old Canadian male was $624.96. This means that a 55-year-old Canadian male could pay Canada Life $100,000 on that date, in exchange for receiving a continuous stream of monthly payments of $624.96 for as long as he remains alive. This is the standard life-only annuity. Our database for the Canadian SPIA market also provides SPIA values for a wide range of guaranteed periods. Thus, a guaranteed period for a given SPIA will stipulate the number of years that the SPIA must make its stated monthly payment (perhaps to a beneficiary), even if its holder is no longer alive. Canadian SPIAs are typically quoted for ages 55–80 at five-year intervals (ages 55, 60, 65, 70, 75, and 80) and for guaranteed periods of zero to twenty-five years also at five-year intervals (0, 5, 10, 15, 20, and 25 guaranteed years). Canadian providers stopped offering SPIAs with guaranteed periods past age 90 around the middle of 2002, due to regulatory changes. We emphasize that most SPIAs currently offered and sold in Canada are in nominal terms and are not indexed to inflation, so they leave buyers exposed to inflation risk. (One can obtain real quotes, in addition to other variations like impaired annuities, on special request directly from a limited number of insurance companies.)

In general, the quoted monthly payments for SPIAs increase with age, decrease with the length of the guaranteed period, and are lower for females. For instance, a quote for a 55-year old will be in the range of $500–600 per month, while a quote for an 80-year old will be in the range of $800–1200 per month. The drop in monthly payments as the guaranteed period increases by five years can range from as low as a few dollars for younger ages to upward of over $100 for older ages. The Canadian SPIA market is fairly competitive with a spread smaller than in some other markets: the spread between the highest and lowest quotes in our database is no more than 20 percent and can often at times be 5 percent.

In Canada, as in the United States and other countries, income annuities can be purchased using money from either registered (i.e., tax sheltered) retirement funds[2] or non-registered funds. For annuities purchased from a registered fund, where the proceeds used have not yet been subject to taxation, the annuity income is taxed as regular income and is taxable in the year that the payment is received. This is the same as in the United States, where annuity payments once received are taxed as regular current income if the annuity was purchased with funds from a qualified pension plan or IRA-funding vehicle since these are after-tax dollars.

For annuities purchased with non-registered funds, the tax treatment depends on whether the annuity is prescribed (on a cash basis) or non-prescribed (on an accrual basis). For prescribed annuities, taxation of interest income is not subject to accrual (a larger portion of the annuity payment is counted as interest income in earlier years). Instead, the total expected interest to be earned over the life of the annuity is spread evenly over all payments and taxed by calendar year. For non-prescribed annuities, taxation of interest income is subject to accrual and the annuity purchaser is provided a tax slip for the taxable interest portion of all payments received in a policy year. This differs from the United States, where all annuities purchased with after-tax dollars are taxed based on an exclusion ratio and recovery of basis format. Under this format, the US annuity holder must subject a portion of every annuity payment once received to taxation as current income based on the exclusion ratio which is determined by the ratio of the basis (initial premium paid) of the annuity over the expected value of annuity. Once the annuity holder has recovered the entire basis for his annuity through annuity payments, any remaining payments are taxed entirely as regular income. The tax treatment of US non-qualified annuities is discussed in Brown et al. (1999), where they compute after-tax MWRs as well.

In Canada, the tax treatment for prescribed annuities is more favorable, though two main differences exist between qualifying for prescribed and non-prescribed status. To qualify for prescribed tax status, the annuity must be level (not indexed) and must be owned by the same individual who is to receive the annuity payments (this excludes corporations from being the owner of the annuity). Hence, non-prescribed status must be applied if the individual wishes to obtain an annuity with non-level payments (indexing of any kind, accelerated annuities, and/or annuities with additional medical benefit payments), or he wishes the annuity to be held in ownership by a corporation. For annuities purchased with non-registered funds, the tax treatment of annuities provides the advantage of deferred taxation on interest income. This advantage does not carry through to annuities purchased with registered or qualified funds as interest income on these funds is already subject to deferred taxation.[3]

Canadian money's worth ratios from 2000 to 2009

The concept of an MWR for annuities was first introduced by Friedman and Warshawsky (1988) to measure how much value an annuity provides, in relation to its cost. It is defined precisely as the expected present discounted value of the payout stream of an annuity, divided by its present-day premium cost. Mitchell et al. (1999) estimated that the MWR for US annuities was approximately 70–90 percent of the premiums paid, depending on the year (1985, 1990, or 1995), the yield curve applied (treasury or corporate), and whether population or annuitant mortality rates were used. While this might be seen as showing that annuities were not a good investment, since they returned on average less than similarly riskless or low-risk investments, the authors further showed that, because annuities provide insurance against longevity risk, they may still be desired by the public despite this deep discount. Higher MWRs were discovered in the United Kingdom by Murthi et al. (1999), of around 88–90 percent according to population mortality tables and around 95–97 percent according to annuitant pool mortality tables. More recent studies have concluded that annuity MWRs are often quite high, and even close to 100 percent when assessed using a risk-free yield curve, as in James and Vittas (2001) and James and Song (2002). Cannon and Tonks (2004) use a very long time series of UK annuity data from 1957–2002 and also show historical MWRs close to 100 percent. Fong (2002) and Fong et al. (2010) report that the MWR of annuities in Singapore is around 100 percent. Doyle et al. (2004) found that the MWR of annuities is close to 95 percent for both Singapore and Australia. Similarly, Gaudecker and Weber (2004), Thorburn et al. (2007), and Ruiz and Mitchell (2011) discover that MWRs are close to 100 percent for Germany and Chile.

To examine the value of SPIA products on offer in the Canadian marketplace, we calculate the MWRs for an average across annuity providers of quotes from mid-2000 to mid-2009 (see also Shao 2010). Specifically, we construct pretax MWRs using the Canadian risk-free zero-coupon government treasury yield curve provided by the Bank of Canada, together with mortality rates projected for the annuitant population by the Society of Actuaries (1996 US annuity 2000 tables with Projection Scale AA). The annuity quotes are obtained from a CANNEX annuity database which compiles private annuities quotes across Canada for annuities purchased out of registered funds.

Figure 4.1 shows the MWRs over time calculated for an average of annuity providers on annuities sold to 65-year-old males and females with no guaranteed periods. From these we can see that during most of the 2000–2009 period, the MWRs (for both sexes) were fairly stable, but during the later period – when the financial crisis of 2007/8 occurred – the MWRs spiked. The spike started around 2007 and peaked around 2008; it was coming back down as of early 2009 (the very end of the time window), although it was still significantly above pre-2007 levels. Figure 4.1 also shows that Canadian MWRs calculated using the risk-free treasury yield curve, roughly around 100–105 percent, are consistent with the more recent studies of MWR across the globe. This implies that annuity providers are either barely making any money or losing money selling annuities.

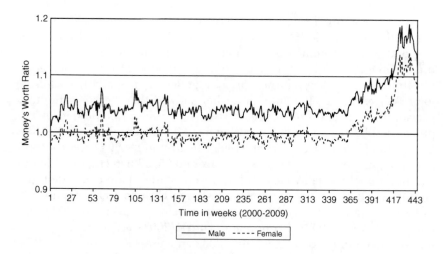

Figure 4.1 Money's worth ratio (MWR) for annuities purchased at age 65 with no guaranteed periods. *Source*: Authors' calculations; see text.

Naturally, this cannot persist for long, so it must be the case that the insurers are assuming an asset return of something greater than the risk-free rate; consequently, this implies they are investing in riskier assets than riskless government debt.

To take into account the more realistic investing behavior of annuity providers, Mitchell et al. (1999) recalculated annuity MWRs using an upward-shifted yield curve which they term the corporate yield curve. Following this methodology, we also recalculate our MWRs using a Canadian risk-free treasury curve shifted up by 178 basis points for all maturities, to account for the monthly historical bond yield difference (estimated 1952–2009) between high-grade corporate bonds (BAA corporate bonds) and riskless government bonds (ten-year US treasuries). Figure 4.2 graphs the MWRs in Figure 4.1 using this upwardly shifted treasury curve. The results show that accounting for higher yielding (but still fairly safe) high-grade corporate bond investments raises the MWRs to more believable levels of 85–90 percent (believable in the sense that annuity providers will then not lose money by selling annuities). More importantly, Figure 4.2 confirms the MWR patterns over time in Figure 4.1. Thus, during most of 2000–2009, the MWRs are fairly stable but then they spike up dramatically during the crisis of 2007–8, with the spike starting around 2007, peaking around 2008. Again, it comes back down as of early 2009, albeit not back to pre-2007 levels.

The spiking of the MWR during the financial crisis of 2007–8 is a result of the fact that annuity providers did not adjust their annuity quotes, on

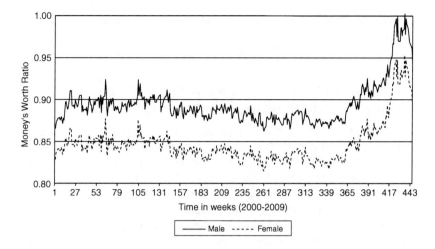

Figure 4.2 Adjusted money's worth ratio (MWR) for annuities purchased at age 65 with no guaranteed periods. *Source:* Authors' calculations; see text.

average, to compensate for the dramatic downward movement in the risk-free zero-coupon yield curve. This occurred during the 2007–8 financial crisis, during which the Canadian government lowered interest rates to combat the aftereffects of the crisis. A closer look at the individual annuity quotes offered by companies from 2000 to 2009 suggests that, while annuity providers did downwardly adjust annuity quotes over time to compensate in part for improvements in mortality over time, annuity quotes stayed surprisingly flat during the 2007–9 time window despite the fact that the interest rate environment changed dramatically. This revelation suggests that either the funding vehicles used by the SPIA providers were not very sensitive to changes in the risk-free yield curve or that the annuity industry by and large ignored the fallout from the 2007–8 financial crisis. In other words, if the Canadian SPIA industry is not basing long-term asset returns on the risk-free yield curve, it runs the danger of underfunding like many pension funds around the world.

To sum up thus far, there are two main takeaways from our analysis of the Canadian SPIA market. First, the MWRs of Canadian SPIAs represent a fairly good deal for the annuity purchaser. Should the annuity purchaser believe that his annuity payments are indeed risk-free, the SPIA with an MWR of around 100 percent (when evaluated with the risk-free government treasury yield curve) represents a very competitive investment compared to similar risk-free government bonds. Second, the MWRs' patterns for Canadian SPIAs over the 2007–8 financial crisis are a worrying sign of the future health of Canadian SPIA providers, in that it suggests annuity providers could be facing significant risk of underfunding their liabilities.

The introduction of the guaranteed lifetime withdrawal benefit product in Canada

The Guaranteed Lifetime Withdrawal Benefit (GLWB) annuity was introduced to Canada in late 2007 by Manulife Financial (the parent company of John Hancock in the United States), which at the time was the largest insurance company in Canada based on market capitalization. The initial GLWB product was modeled on the variable annuity (VA) design in the United States. VAs in the United States were initially marketed and promoted for the favorable tax treatment and death-guarantees they enjoyed. Over time, these products moved to include riders with features of minimum income stream investors could receive, and these features became critical selling points on their own.

Essentially, a GLWB rider allows investors to lock in a minimal income for life – like a SPIA or deferred income annuity – without tying up or surrendering their capital irreversibly (Milevsky and Salisbury 2006). Thus, they provide savers with (some of) the retirement longevity protection of a traditional annuity, without forcing them to surrender upside potential or liquidity. The best way to think of them is as a mutual fund with a complex path-dependent put option that allows for a minimal withdrawal. Obviously, the guaranteed withdrawal level is (much) less than what a SPIA would have offered, otherwise there would be blatant arbitrage opportunities for individuals.

Here is a synopsis of the mechanics. The individual policyholder (in the pure case, a pensionless retiree) deposits or rolls over a sum of money into an investment portfolio which is then allocated (usually by the individual) into a number of subaccounts that contain stocks, bonds, and other generic investments. The portfolio then grows (or shrinks) over time, depending on the performance of the underlying investments. Any capital gains are tax-deferred and eventually treated as ordinary income (note that in Canada there is no tax deferral of gains). Then, at some future date, usually under the control of the policyholder, the annuitant can start taking guaranteed withdrawals from the account. We think of this income like a systematic withdrawal plan (SWiP) at a nominal (i.e., not inflation-adjusted) nondecreasing level. The income is guaranteed to never decline for the remaining life of the annuitant (and his spouse in the case of a joint product). Thus, in contrast to a SWiP, if the underlying investment portfolio (a.k.a. account value) ever reached zero, the guaranteed income would continue, as long as one member of the couple lives.

The guaranteed withdrawal rate is determined by the company issuing the GLWB at the time of sale. The guarantee *amount* is the product of multiplying a guaranteed *rate* by the guaranteed *base*, determined at the point of first withdrawal. In the case of the current offering of Canadian products, the rate is between 4 and 6 percent, depending on the age at initial withdrawal. Moreover, if the investment portfolio happens to grow even while undergoing these withdrawals, the guaranteed base might reset to a higher level and hence generate even greater withdrawals. As far as estate values are concerned, upon the second death, whatever is left over in the account goes to the heirs, with the requisite tax implications (and depending on whether the GLWB was inside a tax shelter).

GLWBs as described earlier exist in a variety of alternative formats, and they are often bundled with an array of other guarantees, ratchets, or step-ups linked to death benefits and life insurance. But specifics aside, the basic GLWB guarantees that some withdrawals will continue for life, regardless of whether the underlying account has the funds to support them. In other words, fees and periodic withdrawals are deducted from the VA account, as long as there are funds available. But if those periodic withdrawals ever fully deplete this account, the underwriter steps in and pays for the remaining withdrawals over the lifetime of the investor. Thus, it will convert into a pure income annuity or SPIA if the account is ever depleted.

The periodic withdrawals provide downside protection, but there is still upside potential for the underlying account to grow if markets perform well. The investor preserves liquidity, since the underlying account value may be withdrawn at any time (less any surrender charges). Unlike a traditional income annuity, if the investor dies, his or her heirs will inherit the remaining account value.

As of early 2010, the large majority of these sales in Canada (also known as segregated funds) now include GLWB riders, which anecdotally have become central to the sales pitch and a key reason that consumers purchase this product. To the insurance companies manufacturing the new generation of VAs, these are viewed as a private sector replacement for defined benefit pensions, in an increasingly defined contribution world. Whether or not the GLWB is better than SPIAs from the consumer's perspective depends on the relationship between the pricing of the guarantee, the retiree's optimal consumption strategy, and the existence of bequest motives. Below, we make the case that it is often optimal to devote some retirement wealth to these instruments.

In sum, the latest generation of (what used to be expensive tax-deferred) VA contracts has been financially engineered to provide an assortment of lifetime income guarantees intended to protect the policyholder against what the industry has coined the 'sequence of returns risk' and 'longevity risk'. These refer to the chance that a retirement portfolio from which cash is being withdrawn suffers early losses and the retiree lives longer than average. The common denominator of all these insurance riders is that they contain an implicit put option on financial markets, plus some form of longevity insurance akin to a pure life annuity. Of course, using the concept of the put–call parity, these can also be viewed as call options to annuitize at some variable strike price. The (anecdotal) sales 'pitch' for these products revolves around the idea that these guarantees should induce investors to take on more financial risk than they normally would if they did not have these guarantees. Evidence of this is provided by Milevsky and KyryChencko (2008).

The longevity-put can be selected (or not) when the VA policy is initially purchased. This rider gives the holder the ability to annuitize some minimally guaranteed amount at some contractually guaranteed rate. Thus, for example, if a $10,000 premium is placed into a VA, the insurance company might guarantee that at least $15,000 can be received for life, starting in ten years. The purchase price (or annuity factor) would be specified within the contract; for example, $20 per dollar of lifetime income. So, essentially, this contract would guarantee a life annuity of at least $15,000/$20 = $750 per year in the worst-case scenario. And, if the market value of the (subaccounts within the) VA is worth more than guaranteed $15,000 in ten years time, the policyholder can withdraw at the (greater) market value. As of mid-2009, several companies offer GLWB products in Canada including Empire Life, Desjardins Financial, Industrial Alliance, Manulife Financial, SunLife Finance, and Canada Life. Table 4.1 provides a table illustrating the most important dimensions along which GLWB products can differ from each other.

As noted earlier, questions then arise regarding how much of his wealth the consumer should optimally allocate to these products. For instance, how much of the retiree's nest egg should be invested in an annuity product versus regular mutual funds? What proportion, if any, of a portfolio should be allocated to a VA with a GLWB? Or what if the consumer seeks to figure out at what age she should purchase an annuity or begin lifetime income on an existing VA product? These are definitely not portfolio asset allocation questions, but rather they are what we term product allocation issues which have not received sufficient attention from academics and practitioners to date. For this reason, it may be useful to explore the product allocation aspects of retirement income planning, as they pertain to the allocation between basic SPIA products and GLWBs.

We think of this issue as an optimization problem along a frontier that is defined by the trade-off between sustainability and bequest, and review the products to generate income during retirement that are available for client portfolios. Conceptually one can group the entire universe of retirement income-generating products into three distinct 'silos'. In the first silo, we place traditional mutual funds, exchange traded funds (ETFs), separately

TABLE 4.1 Typical guaranteed lifetime withdrawal benefit (GLWB) product features

Product feature	Options
Minimum single premium initial deposit	Ranges from $5,000 to $100,000
Investment asset allocation options	Complete flexibility to select any funds or restricted model portfolios
Highest allowable equity/risk exposure	Ranges from 50 to 95%
Total maximum (investment + insurance) fees	Anywhere from 1 to 5%
Phantom interest credit to guaranteed base	Ranges from 0 to 10%
Earliest timing of guaranteed withdrawals	Immediately to ten years
Guaranteed early withdrawal rate at age 62	Ranges from 4 to 6%
Guaranteed late withdrawal rate at age 77	Ranges from 5 to 8%
Frequency of guaranteed base value reset	Annual, quarterly, monthly, daily
Ability to increase withdrawal rate with age	Some products offer increasing bands
Inflation or COLA for guaranteed income	Most do not
Credit strength of entity issuing guarantee	Anywhere from A to AAA

Note: Some products imposed a surrender charge on excess withdrawals.

Source: Authors' calculations; see text.

managed accounts, and other conventional accumulation-based instruments. They contain no bells, no whistles, and no guarantees. From these, retirement income is generated by periodically selling an appropriate number of units; one can think of this as reverse dollar cost averaging (DCA), otherwise known as a SWiP. There is no longevity insurance or downside protection.

A second set of products include defined benefit pensions and income annuity products, including variable, fixed, and inflation-adjusted payments that offer a lifetime income at a very cheap economic price. In this silo, too, there are no bells or whistles, but high mortality credits come at the cost of complete irreversibility and loss of liquidity. We label anything in this silo a lifetime payout income annuity (LPiA). This is the traditional longevity insurance addressed in many research articles. And in the third silo, we place all of the remaining financially engineered products that are not-quite-pensions and not-quite-SWiPs. These are the protected investments and longevity-put options, including, of course, VAs with GLWB.

Consider the case of a retiree, aged 65 and in good health, who wants to start withdrawing (say) 4.5 percent of the current value of her portfolio, inflation-adjusted each year, to generate income for the rest of her life. We assume she has no preexisting income from a pension (and ignore social security for the moment), nor does she intend to borrow against home equity using a reverse mortgage. The $4,500 desired per $100,000 initial nest egg is a reasonable spending rate according to most sustainability studies. From a strategic point of view – balancing the desire for bequest versus personal income sustainability – one can make an argument that approximately one-third of her investable nest egg should be allocated to pure pensions (i.e., she should use a third of her money to buy a SPIA), one-third to conventional mutual funds and/or managed accounts (i.e., she should keep things as is), and the final third to protected investments (e.g., VAs with a GLWB). As we show elsewhere, this particular allocation produces an optimized balance between the goals of personal retirement income sustainability and leaving a financial legacy for the client's descendants. More technically, this allocation will induce the most efficient 85 percent income sustainability ratio while still maintaining a 20 percent financial legacy in present value terms. We must add that this hypothetical model client was assumed to have no preexisting pension, whereas in the real world, one must add the discounted value of pension and social security benefits to arrive at a mark-to-market 'value' of the retirement nest egg. If only one-third of this broadly defined nest egg should be annuitized, and the discounted value of her social security benefits is more than twice her liquid investable net worth at retirement, she already has all the annuitized income she needs.[4]

The approximately one-third of the client's portfolio allocated to GLWB-type products will swing like a pendulum between the pure SPIA and the pure investment silos depending on market conditions. When times are good, the pendulum behaves like a mutual fund and increases in value during bull markets. Of course, it never quite catches up to the traditional investment silo because of the higher fees and insurance costs. When times are bad and markets are falling, the pendulum swings in the other direction and behaves more like a SPIA or pure pension. Anyone who purchased a GLWB in late 2007 will understand firsthand how this process has worked. The GLWB has converted into a traditional income annuity, which pays a percentage of the base for the life of the annuitant. The bear market essentially 'pensionized' the VA of segregated funds.

Conclusion

Our overview of the available retirement income products in Canada has focused most on single-premium immediate annuities as well as GLWB products, which are options (or derivatives) on life annuities. We find that the money's worth values in Canada do not differ substantially from those reported in other countries, although our MWRs are marginally higher and exhibit a guarantee-dependent relationship that remains unexplained. We also note a large spike in MWR values around the financial crisis of

2007–8 during which the values exceeded one by substantial margins; buyers of SPIAs during the financial crisis received a surprisingly high MWR, probably because the crediting (pricing) rate used by insurance companies was tied to long-term and slower moving yields on their corporate and commercial bonds portfolio. We also evaluate how much a retiree might optimally allocate to GLWB and discuss sensible product allocation, where the retiree spreads her assets across conventional (low-cost) mutual funds, income annuities, and GLWB products, with the exact allocation depending on the individual preference for bequest versus personal consumption. The development of these products suggests that the Canadian market for annuities will continue to grow in size and innovativeness.

Notes

[1] These companies have included AIG Life of Canada (now BMO Life), Canada Life, Clarica, Desjardins Financial Security, Empire Life, Equitable Life, Great-West Life, IAPacific Life, Imperial Life, Industrial Alliance, London Life, Manulife Investments, Maritime Life, NN Life, North West Life, Royal & Sun Alliance, SSQ Financial Group, Standard Life, Sun Life Assurance Co., and Transamerica Life.

[2] These include Registered Retirement Saving Plans or RRSPs, Locked-in RRSPs, Registered Retirement Income Funds or RRIFs, Locked-In Retirement Funds or LRIFs, Life Income Funds or LIFs, or pension funds.

[3] Interested readers should consult Charupat and Milevsky(2001) for a discussion of how the favorable Canadian tax treatment of income annuities compares to that in the United States, along with the apparent tax arbitrage opportunity this creates using a formal pricing model.

[4] Naturally, the 'one-third thrice' model allocation depends on a number of assumptions, both implicit and explicit. For example, to generate these values, we assume a GLWB guarantees income of 5 percent for life at an extra (above management fee) cost of seventy-five basis points per year. If a specific GLWB charged more or promised less, the optimal allocation would be below one-third. In addition, if the retiree sought greater sustainability than (in this example) 85 percent, then she would annuitize more. If she wanted to leave a larger financial legacy, then she would annuitize less.

References

Brown, J., O.S. Mitchell, J. Poterba, and M. Warshawsky (1999). 'Taxing Retirement Income: Non-Qualified Annuities and Distributions from Qualified Accounts,' *National Tax Journal*, 3: 563–91.

Canadian Life and Health Insurance Association (CLHIA) (2009). *Industry Information*. Toronto, Canada: CLHIA. http://www.clhia.ca/e3a.htm

Cannon, E. and I. Tonks (2004). 'UK Annuity Rates, Money's Worth and Pension Replacement Ratios 1957–2002,' *Geneva Papers on Risk and Insurance*, 29: 371–93.

Charupat, N. and Moshe A. Milevsky (2001). 'Mortality Swaps and Tax Arbitrage in the Canadian Insurance Market,' *Journal of Risk and Insurance*, 68(2): 124–47.

Doyle, S., Olivia S. Mitchell, and John Piggott (2004). 'Annuity Values in Defined Contribution Retirement Systems: Australia and Singapore Compared,' *Australian Economic Review*, 37: 402–16.

Fong, W.M. (2002). 'On the Cost of Adverse Selection in Individual Annuity Markets: Evidence from Singapore,' *Journal of Risk and Insurance*, 69: 193–208.

Fong, Joelle H.Y., Olivia S. Mitchell, and Benedict S.K. Koh (2010). 'Longevity Risk and Annuities in Singapore,' in O.S. Mitchell and R.L. Clark, eds., *Reorienting Retirement Risk Management*. Oxford, UK: Oxford University Press, pp. 156–76.

Friedman, B. and M. Warshawsky (1988). 'Annuity Prices and Saving Behavior in the United States,' in Z. Bodie, J. Shoven, and D. Wise, eds., *Pensions in the US Economy*. Chicago, IL: University of Chicago Press, pp. 53–77.

Gaudecker, H. and C. Weber (2004). 'Surprises in a Growing Market Niche: An Evaluation of the German Private Life Annuities Market,' *Geneva Papers on Risk and Insurance*, 29: 394–416.

James, E. and D. Vittas (2001). 'Annuities Markets in Comparative Perspective: Do Consumers Get Their Money's Worth?,' in OECD 2000 Private Pensions Conference. Paris, France: OECD, pp. 313–44.

—— X. Song (2002). 'Annuities Markets Around the World: Money's Worth and Risk Intermediation,' SSRN Working Papers Series. Chicago, IL: SSRN.

Milevsky, Moshe A. and V. KyryChencko (2008). 'Portfolio Choice with Puts: Evidence from Variable Annuities,' *Financial Analysts Journal*, 64: 80–95.

—— T. Salisbury (2006). 'Financial Valuation of Guaranteed Minimum Withdrawal Benefits,' *Insurance: Mathematics and Economics*, 38(1): 21–38.

Mitchell, O.S., J.M. Poterba, M.J. Warshawsky, and J.R. Brown (1999). 'New Evidence on the Money's Worth of Individual Annuities,' *American Economic Review*, 89: 1299–318.

Murthi, M., Orszag, J.M., and P.R. Orszag (1999). 'The Value for Money of Annuities in the UK: Theory, Experience and Policy.' Report for World Bank Annuity Project and Centre for Pensions and Social Insurance Research Report 1999–2009. Washington, DC: The World Bank.

Ruiz, Jose and Olivia S. Mitchell (2011). 'Pension Payouts in Chile: Past, Present, and Future Prospects,' in O.S. Mitchell and J. Piggott, eds., *Revisiting Retirement Payouts: Market Developments and Policy Issues*. Oxford, UK: Oxford University Press.

Shao, L. (2010). The Money's Worth Ratio of Single Life Immediate Annuities in the Canadian Private Annuities Market. Ph.D. dissertation, York University, Toronto, Canada.

Thorburn, C., R. Rocha, and M. Morales (2007). 'An Analysis of Money's Worth Ratios in Chile,' *Journal of Pension Economics and Finance*, 6: 287–312.

Chapter 5

The United States Longevity Insurance Market

Anthony Webb

Although the annuity market in the United States is well developed by international standards, households rarely voluntarily annuitize any of their wealth. Most of the longevity insurance enjoyed by American households is provided by Social Security and defined benefit (DB) pensions. Social Security pays benefits in the form of a lifetime inflation-protected annuity, while DB pensions, until recently, typically paid benefits in the form of a nominal annuity. While these sources of longevity insurance are declining in importance over time, it is also true that only a very small proportion of households voluntarily annuitize, and a majority appears to show a strong preference for converting annuity income into lump sums.

In what follows, we first discuss theoretical calculations of the value of annuitization. We argue that, once account is taken of pre-annuitized wealth, longevity risk pooling within marriage, and the risk posed by uninsured medical costs, the value of annuitization may be less than sometimes believed. Next, we consider why households appear to be so reluctant to annuitize. Then, we turn to a discussion of the US annuity market in more detail, along with product innovations. We conclude by considering policy options to increase annuitization rates.

Theoretical calculations of the value of annuities

In the absence of annuities, households must trade off the risk of outliving their wealth against their desire to maximize lifetime consumption. An annuity is said to be actuarially fair, or to have a money's worth ratio (MWR) of one, if the benefit stream discounted by an interest rate and annual survival probabilities equals the premium paid. An actuarially fair annuity enables a risk-averse household facing an uncertain life span to increase lifetime consumption, because it is able to offer a rate of return in excess of that obtainable on equivalent unannuitized investments. But in practice, annuities are not actuarially fair; they also involve a loss of liquidity. This lack of liquidity may be a particular disadvantage in the

United States, where most households face substantial uncertainty as to the level of their out-of-pocket health care costs.

A series of papers has attempted to calculate the actuarial unfairness of annuities around the world, to investigate whether the longevity insurance they provide is sufficient to outweigh that actuarial unfairness, and to determine optimal annuitization strategies. The latter calculations require computationally intensive numerical optimization techniques, and it is only in the past two or three years that models have begun to incorporate the level of realism required to support financial planning recommendations. A first paper to calculate the value of annuities and take account of the value of the longevity insurance they provide was by Mitchell et al. (1999). Assuming constant relative risk aversion (CRRA) utility with plausible coefficients of risk aversion, they calculated that the value of the longevity insurance to single individuals with no pre-annuitized wealth greatly exceeded plausible estimates of the actuarial unfairness of annuities. The value of this longevity insurance was lower, but it was still substantially greater than the estimates of actuarial unfairness, when an assumed 50 percent of wealth was held in pre-annuitized form – for example, through Social Security and DB pensions. The small size of the US annuity market was therefore somewhat puzzling. Brown and Poterba (2000) extended the analysis to married couples, and they found that longevity risk pooling within marriage substantially reduced the value of annuitization.

A follow-on study by Dushi and Webb (2004) analyzed data from the Health and Retirement Study, a panel of Americans born between 1931 and 1941, and it found that the average household held much more than half of its wealth in pre-annuitized form. Again assuming CRRA utility, the value of annuitizing the small remaining proportion of wealth held in unannuitized form was now barely sufficient to offset the actuarial unfairness of annuities.[1] Those that did annuitize were found to be better off delaying until their late 70s or early 80s.

These earlier models assume that the household faces no uncertainty regarding the marginal utility of consumption during retirement, and that the household has no bequest motive. It is unclear to what extent most households have a bequest motive, and we believe it is unlikely that the marginal utility of consumption remains constant during retirement. Households may prefer greater consumption at younger ages, when they are better able to enjoy leisure pursuits, and marginal utility may spike in the event of uninsured medical expenses. Models are only now being developed (Pang and Warshawsky 2008; Turra and Mitchell 2008; Yogo 2009) that incorporate the risk of incurring uninsured medical expenses. But these sophisticated models do not as of yet fully incorporate the house, an asset that plausibly functions as self-insurance against one of the largest sources of uninsured medical costs, namely the cost of long-term care.

These earlier models are also sensitive to assumptions made regarding interest and mortality rates. One alternative would be to use population mortality tables, but many high-mortality households have little annuitizable wealth. Conversely, households that actually purchase annuities tend to have much lower than average mortality. The results also depend upon the assumed interest rate on alternative investments. One alternative might be to use the Treasury STRIP interest rate, on the grounds that a portion of annuity payments is protected by state-level guarantees, but one might choose the term structure of high-grade corporate bonds if that is the household's alternative investment. One must also decide whether to take the average of the prices charged by all insurance companies, or to assume that the household shops around, and what assumptions to make about the level of management charges on alternative investments.

From a modeling standpoint, then, it is possible to construct a model in which many households might choose not to annuitize. Nevertheless, the almost total absence of voluntary annuitization in practice is still somewhat puzzling. In 2007, immediate annuity sales excluding structured settlements totaled only $6.8 billion in the United States compared with the approximately $458 billion of initial Social Security benefit claims in 2008 expected present value.[2] This has led to a considerable discussion of both rational and behavioral explanations for non-annuitization. Brown (2007) summarizes the principal candidates, and the behavioral reasons appear to go beyond mere inertia. Evidence from the Health and Retirement Study suggests that many near-retirement-age respondents state a preference for receiving a lump sum in place of the annuity from Social Security, even when the lump sum is favorably priced relative to its actuarial value (Brown 2009). One explanation might be that households are simply incapable of making the necessary actuarial calculations, but it is also possible that households frame the decision not as an opportunity to retain valuable longevity insurance but as a risky gamble that the household will lose if it dies young. A controlled experiment by Agnew et al. (2008) supports this view. Individuals who received a presentation that emphasized the benefits of annuities were significantly more likely to annuitize than those who received a presentation emphasizing the benefits of unannuitized investments. Yet, the authors found that the financially literate were actually less likely to annuitize. Perhaps the more financially sophisticated, or those who believe they are more financially sophisticated, overestimate their investment abilities or are less willing to relinquish control over their investments. It is noteworthy that the one annuity type that has enjoyed substantial sales is the deferred annuity, a product with a cash surrender value, even though it provides a lower retirement income than an immediate annuity.

The declining role of Social Security and DB pensions

US nationals have traditionally obtained most of their longevity insurance from Social Security and DB pensions. Both of these sources of retirement income are declining in relation to preretirement income. Social Security is a mainly pay-as-you-go social insurance program funded by a payroll tax. Retired worker benefits can be claimed at any age from 62 to 70, and they receive an inflation-indexed annuity. The benefits of individuals claiming before their full retirement age are actuarially reduced, and those of individuals claiming after their full retirement age are actuarially increased. The normal retirement age was 65 for individuals born before 1938, but it has been gradually increased to 67 for individuals born after 1959. This increase is equivalent to a 13.3 percent cut in benefits for individuals who claim benefits at age 65.

Increased female labor force participation has further reduced Social Security replacement rates. Married women are entitled to claim the greater of their own retired worker benefit and a spousal benefit, which, if claimed at the wife's full retirement age, equals one half of the husband's benefit payable at his full retirement age.[3] If the wife is still better off claiming spousal rather than retired worker benefit, an increase in female earnings reduces the replacement rate by increasing the denominator (the household's earnings), but not the numerator (Social Security benefits).

In the long run, Social Security replacement rates may fall still further.[4] Prior to 1984, Social Security benefits were not subject to income tax. From 1984 until 1993, 50 percent of benefits became potentially taxable for single individuals with incomes of more than $25,000 and married couples with incomes over $32,000. Beginning in 1994, the maximum taxable proportion was increased to 85 percent. Importantly, the tax thresholds were not indexed, so increases in nominal incomes result in an increasing proportion of retirees facing taxation of benefits.

Historically, DB pensions have been an important source of longevity insurance in the United States, traditionally providing benefits in the form of a nominal annuity. But there has been a dramatic increase in the proportion of DB pension plans that offer a lump-sum option – up from 15 percent in 1995 to 52 percent in 2005 (BLS 1995, 2005). Although DB pension plans over the past twenty years still predominate in the public sector, they have largely been displaced in the private sector by 401(k) and other defined contribution (DC) plans. Figure 5.1 shows the percentage of private sector workers with pension coverage who have a DB, DC, or both types of plan.

Brown and Warshawsky (2004) forecast future DB pension plan coverage and annual benefit payments from a base year of 1999, using the Pension Benefit Guaranty Corporation Pension Insurance Modeling System. They

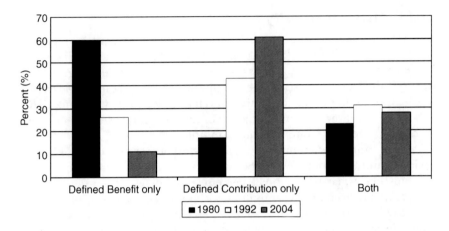

Figure 5.1 Fraction of workforce covered by pension plan of given type over time. *Source:* Authors' calculations; see text.

forecast that the number of active plan participants will remain stable at 11 million over the twenty-year period, while annual benefits will increase in inflation-adjusted terms from $94 billion in 1999 to $160 billion in 2019. If a large proportion of participants exercises the newly acquired right to take benefits in the form of a lump sum, then benefits could actually fall in real terms, even without an accelerated decline in DB pension plan coverage.

The extent to which the displacement of DB by DC pension plans reduces annuitization rates will also depend on the extent to which individuals voluntarily annuitize their DC plan balances. This is because, in contrast to other countries (e.g., the United Kingdom, which, prior to April 2006, required participants in DC plans to annuitize their plan balances by age 75 at the latest), there is no legal requirement for participants to annuitize at any age. After attaining age 59½, individuals may withdraw their balances without penalty. Starting in the year that they attain age 70½, they must take a 'required minimum withdrawal' of an amount equal to their plan balance divided by their remaining life expectancy, as specified in unisex life tables published by the Internal Revenue Service (2009).

Currently, only 20 percent of plans offer an annuitization option and only 2 percent of participants exercise it (Reno et al. 2005).[5] But Brown (2001) found that 48 percent of Health and Retirement Study households stated that they expected to annuitize at least part of their DC account balances. The first cohort with substantial DC account balances has yet to reach the point when mortality credits become substantial, and it is possible – but probably unlikely – that the remaining households will eventually act in accordance with their stated intentions.

The individual annuity market

The United States is one of the few countries with a significant private annuity market.[6] Poterba (2001) documents the history of annuities in the United States. Published statistics on the current size and recent growth of the individual annuity market give a highly misleading picture of the extent to which households are voluntarily purchasing longevity insurance. This is because the overwhelming majority of annuity purchases are so-called deferred, as opposed to immediate, annuities.

Deferred annuities are investment products that give the policyholder the option to annuitize, but they also permit prior withdrawal of the investment.[7] It seems likely that only a small percentage of deferred annuity holders will eventually exercise the annuitization option. For instance, Brown and Poterba (2006) report that only about 1 percent of holders currently receive annuity payments. Reno et al. (2005: 78) report that in 2004, about $10 billion of deferred annuities was converted into immediate annuities. They typically give the right to receive a guaranteed minimum payment for life. For example, 5 percent of the premium, a right that has provided considerable protection during the recent market downturn. But they lack the essential feature of immediate annuities that enables them to give an enhanced income return over similar unannuitized investments, namely the reallocation of wealth from those who die young to those who live unusually long. In consequence, they offer a lower guaranteed lifetime income than an immediate annuity, but they also have a cash surrender value. The amount of that surrender value will depend on withdrawals taken, investment returns, the guarantees provided, and the insurance company charges associated with both investment management and the provision of these guarantees. Trading off lower income in return for the option to surrender for cash may be attractive to households with a bequest motive and who place some value on liquidity.

Although voluntary purchases of immediate annuities have increased in recent years, the increase has been insignificant in relation to the amounts of longevity insurance provided by Social Security and DB pensions. Table 5.1 reports sales of various annuity types, in billions of dollars, from 1996 onward. Sales of variable deferred annuities predominate. Total immediate annuity sales increased from $3.0 billion in 1996 to $6.8 billion in 2007. Variable immediate annuity sales represented 5 percent of total immediate annuity sales in 1996. This proportion peaked at 21 percent in 2000 before steadily dropping over the decade to a low of 1 percent by 2008. Industry representatives have attributed the decline in variable immediate annuity sales to competition from deferred annuity products with income and withdrawal guarantees.

The taxation of annuities depends on whether they are purchased with taxed (non-qualified) or tax-deferred (qualified) wealth (such as IRA or 401(k) balances). If they are purchased with tax-deferred wealth, both the

TABLE 5.1 Annuity sales by product types for the period 1996–2008 (dollars in billions)

Annuity type	1996	1997	1998	1999	2000	2001	2002	2003	2004	2005	2006	2007	2008
Total variable annuities	74.3	88.2	99.8	123.0	137.4	113.3	15.0	129.4	132.9	136.9	160.4	184.1	155.6
Variable immediate annuities	0.2	0.2	0.3	0.5	0.8	0.7	0.6	0.5	0.3	0.3	0.4	0.3	0.1
Variable deferred annuities	74.1	88.0	99.5	122.5	136.6	112.6	14.4	128.9	132.6	136.6	160.0	183.8	155.5
Total fixed annuities	38.0	38.2	32.0	41.7	52.7	74.3	103.3	89.4	87.9	79.5	78.3	73.0	109.4
Fixed immediate annuities	2.8	2.8	2.1	2.4	3.0	3.6	4.8	4.8	5.3	5.3	6.1	6.5	8.0
Fixed deferred annuities	32.8	32.7	26.6	35.3	44.7	64.7	92.6	78.6	76.6	68.3	66.3	60.3	95.1
Structured settlements	2.4	2.7	3.3	4.0	5.0	6.0	5.9	6.0	6.0	5.9	5.9	6.2	6.3
Total immediate annuities	3.0	3.0	2.4	2.9	3.8	4.3	5.4	5.3	5.6	5.6	6.5	6.8	8.1

Source: Beatrice and Dinkwater (2007) and LIMRA International (2008*b*).

income and the capital components of the annuity income are subject to tax. But if they are purchased with taxed wealth, the portion of the annuity payments that represent the return of that capital is excluded from tax.[8] Table 5.2 analyzes immediate annuities between qualified and non-qualified sales. There appears to be no clear trend pattern in the data.

Annuity money's worth in the United States

James and Song (2002) calculated the MWR for the United States and seven other high- and middle-income countries, and the author found that the MWRs for the average annuitant exceed 95 percent in almost every country when discounting at the risk-free Treasury rate. Among annuitants, the money's worth for the United States, the United Kingdom, and Canada, which operate in the freest markets, was found to be less than that of Switzerland (120 percent) and Israel (109 percent), which operate in quasi-mandatory, heavily regulated systems. Gong and Webb (2010) found that money's worth figures exceeded 100 percent of the premium paid to households with annuitant mortality when the income flow was discounted using either the Treasury STRIP or the term structure of the AA corporate bond interest rate.[9] They were around 100 percent for households with population-average mortality when the Treasury STRIP interest rate was used, and came close to 100 percent when the AA corporate bond interest rate was used. The money's worths were higher than those calculated by Mitchell et al. (1999) using 1995 data, perhaps because Gong and Webb (2010) use institutional prices, though it may also reflect a long-term trend toward higher money's worths documented by James and Song (2002).

Annuity product innovation

A number of product innovations in both the immediate and deferred annuity market have appeared recently. Next, we review these in the immediate annuity market, though sales have been modest, and to date most are for traditional nominal annuities.

Variable immediate annuities

Traditional fixed annuities have bond-like investment characteristics, in that they provide a guaranteed fixed income. In contrast, variable immediate annuities provide a lifetime income, the amount of which depends on the performance of an underlying fund. If the return on the underlying fund exceeds a certain target rate, typically around 4 percent, the annuity income increases. If the return falls short, the annuity income declines.

Table 5.2 Immediate annuity qualified and non-qualified sales 2001–6

Annuity type	2001		2002		2003		2004		2005		2006	
	Amount	% of total	Amount	% of total	Amount	% of total	Amount	% of total	Amount	% of total	Amount	% of total
Variable immediate[a]												
Qualified	481	67.9	378	62.2	237	45.8	146	52.1	87	29.5	145	39.7
Non-qualified	227	32.1	229	37.8	281	54.2	134	47.9	208	70.5	220	60.3
Total	708	—	607	—	518	—	280	—	295	—	365	—
Fixed immediate[a]												
Qualified	1.8	50	1.5	31	1.2	25	1.2	23	1.4	26	1.9	31
Non-qualified	1.8	50	3.3	69	3.6	75	4.1	77	3.9	74	4.2	69
Total	3.6	—	4.8	—	4.8	—	5.3	—	5.3	—	6.1	—

[a] Amounts of variable immediate annuities measured in millions of dollars; amounts of fixed immediate annuities measured in billions of dollars.

Source: Beatrice and Dinkwater (2007) and LIMRA International (2008a).

Variable immediate annuities overcome an argument in favor of deferred annuitization (Milevsky 1998; Milevsky and Young 2007), namely that at younger ages, households are better off foregoing mortality credits in order to obtain the benefit of the equity premium. With variable immediate annuities, households can enjoy both.

There would seem to be a strong case that retired households should invest at least part of their wealth in variable immediate annuities. According to both economic theory and the recommendations of financial planners, households should invest mainly in stocks when young and rebalance in favor of bonds as they age.[10] Most life-cycle funds have a significant equity allocation at the age of retirement. It is unlikely to be optimal to switch from a mixed equity/bond portfolio the day before the household annuitizes to zero equity exposure the day after. But as mentioned earlier, sales of variable immediate annuities remain extremely small.

Medically underwritten annuities

There is a strong relationship between longevity and socioeconomic status (Attanasio and Hoynes 2000). In theory, this ought to provide an incentive for insurance companies to try to select 'better' – that is, high-mortality – risks, much as providers of life insurance try to screen out high-mortality lives. In practice, and with the exception of medically underwritten annuities providing larger payouts to individuals able to demonstrate that they have shorter than average life expectancy due to health-related conditions, the only underwriting seen in the United States is by sex. In 2004, medically underwritten annuities comprised only 4 percent of the total market (Drinkwater et al. 2006). These products have the potential to improve welfare if purchasers of medically underwritten annuities would otherwise have chosen not to annuitize.

In one state (Montana), insurance companies are refusing to use unisex pricing. The state of Massachusetts has recently enacted a similar law that prohibits the use of sex-distinct mortality tables for individual or group annuities or pure endowment contracts (Currin 2008).

Zip-code underwriting

There are substantial geographic variations in average longevity. Zip-code or post-code pricing allows insurers to manage longevity risk and reduce adverse selection by exploiting this relationship. Post-code pricing was introduced in the UK market in 2007, and several major insurance companies have announced plans to issue post-code annuities (Hill 2008). Those living in less affluent neighborhoods will be offered up to a 5 percent increase in annuity rates (Milner 2008). As yet, no company uses zip-code pricing in the United States.

Inflation-protected annuities

An individual purchasing a nominal annuity faces the risk of his income being eroded by the effects of inflation. At a 2.5 percent inflation rate, a couple aged 65 faces a 31 percent risk of surviving long enough to see their real income halved (assuming population mortality for the 1945 cohort). Households can, of course, purchase increasing nominal annuities, but these do not protect against unexpected inflation. The overwhelming majority of purchasers choose a level nominal annuity, possibly because these offer the highest initial income.

Treasury inflation-protected securities (TIPS) have existed in the United States since 1997, but the market for inflation-protected annuities has been slow to develop. TIAA-CREF has for some time offered a variable immediate annuity invested in TIPS, but it is not a true inflation-indexed annuity because changes in real interest rates could affect the value of the investment and, therefore, the payouts from the annuity. Irish Life was the first company to offer a true inflation-indexed annuity (Brown et al. 2002). Although additional companies have entered the market, the size of the inflation-protected immediate annuity market remains very small. It was estimated that sales of inflation-indexed immediate annuities were less than $200 million a year, representing less than 3 percent of total immediate annuities sold in 2006 (Woolley 2006).

Gong and Webb (2010) calculate that inflation-indexed annuities have similar money's worths to those of nominal annuities. They should therefore be attractive to households seeking to hedge inflation risk. The lack of demand to date may reflect a preference for higher real income early in retirement, or a lack of awareness of the likely effect of inflation on the real income provided by a level nominal annuity.

Advanced life deferred annuity

Annuities are most effective when used to finance consumption at advanced old age. Consider a consumer aged 60 who wants to enjoy $1 of consumption at age 100. Assume that the probability of survival to 100 is 1 percent, the real interest is 3 percent, and the insurance company applies a 100 percent markup on actuarially fair rates. One option for the household would be to deposit 31 cents in a bank account. With accumulated interest, that amount would provide the required $1.00 at age 100. But the consumer would do much better by purchasing an annuity paying out $1 at age 100, conditional on survival to that age. An insurance company applying a 100 percent markup would sell that annuity for less than 1 cent.

The advanced life deferred annuity (ALDA) by Milevsky (2005) envisages an inflation-protected annuity that would be purchased at retirement or even earlier. But in contrast to a traditional annuity, income payments start only at some advanced age, providing insurance against the risk of living exceptionally long. The deferral period reduces the cost of the longevity insurance provided by the ALDA just as a large deductible can reduce the cost of homeowner's insurance. Although a few insurance companies have very recently begun to offer ALDA-type products with benefits fixed in nominal terms, no company has thus far launched the type of inflation-protected product proposed by Milevsky.

Gong and Webb (2010) compare retirement wealth decumulation strategies based on an inflation-protected ALDA with three alternatives: buying of an inflation-protected annuity immediately on retirement, postponing the purchase of an annuity until some advanced age, or undertaking an optimal decumulation of unannuitized wealth. They show that the ALDA approach has three important advantages. First, it enables households to preserve liquidity at least until the ALDA payments commence, because the purchase cost is a fraction of the cost of immediate annuities, thus overcoming a potentially important psychological barrier to annuitization. A consumer planning to smooth consumption through his retirement would need to allocate only 15 percent of his age 60 wealth to an ALDA with payments commencing at age 85, holding the remainder of its wealth in unannuitized form, to finance consumption from age 60 to 85. Second, although a risk-averse consumer facing an uncertain life span would prefer the full longevity insurance provided by an actuarially fair annuity to the partial longevity insurance provided by an actuarially fair ALDA, the consumer would prefer the ALDA to full annuitization at plausible projected levels of actuarial unfairness. The intuition is simply that the consumer buys and gets almost as much longevity insurance. An ALDA also dominates an optimal decumulation of unannuitized wealth. Third, ALDAs have the potential to improve and simplify the process of retirement wealth decumulation, using simple rules of thumb that perform almost as well as the optimal and can be applied to the management of wealth decumulation over a period ending on the date that the ALDA income commences. In contrast, widely advocated rules for managing the decumulation of unannuitized wealth over an entire lifetime are highly suboptimal. Nevertheless, it is understood that ALDA sales have, as yet, been only modest.

Life care annuity

Annuities involve a loss of liquidity, which need not be a serious drawback if the consumer's financial needs are known in advance. But US households are exposed to substantial uninsured medical and long-term care costs, meaning that a need for liquidity might therefore lead to annuitization. Warshawsky et al. (2001) propose an annuity structure to address this issue by providing increased benefits in the event of the annuitant requiring long-term care. They argued that a combination product might be less affected by adverse selection than products sold separately. In fact, though combined annuity/long-term care products have been in the market for about eight years, they have achieved only modest sales to date. A recent study of long-term care insurance professionals has nonetheless suggested that the market is headed for moderate to strong growth over the next few years (Matso Lysiak 2007).

Aggregate mortality risk sharing

An annuity provider faces three kinds of mortality risk. The first is that it could obtain a bad draw of mortality outcomes from a given risk pool. The insurer can largely eliminate this risk by increasing the size of the risk pool. The second is that the insurer may experience a greater-than-expected level of adverse selection, for example, if other insurers develop a means of selecting the 'better,' that is, higher mortality risks. The third is that the average mortality of the whole population may decline more rapidly than expected.

From the perspective of the insurance company, aggregate mortality risk is far greater than the risk of having a single bad draw from the annuitant pool. Of course, the opposite is true from the perspective of the annuitant. One approach might therefore be for the annuitant to share aggregate mortality risk with the annuity provider. For the annuitant, the risk of outliving his wealth far exceeds the risk of a small reduction in his annuity income in the event of average mortality rates decreasing more rapidly than expected. The Teachers Insurance and Annuity Association (TIAA) actually has such a product on offer, selling participating annuities through its companion organization College Retirement Equities Fund (CREF). Here, annuity payments are linked to participant's mortality, and historical experience is used as a guide in the annual adjustment to the mortality participation factor (Piggott et al. 2005).

Conclusion

In this chapter, we have reviewed prospects for the market for longevity insurance in the United States. While the US annuity market is well developed in terms of product diversity, the evidence suggests that most consumers do not voluntarily annuitize much of their financial wealth at or near retirement. Accordingly, a question arises as to whether annuities might be further encouraged or mandated. Mandatory annuitization would reduce annuity prices if consumers at high risk of early death were required to annuitize and join the risk pool, though the gains may be small empirically, if high-mortality-risk households have little liquid wealth (Dushi and Webb 2004). Mandating would also adversely affect those households that would rationally prefer not to annuitize, even at the more favorable rates made possible by compulsion; indeed Gong and Webb (2010) calculate that some 16 percent of households in the US Health and Retirement Study would be made worse off (in expected utility terms) if annuities were mandated on actuarially fair terms. Furthermore, experience in the United Kingdom suggests that mandatory annuitization is quite unpopular.

Encouraging annuitization would be an alternative policy, either by making them the default option in 401(k) plans or by requiring 401(k) plans to offer an annuitization option. In fact, this may be compared to the success of automatic enrollment in 401(k) plans, as mentioned by Brown and Warshawsky (2004). But circumstances are very different at retirement. While consumers could favor automatic enrollment as a means to overcome their own tendency to procrastinate around saving for retirement, it is far from clear that most consumers understand the importance of annuities as an appropriate tool for managing wealth decumulation. Also, there is agreement that defaulting workers into contributing to their employer's 401(k) plan does little harm; anyone saving more than desired can reduce saving subsequently. By contrast, the annuitization decision is usually irreversible, and there is no consensus on what might represent an appropriate default. For instance, households might be required to annuitize only enough wealth to pay for basic subsistence (as in Singapore; see Fong et al. 2010). This would, of course, require providers to have access to information on the retiree's entire portfolio. Other questions would also have to be addressed, including the age at which consumers might be defaulted into annuities, whether the produce should be a level or rising nominal, inflation-protected, or variable annuity. Similarly, policymakers would need to evaluate whether spousal consent should be required before a married individual elected a single life annuity (similar to the consent required of DB plan participants).

In sum, it seems clear that financial products affording consumers' protection against longevity risk will become increasingly important in the United States in the future. Nevertheless, more work must be done on both the demand and the supply side, to ensure that the industry creates products that are both effective and suitable for the marketplace.

Notes

[1] The assumption regarding the way in which consumption enters the utility function can substantially affect the results. For example, the value of annuitization would be much higher if one were to assume that pre-annuitized wealth met basic living expenses that did not enter the utility function.

[2] Author's calculations, assuming population mortality for the 1944 birth cohort, a 3 percent interest rate, and the number of new benefit claims reported in SSA (2009).

[3] Married men can also claim a spousal benefit if their earnings are sufficiently large in relation to those of their wives.

[4] The Social Security Trustees project that in the absence of tax increases or benefit cuts, the Social Security Trust Fund will be exhausted by 2042, at which point benefits, including benefits in payment, would be cut by approximately 30 percent.

[5] The remaining 80 percent can still access the annuity market by rolling over their 401(k) balance into an Individual Retirement Account (IRA) offering an annuity option.

[6] Other countries are Canada, Chile, the Netherlands, Switzerland, and the United Kingdom (Mackenzie 2006: 24).

[7] For a review, see Brown and Poterba (2006). Many deferred annuities appear to have high investment management, insurance, and surrender charges.

[8] For further information, see http://www.irs.gov/publications/p939/ar02.html#d0e819

[9] The authors used institutional rates supplied by Hueler Associates that are slightly more favorable than retail rates. Population mortality was obtained from Social Security cohort life tables, and annuitant mortality was projected using Projection Scale AA.

[10] Financial planners often argue that younger households should hold a greater proportion of their financial assets in stocks because stocks are relatively less risky over long horizons, a questionable claim. A more convincing justification (Jagannathan and Kocherlakota 1996) is that a large proportion of the wealth of younger households is held in relatively low-risk human capital.

References

Agnew, Julie R., Lisa R. Anderson, Jeffrey R. Gerlach, and Lisa R. Szykman (2008). 'Who Chooses Annuities? An Experimental Investigation of the Role of Gender, Framing, and Defaults,' *American Economic Review*, 98(2): 418–22.

Attanasio, Orazio and Hilary Hoynes (2000). 'Differential Mortality and Wealth Accumulation,' *Journal of Human Resources*, 35(1): 1–29.

Beatrice, Dan and Matthew Drinkwater (2007). *The 2006 Individual Annuity Market: Sales and Assets*. Windsor, CT: LIMRA International. http://www.limra.com

Brown, Jeffrey R. (2001). 'Private Pensions, Mortality Risk, and the Decision to Annuitize,' *Journal of Public Economics*, 82(1): 29–62.

—— (2007). 'Rational and Behavior Perspectives on the Role of Annuities in Retirement Planning.' Working Paper 13537. Cambridge, MA: National Bureau of Economic Research.

—— (2009). 'Financial Education and Annuities,' *OECD Papers*, 2008(3): 171–214.

Brown, Jeffrey R. and James M. Poterba (2000). 'Joint Life Annuities and the Demand for Annuities by Married Couples,' *The Journal of Risk and Insurance,* 67 (4): 527–53.

———— (2006). 'Household Demand for Variable Annuities,' in J.M. Poterba, ed., *Tax Policy and the Economy,* Vol. 20. Cambridge, MA: The MIT Press, pp. 163–92.

—— Mark J. Warshawsky (2004). 'Longevity Insured Retirement Distributions from Pension Plans: Market and Regulatory Issues,' in W. Gale, J. Shoven, and M. Warshawsky, eds., *Public Policies and Private Pensions.* Washington, DC: The Brookings Institution, pp. 332–78.

—— Olivia S. Mitchell, and James M. Poterba (2002). 'Mortality Risk, Inflation Risk, and Annuity Products,' in O.S. Mitchell, Z. Bodie, B. Hammond, and S. Zeldes, eds., *Innovations in Retirement Financing.* Philadelphia, PA: University of Pennsylvania Press, pp. 175–97.

Bureau of Labor Statistics (BLS) (1995). *Employee Benefits in Medium and Large Private Establishments – Table 113.* Washington, DC: Bureau of Labor Statistics. http://www.bls.gov/ncs/ebs/sp/ebbl0015.pdf

——(2005). *National Compensation Survey: Employee Benefits in Private Industry in the United States – Table 51.* Washington, DC: Bureau of Labor Statistics. http://www.bls.gov/ncs/ebs/sp/ebbl0022.pdf

Currin, Cailie (2008). *Gender Equity in MA Annuities.* Greenwich, NY: Currin Compliance Services, LLC. http://www.lifeinsurancelawblog.com

Drinkwater, Matthew, Joseph Montminy, Eric T. Sondergeld, Christopher G. Rahamn, and Chad R. Runchey (2006). *Substandard Annuities.* Schaumburg, IL: LIMRA International and the Society of Actuaries, in collaboration with Ernst and Young, LLP. http://www.soa.org/files/pdf/007289-Substandard%20annuities-full%20rpt-REV-8-21.pdf

Dushi, Irena and Anthony Webb (2004). 'Household Annuitization Decisions: Simulations and Empirical Analyses,' *Journal of Pension Economics and Finance,* 3 (2): 109–43.

Fong, Joelle H.Y., Olivia S. Mitchell, and Benedict S.K. Koh (2010). 'Longevity Risk and Annuities in Singapore,' in R.L. Clark and O.S. Mitchell, eds., *Reorienting Retirement Risk Management.* Oxford, UK: Oxford University Press, pp. 156–78.

Gong, Guan and Anthony Webb (2010). 'Evaluating the Advanced Life Deferred Annuity – An Annuity People Might Actually Buy,' *Insurance: Mathematics and Economics,* 46: 210–21.

Hill, Jennifer (2008). *UK Insurer Aviva Joins Postcode Annuity Fray.* London, UK: Reuters. http://uk.reuters.com/article/idUKL1383215920080613

Internal Revenue Service (2009). *Individual Retirement Arrangements.* Publication 590. Washington, DC: Internal Revenue Service.

Jagannathan, Ravi and Narayana Kocherlakota (1996). 'Why Should Older People Invest Less in Stocks That Younger People?,' *Federal Reserve Bank of Minneapolis Quarterly Review,* 20(3): 11–23.

James, Estelle and Xue Song (2002). 'Annuities Markets Around the World: Money's Worth and Risk Intermediation.' American Economic Association Meetings and CERP Working Paper 16/01. Turin, Italy: Center for Research on Pensions and Welfare Policies.

LIMRA International (2008a). *US Individual Annuities Second Quarter 2008 Report.* Windsor, CT: LIMRA International. http://www.limra.com

—— (2008b). *US Individual Annuities Fourth Quarter 2008 Report.* Windsor, CT: LIMRA International. http://www.limra.com

Mackenzie, George A. (2006). *Annuity Markets and Pension Reform.* New York, NY: Cambridge University Press.

Matso Lysiak, Fran (2007). *Combo Deal: Hybrid Long-term-Care/Annuity Products are Life Insurers' Newest Weapon in Their Battle for Retirement Assets.* Oldwick, NJ: A.M. Best Company. http://www.thefreelibrary.com/Combo+deal%3a+hybrid+long-term-care%2fannuity+products+are+life+insurers'...-a0160641464

Milevsky, Moshe A. (1998). 'Optimal Asset Allocation Towards the End of the Life Cycle: To Annuitize or not to Annuitize?,' *The Journal of Risk and Insurance*, 65(3): 401–26.

—— (2005). 'Real Longevity Insurance With a Deductible: Introduction to Advanced-Life Delayed Annuities (ALDA),' *North American Actuarial Journal*, 9(4): 109–22.

—— Virginia R. Young (2007). 'Annuitization and Asset Allocation,' *Journal of Economic Dynamics and Control*, 31(9): 3138–77.

Milner, Leah (2008). *Prudential Postcode Annuity Move marks Tipping Point, says Hargreaves Lansdown.* Adad, London, UK: Centaur Media. http://www.money-marketing.co.uk/news/prudential-postcode-annuity-move-marks-tipping-point-says-hargreaves-lansdown/171014.article

Mitchell, Olivia S., James Poterba, Mark J. Warshawsky, and Jeffrey R. Brown (1999). 'New Evidence on the Money's Worth of Individual Annuities,' *American Economic Review*, 89(5): 1299–318.

Pang, Gaobo and Mark Warshawsky (2008). 'Optimizing the Equity – Bond-Annuity Portfolio in Retirement: The Impact of Uncertain Health Expenses.' Pension Research Council Working Paper 2008-05. Philadelphia, PA: Pension Research Council.

Piggott, John, Emiliano Valdez, and Bettina Detzel (2005). 'The Simple Analytics of a Pooled Annuity Fund,' *The Journal of Risk and Insurance*, 72(3): 497–520.

Poterba, James (2001). 'The History of Annuities in the United States,' in J. Brown, O.S. Mitchell, J. Poterba, and M. Warshawsky, eds., *The Role of Annuity Markets in Financing Retirement.* Cambridge, MA: MIT Press, pp. 23–56.

Reno, Virginia P., Michael J. Greatz, Kenneth S. Apfel, Joni Lavery, and Catherine Hill (2005). 'Uncharted Waters: Paying Benefits from Individual Accounts in Federal Retirement Policy.' Study panel final report, January. Washington, DC: National Academy of Social Insurance.

Social Security Administration (SSA) (2009). *Annual Statistical Supplement to the Social Security Bulletin, 2009.* Washington, DC: Social Security Administration. http://www.ssa.gov/policy/docs/statcomps/supplement/

Turra, Cassio and Mitchell, Olivia S. (2008). 'The Impact of Health Status and Out-of-Pocket Medical Expenditures on Annuity Valuation,' in John Ameriks and Olivia S. Mitchell, eds., *Recalibrating Retirement Spending and Saving.* Oxford, UK: Oxford University Press, pp. 227–50.

Warshawsky, Mark J., Christopher M. Murtaugh, and Brenda C. Spillman (2001). 'In Sickness and in Health: An Annuity Approach to Financing Long-Term Care and Retirement Income,' *The Journal of Risk and Insurance*, 68(2): 225–54.

Woolley, Scott (2006). *Retire Relaxed*. New York, NY: Forbes Magazine. http://www.forbes.com/forbes/2006/1211/158.html

Yogo, Motohiro (2009). 'Portfolio Choice in Retirement: Health Risk and the Demand for Annuities, Housing, and Risky Assets.' NBER Working Paper 15307. Cambridge, MA: National Bureau of Economic Research.

Chapter 6

Too Much Risk to Insure? The Australian (non-) Market for Annuities

Hazel Bateman and John Piggott

Products and policies which provide protection against longevity risk – the risk that an individual might outlive his or her resources – are increasingly important in an era characterized both by increased life expectancy and increased uncertainty surrounding longevity. Yet the reality is that, as privately managed defined contribution (DC) retirement saving gains greater importance globally, both governments and the private sector are retreating from the provision of longevity insurance. The lack of formal structures and products offering such insurance does not mean that the risk has decreased, even though its financial implications may not find their way to the balance sheets of commercial or government institutions. Rather, the absence of organized longevity insurance structures suggests that when the outcomes are realized, the response will be arbitrary and likely to be driven by political exigency. Rewards for careful planning on the part of individuals, or of careful management by financial institutions, may be compromised by short-term policy reaction to circumstances which, in the large, can be anticipated now but for which current structures do not encourage planning.

Nowhere is this more true than in Australia, where heavy reliance for income replacement in retirement is placed on a mandatory DC structure, administered through private institutions. Accumulations are available as lump sums or income streams, free of any tax on withdrawal at age 60, and the tax, social security, and regulatory framework make it easier and less expensive to choose non-annuitized benefits.[1] The demand for immediate annuities, and particularly life annuities, in Australia has always been small and incentives to take annuitized products, introduced in conjunction with the private mandatory arrangements, have been gradually withdrawn. As a result, the market for life annuities has virtually disappeared. In 2001, only 1,927 life annuities were sold in Australia. By 2009, this had fallen to fewer than twenty.

While a relatively generous and widely accessed safety net exists, there are therefore no structures in place in Australia to encourage or mandate income replacement accumulations to be taken as annuitized benefits. Australia is the only country which relies predominantly on a mandatory privately administered DC structure for income replacement, not to have incentives or mandates in place for longevity insurance.

Nevertheless, there is cause for optimism, with some formative steps toward a revitalized market for longevity insurance products. The Australian wealth management industry (AFTS 2009) is actively developing new longevity products, while the government, in response to recent reviews of the superannuation industry, is looking at ways to both increase consumer demand and reduce supply-side constraints. With appropriate policy settings, better policy coordination, and private–public collaboration, it may be possible to resurrect the longevity insurance market without a need for compulsory annuitization.

For such a small market, the Australian retirement income product market commands extraordinary academic attention, perhaps because of its unique position as the only retirement market in the English-speaking world which operates in the context of a mandatory funded DC-type second pillar. Analysis has included the effectiveness of the tax-transfer provisions for retirement income products (Bateman et al. 1993; Bateman and Kingston 2007; Bateman and Thorp 2008), money's worth estimates (Knox 2000; Doyle et al. 2004; Bateman and Ganegoda 2008), optimal timing of annuitization (Kingston and Thorp 2005), and supply-side constraints in the annuity market (Purcal 2006). Brunner and Thorburn (2008) provide an overview of the market for retirement income products. Yet, no one predicted the collapse of the Australian life annuity market over 2008–9.

The chapter does four things. First, we lay out the current state of retirement policy in Australia. Second, we describe the retirement product market in Australia and summarize trends by product type. We then relate the supply and demand for these products to policy change and to changes in longevity. It is clear that the market for life annuities, while small, has been very responsive to changes in the regulatory environment.[2] Finally, we report current progress and suggest ways forward that may provide the potential for a revival of the annuity market.

The Australian retirement income policy structure[3]

Australian retirement policy differs from that characterized by the proto-typical OECD structure. It comprises a means-tested safety net; a mandatory, privately administered DC-type income replacement scheme (the Superannuation Guarantee); and some additional concessions for further retirement saving. Each of these components is described briefly.

The Age Pension

Retirement provision in Australia relies heavily on an Age Pension, financed from general revenue, which currently pays 27.7 percent of male full-time earnings for a single pensioner, and 41.3 percent for a retiree couple. Net replacement rates are higher as the Age Pension is exempt from income tax, and payments are indexed to the greater of the growth of the consumer price index (CPI), a pensioner and beneficiary living cost index, and male average earnings, which ensures that it at least retains its relativity to wages. Eligibility for the Age Pension brings with it access to other benefits, including a pension supplement, a pensioner concession card, a Health Card, and rent assistance.[4] The access age is currently 65, but following a review of public pensions in 2008–9, it will rise to 67 over the period 2017–23 (Australian Government 2009; Harmer 2009).[5]

The Age Pension is available to all eligible residents regardless of work history, but is means-tested. The means tests, applying to both income and assets, have the effect of excluding the best-off quartile of age 65+ residents from receiving pension benefits. Rather, more than half of this group receives the full pension, with the remainder facing tapers on the means tests which reduce their entitlement below the full pension level. The income and assets tests are comprehensively defined, although the value of the retiree's owner-occupied home is excluded from the assets test. Until recently, differential application of these tests to retirement assets and benefits provided a mechanism for encouraging different types of retirement benefit products.

One way of thinking about the Australian Age Pension is to view it as a poverty alleviation instrument which excludes the rich, rather than a safety net targeting the poor. It is still the major source of income for most retirees, and along with the owner-occupied home, it is the major asset with which they enter retirement.

The Superannuation Guarantee

The Age Pension is supplemented by a mandatory predominantly DC retirement saving program. The minimum contribution rate is 9 percent of earnings, payable by an employer, although the 9 percent is gross of taxes and fees. Known as the Superannuation Guarantee (SG), this arrangement was legislated in 1992, after a period of several years when a 3 percent pay-in was negotiated through centralized bargaining arrangements.

The rationale behind the SG can be provided easily enough, although it is unclear whether this rationale actually underpinned the policy initiative. If an unfunded transfer is to be provided to the elderly to alleviate old-age poverty, then compulsory saving will go some way to correcting the resulting price distortion which might be expected to lead some to save less. This idea, attributed initially to Hayek (1960) and elaborated elsewhere (e.g., Hubbard et al. 1995), has been formally incorporated into a mandatory saving model by von Weizsaecker (2003).

The SG contribution rate was phased in over time, with the 9 percent pay-in finally reached in 2002. Access age is 55, increasing to 60 for those born after July 1964.[6] It follows that for most of the 50 percent of employees who enjoyed no superannuation entitlements before mandation, the SG will not yield substantial lifetime income streams. It will be another twenty-five years before full working life contributions will be available to retiring cohorts.

Superannuation saving is subject to a complex tax regime. The tax treatment of contributions differs by contribution type (e.g., employer, employee, self-employed), with employee contributions generally paid out of after-tax income and employer contributions generally tax deductible to employers, but taxed as income in the hands of the superannuation (pension) fund.[7] Superannuation fund earnings are taxed but at different rates depending on the income type. Prior to the Simpler Super reforms of 2006–7, differential tax treatment across retirement benefit products provided another mechanism to encourage particular types of retirement income streams (Australian Treasury 2006; Bateman and Kingston 2007). But all superannuation benefits taken after age 60 have been free of tax since July 2007.[8] This last change has meant that tax incentives toward income streams relative to lump sums, and between different kinds of income streams, have almost disappeared for this age group, although those retiring before age 60 will still face differential tax rates depending on benefit type.

Voluntary retirement saving

Many people have more than 9 percent of earnings contributed to their accounts, either because employers choose to make more than the minimum contribution or because employees supplement the 9 percent with contributions of their own. This may be thought of as voluntary employment-related saving. One of the advantages of the SG is that it has encouraged further voluntary saving of this type. Voluntary contributions are encouraged by the overall concessional tax treatment of superannuation saving, the government co-contribution scheme which provides a government contribution of 150 percent of the employee or self-employed contribution for low- and middle-income earners, and tax rebates for spouse and child contributions.[9] As well, some employees can take advantage of 'salary sacrifice' arrangements under which their (employee) contributions are treated as employer contributions for tax purposes (and are therefore subject to the 15 percent tax rate applying to employer contributions as opposed to the contributor's marginal tax rate).

While voluntary contributions on average amount to around 7 percent of wages and salaries (Connolly 2007), their distribution is concentrated. Survey data from the Australian Bureau of Statistics (ABS) indicate that, in 2007, only around 25 percent of superannuation fund members made voluntary employee contributions, 13 percent of members made 'salary sacrifice' contributions, and only 20 percent of those eligible made contributions under the government co-contribution scheme (ABS 2009).

Voluntary retirement saving includes not only Superannuation but also other forms of long-term saving through property, shares, managed investments, and, especially, homeownership. Homeownership is the most important non-superannuation asset for most Australians. Owner-occupied housing is worth more than half of the nation's private wealth, and more than 80 percent of retirees own their homes (most of them with no mortgage).

These arrangements may be contextualized by reference to Figure 6.1, which provides a schematic representation of the broad alternatives of retirement saving policy and practice. The boxes on the left may be thought of as three pillars of retirement provision policy, although definitions vary. The alternatives in bold on the right side of the chart indicate Australia's policy choices. Using the taxonomy of Figure 6.1, the three pillars of retirement income provision in Australia comprise the public Age Pension (Pillar 1); mandatory superannuation under the SG (Pillar 2), under which more than 95 percent of Australian employees are currently covered; and voluntary superannuation and other long-term saving through property, shares, and managed funds (Pillar 3). It is important to note that there is neither compulsion nor incentive to take a retirement benefit as an income stream, making Australia unique among those countries relying principally on a mandatory DC plan to deliver income replacement in retirement.

It is also important to appreciate the implications of the long lead time required for a fully funded retirement saving scheme to have its full impact. Current Superannuation accumulations for retirees are quite low, particularly for women. In 2007, average superannuation balances totaled $A87,589 for males and $A52,272 for females, with median balances significantly lower at $A31,252 and $A18,489, respectively.[10] While mean accumulations are higher for those close to retirement, at $A164,679 for persons aged 55–64, this is equivalent to only just over three times average male earnings, and it is considerably higher than the median accumulation for this age group of just $A71,731 (ABS 2009). As a result, around 75 percent of Australians of eligible age receive some Age Pension, with around 60 percent of these paid at the full support rate.

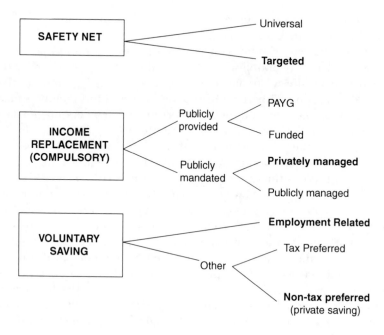

Figure 6.1 Components of retirement income provision. *Source*: Authors' derivations from Bateman et al. (2001).

Retirement accumulations will increase and individual reliance on the Age Pension will continue to fall over time as more retirees leave the workforce with increasing more years of Superannuation coverage. Official projections indicate that, between 2009 and 2050, the proportion of retirees on the full Age Pension will fall from 42 to 28 percent (FaHCSIA 2008; Harmer 2009). With the aging of the population, government estimates suggest that the cost of the Age Pension will rise from 2.7 percent of GDP in 2009–10 to 3.9 percent of GDP over the same period (Australian Treasury 2010). This fiscal burden is quite modest by OECD standards, reflecting the relatively low level of unfunded benefit payable, and the gradual encroachment of funded support into the means-tested areas of the Age Pension.

The market for retirement income products

Pension payout structures from mandatory funded accumulations can take many forms. In Australia, in the absence of mandatory annuities, retirement benefits can be taken as one or a combination of a lump sum or a retirement income stream.[11] Retirement income streams currently available include term and lifetime immediate annuities, and account-based pensions which are a form of phased withdrawal product. As well, hybrid products have been offered from time to time in response to regulatory incentives.[12] All retirement benefits are free of tax for persons aged 60 and above and are equally subject to the Age Pension income and assets tests.

Annuities

Prior to the recent demise of the annuity market, a comprehensive menu of immediate annuities had been available in Australia. These included lifetime and fixed-term annuities offered on a nominal basis, or indexed, single, or joint, and with the options of a guarantee period, reversion, and/ or a return of capital. In absolute terms, the market for annuities in general, and life annuities in particular, was never large, but it has fluctuated in response to policy change. In particular, the removal over 2006–7 of the differential treatment by benefit type under the Age Pension means tests and tax rules led to a severe deterioration of the Australian annuity market. Notably, deferred annuities and variable annuities are now both absent from Australia's retirement income product menu.

Phased withdrawal products

Phased withdrawal products were first introduced in Australia in 1985 and they are now the most popular form of retirement benefit. They were previously provided as products called 'allocated pensions', and they are currently marketed as 'account-based pensions' and 'transition to retirement pensions'. Both products allow retirees to invest their retirement accumulations in an investment portfolio according to their risk preferences, and (subject to drawdown requirements) decide how much income they want to draw down annually.[13] Retirement benefits paid from an account-based pension are tax-free for persons aged 60 and above, and, where minimum age-based annual drawdowns are satisfied (as in Table 6.1), the earnings on the underlying assets are also free of tax.

Transition to retirement pensions was introduced in 2005 with the aim of encouraging partial rather than full withdrawal from the labor force. These benefits are available to pre-retirees with a preservation age between 55 and 60 (i.e., those born on or after July 1, 1960) and must be taken as an income stream subject to a maximum annual drawdown of 10 percent of assets.

Hybrid products

Hybrid products have also arisen from time to time, largely in response to tax-transfer incentives. These include 'life expectancy' term annuities, which received regulatory sanction in 1998, where the term of annuity

TABLE 6.1 Account-based pensions in Australia: minimum drawdowns by age

Age (year)	Percent of account balance
<65	4
65–74	5
75–79	6
80–84	7
85–89	9
90–94	11
95+	14

Source: Supervision (2007).

was required to be at least the life expectancy of the beneficiary, and 'term allocated pensions' or TAPs. TAPs, also known as market-linked income streams, were a form of variable annuity introduced in 2004 in response to changes in the tax, Age Pension means test, and regulatory requirements. They had a similar account structure to a phased withdrawal (then known as an allocated pension), but a similar term structure to a life expectancy term annuity (these are no longer marketed following reforms in 2007 which eliminated tax-transfer preference by benefit type).

Current retirement income product coverage

The take-up of the retirement income products available in Australia is summarized in Tables 6.2 and 6.3. Table 6.2 reports aggregate coverage by type of retirement benefit, while Table 6.3 provides disaggregation by sex and age. From Table 6.2, it is clear that Australian retirees prefer non-annuitized retirement benefits. In 2009, lump sums accounted for 48 percent of benefits paid, and account-based pensions (including transition to retirement pensions) just slightly more at around 95 percent of the remaining 52 percent (or 49 percent) of benefits paid. Term annuities accounted for just 5 percent of total income streams purchased (by assets), while the take-up of life annuities was negligible with only seventeen policies sold in the first nine months of 2009. Longer term trends are discussed later.

Table 6.3 provides a disaggregated picture of retirement income product coverage by sex and age. The columns in the left panel give estimates for all people aged 55+; while the second and third panels increase the catchment

TABLE 6.2 Private retirement benefits in Australia (2009)

Benefit type	Coverage
Lump sum	48% of benefits paid
Income stream	52% of benefits paid
Private market for income stream products	
Life annuity	Negligible: 17 policies sold in the first nine months of 2009 (61 policies sold in 2008)
Term annuity	5% of market for income stream products
Account-based pension[a]	95% of market for income stream products
Superannuation pension[b]	NA

[a] Includes transition to retirement pensions.
[b] A superannuation pension is a lifetime pension provided from some defined benefits superannuation funds. There is no publicly available information on the share of superannuation pensions.
Source: Authors' calculations based on Plan for Life Research (2010) and APRA (2010).

age to 60 and 65. These are important age brackets because of the varying access ages operating in Australian retirement policy.

Nearly a quarter of Australia's population is aged 55+; nearly 20 percent is 60+; and 15 percent is 65+. Yet, only about half the 65+ group thinks of itself as 'retired'. Relatively few continue to work; most of the rest see themselves in caregiving roles, or they do not regard themselves as having had serious labor force attachment throughout their lives. At the risk of some oversimplification, Age Pension support is assumed to begin at age 65, and about 75 percent of this group receives at least some Age Pension.[14] For earlier age groups represented in Table 6.3, the major source of transfer payment is the Disability Support Pension. This is increasingly used as a means of accessing public support in the years immediately before reaching Age Pension eligibility. More than half of Age Pension recipients move to the Age Pension from some other support program.

The lower part of Table 6.3 provides data on private retirement income recipients, drawn from income tax data. These are available from age 55 onward (for persons born before July 1960). At age 60 and above, about 32 percent of retirees enjoy these benefits, but as a proportion of population, coverage is low. Only 17 percent of males aged 60+ have private pensions and annuities, and only 15 percent of the age 65+ population enjoys such access. However, many recipients of annuities and private pensions will also receive some Age Pension. This is an intentional feature of retirement income policy design.

TABLE 6.3 Retirement income product coverage by sex and age in Australia (2006)

	Age 55 and over			Age 60 and over			Age 65 and over		
	Male	Female	Total	Male	Female	Total	Male	Female	Total
Population 2006	2,344,746	2,608,749	4,953,495	1,709,103	1,972,898	3,682,001	1,212,927	1,479,732	2,692,659
Retired population[a]	846,200	843,600	1,689,800	804,000	797,900	1,601,900	702,500	693,100	1,395,600
Public benefits									
Age Pension[bc]	NA	NA	NA	NA	NA	NA	64.2	77.3	71.4
Disability Support Pension[b]	7.5	4.5	5.9	6.0	2.6	4.1	0.5	0.1	0.3
Private benefits[d]									
Retirement income streams[b]	14.3	9.2	11.7	17.3	10.9	13.9	19.4	11.2	14.9

[a] For year 2007 only.
[b] Recipients as a percentage of population.
[c] Assuming the same proportion as 2004 data.
[d] Australian pensions or annuities in 2005–6. People with an annuity/pension offset are largely private sector recipients; those with no offset are mostly public servants due to the tax arrangements of many public sector retirement benefits.

Source: ABS (2009), FaHCSIA (2008), Australian Treasury (2006, 2010).

Policy changes and patterns of demand and supply of retirement income products

Economists since Yaari (1965) have argued that a consumer with no bequest motive should completely annuitize all wealth, yet annuities remain very unpopular. Many explanations have been advanced for this puzzle, including information asymmetry, crowding out, bequest motives, lack of reinsurance opportunities, prudential capital requirements, or behavioral reasons (Brown 2007; Agnew et al. 2008; Brown et al. 2008). Furthermore, supply-side constraints such as a lack of products to hedge the long-term liabilities and uncertainty surrounding mortality risk have made providers reluctant to promote life annuities as a retirement benefit option (Purcal 2006).

In Australia, it is clear that demand for retirement income products has been closely related to policy specification: taxation provisions, Age Pension means-test rules (transfer provisions), and prudential supervision decisions have all combined to generate the specific conditions to be met by each product. And these have changed quite significantly over the past twenty-five years. The evolution of these taxation, transfer, and regulatory requirements is summarized in Table 6.4.

Throughout the 1980s, in conjunction with the introduction of mandatory DC arrangements, tax-transfer reforms were introduced to encourage lifetime annuities. Measures included tax exemption for income on underlying assets; offering a 15 percent tax rebate, which, when compared with the 15 percent tax then imposed on lump sums, gave a 30 percent advantage to life annuity purchase;[15] and a doubling of the retirement accumulation eligible for tax concessions (known in Australia as the Reasonable Benefit Limit) as compared with lump sums. Life annuities were later afforded concessional treatment under the Age Pension income and assets tests. However, almost as soon as they were introduced, these tax-transfer incentives were progressively extended to non-longevity insured products, including phased withdrawals (i.e., allocated pensions) from 1994, life expectancy term annuities from 1998, TAPs in 2004, and transition to retirement pensions in 2005. The 'Simpler Super' reforms of 2006–7 resulted in the removal of all tax-transfer preference by benefit type.

Figures 6.2 and 6.3 summarize trends in the take-up of retirement income products purchased over this period. Figure 6.2 focuses on the split between lump sums and retirement income streams, while Figure 6.3 reports on trends in the market for income stream products, specifically life annuities, term annuities, account-based pensions, and TAPs.

Four trends are evident. First, the figures make clear the recent switch in preference from lump sums to retirement income streams. Second, they indicate a sharp increase in the demand for phased withdrawal-type

TABLE 6.4 Evolution of the tax-transfer treatment of retirement benefits

Period	Taxation of retirement benefits	Age Pension means test treatment of retirement benefits	Product menu
Pre-1983	Tax concessions for lump sums (5% lump sum amount taxed at personal tax rates). Full taxation of retirement income streams at personal tax rates.	Income and assets from superannuation benefits subject to full income and assets tests.	
1983	Specific lump sum taxes introduced (15/30).		First incentives for life annuities
1984	Exemption from tax on income of underlying assets of immediate annuities.		
1988	Significant changes to the taxation of superannuation: • Reduction in lump sum taxes (0/15). • 15% annuity rebate for immediate annuities. • Return of capital excluded from taxable income for immediate annuities. • Introduction of Reasonable Benefit Limits (RBL), with greater RBL for life annuities.		
1990		Concessions introduced for lifetime annuities. • Full exemption from assets test. • Return of capital excluded from income assessed for income test.	
1992			Allocated pension introduced (phased withdrawal with minimum and maximum drawdown requirements).
1994	15% annuity rebate for allocated pensions.		
1998		Age Pension means-test concessions for lifetime annuities extended to life expectancy annuities.	Concept of a life expectancy term annuity.

2004		100% assets test exemption reduced to a 50% exemption and extended to the new term allocated pension (TAP).	Term allocated pension (TAP) – a market-linked income stream introduced.
2005			Transition to retirement pension.
2007	Exemption from tax on all retirement benefits for those aged 60 and above (both lump sums and income streams). • Abolition of Reasonable Benefit Limits. • Abolition of 15% annuity rebate.	Removal of assets test exemption for immediate annuities and TAPs. Full asset test applies to all retirement benefits.	Account-based pension (a revised allocated pension with a minimum drawdown requirement only). TAPs no longer sold.

Source: Authors' calculations; see text.

products (allocated pensions, account-based pensions, and transition to retirement pensions). Third, the figures show the growth and then decline of the market for term annuities, and, finally, they illustrate the disappearance of the small but robust market for life annuities.

Lump sums

Figure 6.2 plots the value of retirement benefits taken from Superannuation funds each year from 1997 as either lump sums or income streams. Traditionally, Australian retirees had a preference for non-annuitized benefits and particularly lump sums: in 1997, income streams accounted for only around 20 percent of retirement benefits taken (by assets). This began to change with the introduction of phased withdrawal products, initially in the form of allocated pensions, and later as 'transition to retirement pensions' and 'account-based pensions'. By 2009, for the first time, income streams dominated lump sums and these income streams are mostly account-based pensions.

Phased withdrawal products

Trends in the demand for account-based pensions (and allocated pensions) are also reported in Figure 6.3. A small spike in sales is evident in 1994 with the extension of the 15 percent annuity rebate to allocated pensions, and a small dip prior to 2004 as retirees switched to term annuities in anticipation of reduced Age Pension means-test preferences

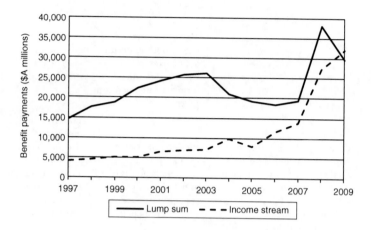

Figure 6.2 Value of retirement benefits: lump sum and income stream (1997–2008). *Source:* Authors' computations from APRA (2007, 2010).

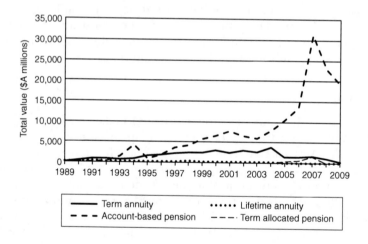

Figure 6.3 Value of private retirement income streams (1989–2008). *Note:* Account-based pensions include transition to retirement pensions. Account-based pensions were previously known as allocated pensions. *Source:* Authors' representations of data from Plan for Life Research (2010).

for these products from September 2004. But, the market for phased withdrawal alternatives expanded rapidly from the mid-2000s. This can almost certainly be attributed to the introduction of the Transition to Retirement legislation of 2005 and the Simpler Super reforms of 2006–7.

The transition to retirement pensions allowed individuals to simultaneously contribute to a superannuation fund, continue to work, and draw down benefits taken as an income stream. This allowed additional contributions to be made from before-tax income (taxed at 15 percent in the hands of the fund), and simultaneous tax-free withdrawals. The tax arbitrage advantages were obvious. Industry estimates indicate that about $A10 billion of the allocated pension market in 2007 can be attributed to this policy mix (Plan for Life Research 2008). The Simpler Super reforms, announced in the May 2006 Budget and implemented in 2006 and 2007, abolished taxes on all retirement benefits taken after age 60, simplified the Age Pension means tests by removing differences by benefit type, and exempted tax on the underlying assets of retirement income streams which satisfied minimum age-based drawdown requirements. As a result, there are now incentives to keep retirement assets in the superannuation system as a retirement income benefit, rather than take it out of the superannuation system as a lump sum. In Australia, this has translated into a rapid increase in the demand for account-based pensions.

Annuities

Prior to the introduction of mandatory accumulations, life annuities were not offered as a marketed product. Yet, in response to tax incentives, a small market for life annuities emerged in the 1980s; this grew slowly in the 1990s in line with advantageous tax arrangements. It reached its peak after the introduction of Age Pension means-test incentives in 1998, in the form of full asset test exemption and income test concessions. Life annuities enjoyed a small niche in the retirement product marketplace until 2004, when their exemption under the asset test was cut to 50 percent. Tax concessions remained and supported a very small number of sales. Later in the decade, after the removal of benefits taxation to retirees over the age of 60 in 2007, all incentives for life annuities ceased (other than for those retiring before age 60). Between 2007 and 2008, the market declined by 90 percent in value, and by two-thirds in terms of number of sales. In the first three quarters of 2009, only seventeen life annuities were sold.

A similar pattern is seen for term annuities, with a gradual increase in demand in line with the gradual extension of the incentives for life annuity purchase to long-term annuities. This was followed by a contraction in demand from 2004 with changes to the asset test and some decline after the withdrawal of the tax-transfer concessions in 2007. The middle part of the decade saw a small upsurge due to the introduction of the 'hybrid' TAP, but changes to means-test rules in 2007 effectively shut this market down.

TABLE 6.5 Patterns of annuity purchase in Australia (2001–9)

Year	Term certain			Term certain with RCV			Lifetime annuities		
	Number	Total value ($A million)	Average value ($A)	Number	Total value ($A million)	Average value ($A)	Number	Total value ($A million)	Average value ($A)
2001	11,072	794	71,677	19,725	1,633	82,799	1,927	166	86,227
2002	15,004	1,096	73,065	20,326	1,896	93,296	1,750	155	88,349
2003	18,606	1,356	72,893	12,530	1,352	107,925	1,477	200	135,674
2004	37,296	2,758	73,951	9,159	1,069	116,731	2,801	280	99,886
2005	7,233	548	75,746	7,664	876	114,307	293	27	93,072
2006	6,566	531	80,810	7,187	946	131,588	341	30	88,446
2007	7,355	790	107,353	6,010	876	145,749	403	37	92,184
2008	999	111	110,951	5,496	1,006	182,997	61	12	195,082
2009	475	51	107,158	2,536	466	183,797	17	4	212,353

Notes: Data for 2009 cover the year to the end of September only.
Source: Authors' calculations based on Plan for Life Research (2010).

Table 6.5 provides a more detailed breakdown of trends and patterns in the annuity market. Purchase over this period was largely accounted for by term annuities, which may be specified to pay back a percentage of the original capital on expiry of the contract, that is, with residual capital value (RCV). Many of the short-term annuities specify an income of interest only, and 100 percent return of capital at the end of the contract, while many of the longer term annuities specify an income comprising both interest and capital. Over the 2001–9 period, short-term annuities were the most popular form of immediate annuity purchased in Australia, relative to genuine longevity and long-term annuities (life and life expectancy products).[16] As illustrated in Table 6.5, of 32,722 immediate annuity policies sold in 2001 (worth $A2.59 billion), only 1,927 were life annuities and 11,702 were term annuities with no RCV. This corresponds to purchase by only 2 percent of Australians retiring that year. By 2008, only 6,556 immediate annuity policies were sold (worth $A1.13 billion) comprising only 999 term annuities with no RCV and 61 life annuities.

Coverage of retirement risks

From an economic standpoint, what is striking about retirement benefits in Australia is not the response in demand for longevity-insured products to changes in policy incentives. Instead, it is that almost no privately chosen Superannuation benefits are longevity insured, no matter what the policy in place. The increasingly popular account-based pensions, while ensuring more provident use of accumulations than a lump sum payout, only offer limited self-insurance against outliving one's resources.

This limitation of phased withdrawals is well recognized, and some analysts (e.g., Walliser 2000) have argued against their use in national DC plans for this reason. Products missing from the Australian market include variable life annuities, hybrid longevity products such as ruin-contingent life annuities, and pooled annuity funds. The benefits of including products of this type on the retirement benefit product menu are clearly illustrated in Mitchell et al. (2006) which assesses retirement income products by coverage of retirement income risks.

Six possible designs for retirement benefit products are assessed as to their degree of coverage of longevity, investment, and inflation risk in retirement. The first three are products currently available in Australia. It is clear that the most popular product – the account-based pension – provides the least coverage against the main risks faced in retirement, while the least popular product – the indexed life annuity – provides the best coverage. Variable life annuities, hybrid longevity products, and pooled annuity funds do not have a presence in the Australian market, yet all three provide better coverage of the key retirement risks than account-based pensions.

Pooled annuity funds

We analyze first the pooled annuity funds or Group Self Annuitization (GSA) products. These provide idiosyncratic risk pooling but leave systematic longevity risk with the annuitizing cohort, or bands of cohorts. Because systematic longevity risk is not covered, organizations other than insurance companies may offer these products. They therefore have potential value in a structure such as Australia's, where large accumulations sit in the individual accounts of those approaching retirement within Superannuation funds – accumulations which the pension funds will lose to other insurance-based organizations, absent some form of retirement product offering. While bilateral negotiation with insurance companies for more formal longevity risk management products is possible and likely, offering this kind of longevity insurance unilaterally has considerable appeal, without the overhead and capital requirements faced by a licensed insurer. Pooled annuity funds provide high coverage against longevity risk and investment risk, and medium coverage against inflation risk.

Variable life annuity

The appeal of a variable life annuity is that it provides retirees discretion over asset allocation and therefore does not require the annuitant to alter his portfolio from whatever it was before retirement – property, equities, bonds – to a portfolio of fixed income assets upon retirement. There is nothing in life cycle theory to suggest that such an abrupt change in asset allocation is optimal, or even sensible, which could be one reason for the lack of appeal of life annuities. Current tax, transfer, and prudential regulations preclude the development of an Australian market for variable annuities (e.g., an annuity with variable payments is not considered an annuity for tax purposes). An exception was the TAP, a form of variable term annuity available in Australia from 2004 to 2007, but this product fell short of providing full longevity insurance.

The standard variable life annuity is likely to provide high coverage against longevity risk and medium coverage against inflation risk. Yet, while the variable annuity product allows access to the returns of a diversified portfolio, the standard product did not insure against a prolonged bear market. While payments may continue until death, they may become vanishingly small, in other words exposing retirees to investment risk.

Hybrid longevity products

The most exciting recent product development is the evolution of variable annuities, which in the United States have been mainly investment vehicles, to embrace a minimum guarantee for life – characterized as hybrid longevity products. Essentially, these products operate as a special type of deferred annuity added to the standard variable annuity, which cuts in not at a prespecified date but in the event that a particular account has been exhausted, either because of market conditions or longevity. As developed by Huang et al. (2009), these ruin-contingency life annuities provide payment contingent on survival.[17]

In the Australian context, this may be thought of as an account-based pension coupled with a wealth-depletion-triggered deferred annuity. To make these worthwhile, the deferred annuity must operate with no surrender value, or RCV, should the holder die before they come into payment. The survivor bonus component is an important piece of the insurance payoff.[18] Such a product is more economical than a standard deferred annuity advocated elsewhere.[19] It may not be needed at all if the market remains strong throughout the life of the individual, and its pricing takes this into account.

While there has been product development along these lines in Australia, it has not been possible to offer an exact copy of the overseas products due to particular regulatory provisions in the Australian market. In late 2009, ING launched a product called 'MoneyforLife' which is essentially an account-based pension with guaranteed minimum lifetime payments. The product is designed to provide insurance against longevity risk and investment risk, and since it is 'account-based' rather than a life annuity, the full value of the product passes to the estate in the event of the product holder's death.[20]

Similar products are under development by other financial service providers, but all have been constrained by legislative provisions relating to the taxation, Age Pension means tests, prudential regulation, and capital adequacy, which require coordination with as many as five different government agencies. Each of these agencies acts in what it sees as a responsible fashion in light of its own mandate, but the overall effect may well be to effectively ban an appealing longevity insurance product. What is needed is a coordinated approach to the regulations and policies impacting on retirement income products, so that greater longevity insurance is encouraged.

Further development of the limited Australian retirement income product market is also constrained by a number of additional barriers including the sparse availability of assets to hedge liabilities associated with life annuities, uncertainties surrounding mortality risk, distribution channels which have been dominated by financial service providers who can make more money selling investment products (even if these are inappropriate), and possibly behavioral biases which lead consumers to make suboptimal decisions (see Agnew et al. 2008; Brown et al. 2008).

The way forward: market potential, product risk sharing, and public–private partnerships

On the face of it, the picture painted here is a bleak one in terms of encouraging longevity insurance. Nevertheless, the Australian market is starting to develop new longevity insurance products which appear to have greater consumer appeal, and which have been selling well in the United States. There is also potential for improvement in policy settings and practice which would significantly expand the longevity insurance market in Australia, although significant reform would be required to achieve this. Properly executed, these may well obviate the need for compulsory annuitization, a course which other nations have considered.

Yet, there are several prerequisites. First, the current policy process with regard to privately offered longevity insurance products must be better coordinated. Several public entities, including the Australian Taxation Office (ATO), the Australian Prudential Regulatory Authority (APRA), the Department of Family, Housing, Community Services and Indigenous Affairs (FaHCSIA), and the Australian Treasury, are influential in creating market opportunities for longevity insurance products. Yet none have the development of this market as among their primary policy goals. Neither is there any meaningful communication between them regarding assessment of proposed products. At the very least, a mechanism to contextualize and coordinate responses to market innovation is required, to provide private sector insurers with a firm basis for product development.

Second, much more sophisticated distribution channels are required for the promotion and sale of longevity insurance products. Most people approaching retirement at present seek the advice of a financial advisor, who in many cases may be naive about longevity risk, and who often is motivated by commission incentives built around investment-style products. A possible mechanism for breaking through this lies with the large Superannuation funds, which do have a relationship with their members. The not-for-profit funds especially, which account for a large proportion of the workforce, may have the capacity to harness their relationships to promote products embracing greater longevity insurance than is presently the case. Other policy suggestions such as limiting commission payments to financial planners may help with increasing net returns, but they seem unlikely on their own to address the retirement protection issue.

Additional policy initiatives may also be considered. Government could also enter the annuity market directly alongside private insurers, to 'kick-start' the market, as has been raised during consultations surrounding the 2007–8 Henry Review of the Australian taxation system. One proposal – the use of relatively small accumulations (because the SG is not yet mature, SG accumulations are frequently small) to 'top up' the Age Pension through a government agency – has considerable political appeal. More immediately, Government debt could be issued in forms which provide natural hedges against longevity (and interest and inflation) risk, essentially allowing insurers to partially immunize their annuity exposure. For example, the issue of long-duration, inflation-indexed bonds would offer an immediate hedge for CPI-indexed annuities.

Conclusion

This chapter has reviewed the parlous state of the market for life annuities in Australia. Australians have traditionally favored non-annuitized retirement benefits, and the market for life annuities has never been large. But, following the withdrawal of tax-transfer incentives for life annuity purchase over 2006–7, the market has all but disappeared and the large increase in retirement benefit products is accounted for solely by phased withdrawal-type products (or account-based pensions in Australia). Fewer than twenty life annuities were sold in Australia in all of 2009. The increasing trend to take phased withdrawal products thus leaves Australian retirees exposed to longevity risk, and Australia as the only country relying predominantly on private mandatory DC accounts not to have incentives or mandates in place for longevity insurance.

Poor coordination between key government policy departments deserves part of the blame for the demise of the market for life annuities. But previous growth and a resurgence of the annuities market has been constrained by supply-side factors. These include the absence of assets to hedge the liabilities associated with life annuities, uncertainties surrounding mortality risks, and possibly the nature of the distribution channels which have been dominated by financial service providers who can make more money selling investment products.

In any event, there is cause for optimism, with some formative steps toward a revitalized market for longevity insurance products. The Australian wealth management industry is actively developing new longevity products of the ruin-contingent variety, while the government, in response to recent reviews of the superannuation industry (AFTS 2009), is looking at ways to both increase consumer demand and reduce supply-side constraints for life annuities. Options canvassed include the issue of long-duration inflation-indexed bonds, and collaboration between the public and private sectors in the offering of longevity products. With appropriate policy settings, better policy coordination, and private–public collaboration, it may be possible to resurrect Australia's longevity insurance market without the need for compulsory annuitization.

Acknowledgments

Financial support from Hitotsubashi University and the Australian Research Council is gratefully acknowledged. We are grateful to Simon Solomon for useful discussions and comments, and Siqi Tang for his fine research assistance. All opinions remain the authors' own.

Notes

[1] Withdrawal at age 60 applies for persons born on or after July 1, 1964. The withdrawal age is 55 for persons born before July 1, 1960, and progressively increases from 55 to 60 for persons born between 1960 and 1964.

[2] The regulatory environment refers to the tax and Age Pension means-test provisions and the prudential regulations.

[3] The discussion of the Australian retirement income arrangements draws on Bateman et al. (2001) and Bateman (2010).

[4] The pension supplement was introduced in 2008. It combines the previous pharmaceutical allowance, utilities allowance, GST supplement, and telephone allowance.

[5] The Age Pension age for females is being gradually increased from age 60 to age 65 by 2014. Between 2017 and 2023, the Age Pension age will increase to 67 for both males and females (see Australian Government 2009).

[6] Under the phase-in arrangements, the preservation age for those born before July 1, 1960 remains at 55, then it increases one year at a time, reaching age 60 for those born after June 30, 1964.

[7] Employee contributions are not tax deductible but may be eligible for tax concessions or government co-contributions. Contributions by the self-employed are tax deductible and from July 2006 will be eligible for the government co-contribution.

[8] This only applies where the Superannuation has been accumulated in a 'taxed' fund, which is the most common case. As well, earnings on assets underlying Superannuation income streams are untaxed where legislated minimum drawdowns apply. Benefits taken prior to age 60 remain subject to tax.

[9] As a consequence of fiscal restraint during the recent global financial crisis, the Superannuation co-contribution matching rate was reduced from 150 to 100 percent for contributions made in 2009–12 and to 125 percent for contributions made for 2012–14.

[10] The exchange rate as of 2010 was $A1 = $US1.133 (Oanda 2010).

[11] For example, term allocated pensions (known as TAPs) were a form of market-linked income stream offered between 2004 and 2007 in response to preferable tax and Age Pension means-test provisions. TAPs had a similar account structure to allocated pensions, but a term structure also to an annuity with a term equal to life expectancy.

[12] As well, some defined benefit pension plans offer superannuation pensions.

[13] The previous allocated pension product had both a minimum and a maximum drawdown requirement.

[14] Table 6.3 shows 71.4 percent. The difference is due to Service Pensions (which are equivalent to an Age Pension but paid to returned servicemen).

[15] The treatment of the principal repayment component of life annuities purchased with tax-preferred accumulations nullified this advantage (Bateman et al. 1993).

[16] Short-term annuities are an attractive and tax-preferred means of preserving superannuation accumulations between preservation age and actual retirement.

[17] Related products are discussed in Kingston and Thorp (2005) and Horneff et al. (2010).

[18] Huang et al. (2009) suggest that such a deferred annuity could be offered as a separate product, which they term a Ruin Contingent Life Annuity (RCLA).

[19] For example, see Bateman et al. (2001).

[20] For details on the ING 'MoneyforLife' product, see http://www.ing.com.au/personal/retirement/ing-moneyforlife.aspx

References

Agnew Julie, Lisa Anderson, Jeffrey Gerlach, and Lisa Szykman (2008). 'Who Chooses Annuities? An Experimental Investigation of the Role of Gender, Framing and Defaults,' *American Economic Review*, 98(2): 418–22.

Australian Bureau of Statistics (ABS) (2009). *Employment Arrangements, Retirement and Superannuation, Australia*. Cat No. 6361.0, April to July 2007 (Re-issue). Canberra, Australia: Australian Bureau of Statistics.

Australia's Future Tax System (AFTS) (2009). *The Retirement Income System: Report on Strategic Issues*. Canberra, Australia: Commonwealth of Australia. http://taxreview.treasury.gov.au/content/downloads/retirement_income_report_stategic_issues/retirement_income_report_20090515.pdf

Australian Government (2009). *Secure and Sustainable Pensions*. Canberra, Australia: Commonwealth of Australia. http://www.centrelink.gov.au/internet/internet.nsf/individuals/budget_secure_pensions.htm

Australian Prudential Regulation Authority (APRA) (2007). *Celebrating 10 Years of Superannuation Data Collection 1996–2006*. Sydney, Australia: Insight Magazine, Issue 2. http://www.apra.gov.au/Insight/upload/Insight_2_2007_web.pdf

——(2010). *Annual Superannuation Bulletin, June 2009 (issued 10 February 2010)*. Sydney, Australia: Australian Prudential Regulation Authority. http://www.apra.gov.au/Statistics/upload/June-2009-Annual-Superannuation-Bulletin-PDF.pdf

Australian Treasury (2006). *A Plan to Simplify and Streamline Superannuation – Detailed Outline*. Canberra, Australia: Commonwealth of Australia. http://simplersuper.treasury.gov.au/documents/outline/html/simpler_super_full.asp

Australian Treasury (2010). *Australia to 2050: Future Challenges*. Canberra, Australia: Commonwealth of Australia. http://www.treasury.gov.au/igr/igr2010/default.asp

Bateman, Hazel (2010). 'Retirement Incomes in Australia in the Wake of the Global Financial Crisis.' Centre for Pensions and Superannuation Discussion Paper 03/10. Sydney, Australia: Australian School of Business, University of New South Wales.

—— Amandha Ganegoda (2008). 'Australia's Disappearing Market for Life Annuities.' Centre for Pensions and Superannuation Discussion Paper 01/08. Sydney, Australia: Australian School of Business, University of New South Wales.

—— Geoffrey Kingston (2007). 'Superannuation and Personal Income Tax Reform,' *Australian Tax Forum*, 22(3): 137–63.

—— Susan Thorp (2008). 'Choices and Constraints over Retirement Income Streams: Comparing Rules and Regulations,' *Economic Record*, 84(s1): S17–S31.

—— —— John Piggott (1993). 'Taxation, Retirement Transfers and Annuities,' *Economic Record*, 69(3): 274–84.

—— —— —— (2001). *Forced Saving: Mandating Private Retirement Incomes*. Cambridge, UK: Cambridge University Press.

Brown, Jeffrey (2007). 'Rational and Behavioral Perspectives on the Role of Annuities in Retirement Planning.' NBER Working Paper No. 13537. Cambridge, MA: National Bureau of Economic Research.

—— Jeffrey R. Kling, Sendhil Mullainathan, and Marian V. Wrobel (2008). 'Why Don't People Insure Late-life Consumption? A Framing Explanation of the Under-Annuitization Puzzle,' *American Economic Review*, 98(2): 304–9.

Brunner, Greg and Craig Thorburn (2008). 'The Market for Retirement Products in Australia.' Policy Research Working Paper 4749. Washington, DC: The World Bank.

Connolly, Ellis (2007). 'The Effect of the Australian Superannuation Guarantee on Household Saving Behaviour.' Reserve Bank of Australia Discussion Paper 2007–08. Sydney, Australia: Reserve Bank of Australia.

Department of Families, Housing, Community Services and Indigenous Affairs (FaHCSIA) (2008). *Annual Report 2007–08*. Canberra, Australia: Australia Department of Families, Housing, Community Services and Indigenous Affairs. http://www.fahcsia.gov.au/about/publicationsarticles/corp/Documents/2008%20Annual%20Report/default.htm

Doyle, Suzanne, Olivia S. Mitchell, and John Piggott (2004). 'Annuity Values in Defined Contribution Retirement Systems: Singapore and Australia Compared,' *Australian Economic Review*, 37(4): 402–16.

Harmer, Jeffrey (2009). *Pension Review Report*. Canberra, Australia: Australia Department of Families, Housing, Community Services and Indigenous Affairs. http://www.fahcsia.gov.au/about/publicationsarticles/corp/BudgetPAES/budget09_10/pension/Pages/PensionReviewReport.aspx

Hayek, Friedrich A. (1960). *The Constitution of Liberty*. Chicago, IL: University of Chicago Press.

Horneff, Wolfram, Raimond H. Maurer, Olivia S. Mitchell, and Michael Z. Stamos (2010). 'Variable Payout Annuities and Dynamic Portfolio Choice in Retirement,' *Journal of Pension Economics and Finance*, 9: 163–83.

Huang, Huaxiong, Moshe A. Milevsky, and Thomas S. Salisbury (2009). 'A Different Perspective on Retirement Income Sustainability: A Blueprint for Ruin Contingent Life Annuity,' *Journal of Wealth Management*, 11(4): 89–96.

Hubbard, R. Glenn, Jonathan Skinner, and Stephen P. Zeldes (1995). 'Precautionary Saving and Social Insurance,' *Journal of Political Economy*, 103(2): 360–99.

Kingston, Geoffrey and Susan Thorp (2005). 'Annuitization and Asset Allocation with HARA Utility,' *Journal of Pension Economics and Finance*, 4(3): 225–48.

Knox, David (2000). 'The Australian Annuity Market.' Policy Research Working Paper 2495. Washington, DC: The World Bank.

Mitchell, Olivia S., John Piggott, Michael Sherris, and Shaun Yow (2006). 'Financial Innovation for an Ageing World,' in C. Kent, A. Park and D. Rees, eds., *Demography and Financial Markets*. Sydney, Australia: Reserve Bank of Australia, pp. 229–336.

Oanda (2010). *Currency Converter*. New York, NY: Oanda. http://www.oanda.com/currency/converter/

Plan for Life Research (2008). *Retirement Monitor, June 2008*. Melbourne, Australia: Plan for Life.

—— (2010). *Immediate Annuity Report, September 2009*. Melbourne, Australia: Plan for Life.

Purcal, Sachi (2006). 'Supply Challenges to the Provision of Annuities.' School of Actuarial Studies Discussion Paper June 2006. Sydney, Australia: University of New South Wales.

Superannuation Industry (Supervision) (2007). *Amendment Regulations (No. 1), Schedule 3*. Sydney, Australia: Commonwealth of Australia.

von Weizsaecker, Jakob (2003). 'The Hayek Pension: An Efficient Minimum Pension to Complement the Welfare State.' CESifo Working Paper 1064. Munich, Germany: CESifo Group Munich.

Walliser, Jan (2000). 'Regulation of Withdrawals in Individual Account Systems.' Social Protection Discussion Paper Series No. 0008. Washington, DC: The World Bank.

Yaari, Menaham E. (1965). 'Uncertain Lifetime, Life Insurance and the Theory of the Consumer,' *Review of Economic Studies*, 32: 137–50.

Chapter 7

Pension Payouts in Chile: Past, Present, and Future Prospects

Jose Ruiz and Olivia S. Mitchell

Chile's funded individual-account defined contribution (DC) pension system, launched in 1981, remains vibrant after almost thirty years. Over the Chilean system's first two decades, analysts and policymakers devoted most of their attention to questions pertaining to coverage, contributions, and investment portfolios. Now, however, as the system moves toward maturity and retirees are increasingly claiming pensions under the program, policymakers are beginning to pay attention to how retirement benefits will be paid.

The goal of this chapter is to review recent developments in the payout market for Chilean pensions, focusing particularly on the role of annuities, and to illustrate what makes the payout market in Chile so different from those in other nations. In what follows, we first offer a brief summary of the Chilean DC pension system as it evolved since 1981. Next, we focus on how participants may elect to take their pension benefits, alternatives that include both a phased withdrawal option and a life annuity. Last, we offer some thoughts on the nature of the Chilean annuity market and discuss prospects for the future.

An overview of the Chilean defined contribution pension system

Chile first instituted a government-run old-age system in the 1920s;[1] in the mid-1950s, this had evolved into three main pension funds organized on occupational lines: one covered most salaried workers, another covered the police, and a third applied to members of the armed forces. Thereafter, additional occupational systems were added, so by the end of the 1970s, the retirement system was a patchwork of more than 150 individual and quite fragmented defined benefit (DB) regimes. This structure produced incomplete coverage (generally attributed to evasion of contributions), as well as low and uneven benefits; ultimately the structure was plagued by massive financing problems. By the end of the 1970s, government subsidies worth 2 percent of GDP were needed to finance the system, and prospects for additional problems loomed.

When Pinochet's military government determined to overhaul the system in the early 1980s, it first raised retirement ages, boosted contribution rates, and eliminated some special schemes. Thereafter, it created the new pension system in 1980, after closing the old systems to new workers who then were required to contribute to a funded DC individual account program.[2] The new mandatory structure was very much in keeping with World Bank recommendations for a multi-pillar arrangement (World Bank 1994). The first-pillar program included a noncontributory, publicly financed, means-tested, pay-as-you-go (PAYGO) welfare-based pension (*pension asistencial*, or PASIS) for the indigent. There was also a state-guaranteed minimum pension guarantee for workers who contributed twenty years into the new DC program but nevertheless ended up with benefits below the government-decreed minimum. The second pillar of the Chilean pension system, by far the better-known feature, consists of a national contributory DC program known as the AFP program, mandatory for wage and salary workers; affiliation remains optional for the self-employed.[3] All covered workers must elect one of the privately managed pension funds, and contribute 10 percent of their monthly earnings to that retirement fund, along with an additional contribution (2–3 percent of monthly wages) to cover administrative costs as well as disability and survivor insurance.[4] Workers can switch between AFPs with advance notice but must hold all of their balance with a single AFP at any given time. At the outset, only government bonds were available for the investment portfolios, and more recently the AFPs have been permitted to offer five funds in the target maturity date spirit. This approach automatically moves workers' assets into more conservative investments as they grow older. There is also a small third pillar in the Chilean system, also an individual funded DC component. In essence, any worker electing to contribute more than the mandated 10 percent amount to his AFP may do so, thus obtaining some additional tax benefits. Relatively few people add additional voluntary contributions in practice.

Figures 7.1 and 7.2 show the time trend in the size of assets under management in the Chilean AFP system, along with the number of contributors and retirees. Figure 7.3 shows the number of people by age claiming different types of pension benefits. We observe that the asset base has been increasing at a rate of over 9 percent per year, such that the pension system now amounts to more than 60 percent of the Chilean GDP. The number of pensioners in the system is around 640,000, of which 37 percent are early retirees, 28 percent are normal retirees, and 35 percent are disability retirees (the latter number is relatively high inasmuch as any

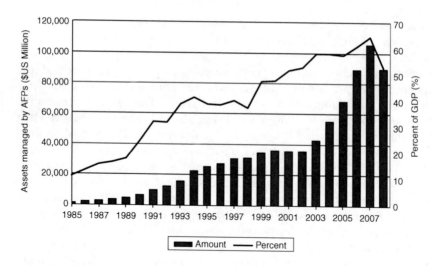

Figure 7.1 Growth of the Chilean AFP pension system. *Source*: Superintendencia de Valores (2010*a*).

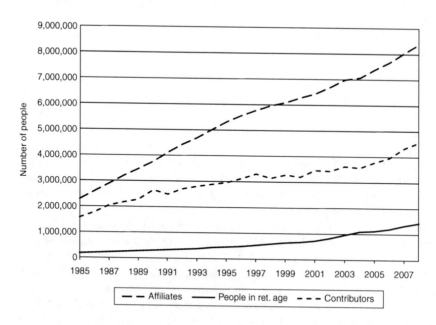

Figure 7.2 Time pattern of affiliates and retirees in the Chilean AFP system. *Source*: Superintendencia de Pensiones (2010*c*).

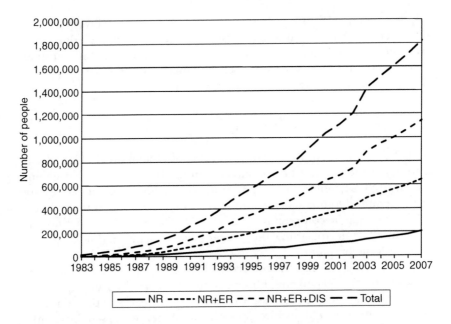

Figure 7.3 Chilean retirees by type, over time. *Source*: Superintendencia de Pensiones (2010*a*).

young system will tend to have a high proportion of disabled participants relative to regular retirees during the early years).

Retirement benefits payable in the Chilean pension system

At retirement, retirees may use their accumulated funds to determine their retirement payout streams. Women may begin their 'normal' payout at age 60, while men must wait until age 65; under certain circumstances (to be explained later), a worker may elect to begin his payments as young as age 55 if he is entitled to receive 'early' payments. Unlike in some countries, receiving the pension does not require one to completely withdraw from the labor force, so some workers remain employed while collecting a pension.

Phased withdrawal payments

The main options for retirement payouts from the AFP system are either (*a*) a 'phased withdrawal' (PW) benefit, or (*b*) a life annuity payout.[5]

In the case of the PW approach, the retiree retains his assets invested at his AFP, whereupon the fund administrator sets the payout according to a government formula that converts the balance into a monthly payout that takes into account the retiree's age, sex, and marital status. Specifically, the PW benefit paid to retiree i in year t is given by:

$$PW_{i,t} = \frac{\text{Balance}_{i,t}}{12 \times \text{NCU}_{i,t}} \tag{1}$$

where $PW_{i,t}$ is the monthly benefit under the PW system which depends on $\text{Balance}_{i,t}$ or the amount he accumulated in the fund as of his retirement date, and $\text{NCU}_{i,t}$ refers to the government's estimate of the 'necessary capital' required to finance one unit of pension payout, given the retiree's sex, age, and family composition (Pino 2005). The NCU term therefore is an annuity factor converting the worker's accumulated pension balance into a periodic payment.

Survivorship pensions are required by law. If the pensioner is male, his widow will receive 60 percent of his pension if he lacks children eligible for survivorship benefits. In the case that a decedent leaves dependent children, his widow would receive 50 percent of her deceased husband's pension while each child receives an additional 15 percent of the benefit. If the pensioner is female, a survivorship pension was paid only to her dependent children and to her surviving husband only if he is disabled.[6]

When the AFP payouts first started, the government lacked good information about workers' survival patterns in retirement. As a result, US annuitant actuarial tables (with some setbacks) were initially used to project PW amounts. Yet, people with very low balances do not purchase annuities, so using annuitant tables to compute payouts for those taking PWs likely overestimated their life expectancies. Over time, new mortality tables for Chile (RV-2004) were devised, based on actual annuitant mortality patterns over the period 1995–2003. Each retiree's PW amount is also recomputed each year using updated mortality patterns and life years remaining, producing a decreasing pattern of real payouts over time.[7]

As with all PW programs, the retiree who elects the PW option retains ownership of his AFP balance as long as it is positive, but he faces both investment risk and longevity risk in that the balance might decline to zero. At the point of converting to the PW mode, the retiree is also charged a flat fee as a percentage of the payout amount (this is current practice; prior to 1987 commissions on assets under management were charged). The AFPs could charge commissions based on a worker's retirement accumulations, but the regulator subsequently prohibited balance fees. As of 2010, the average PW monthly payment for a retiree claiming at the normal retirement age was US$232 and US$556 for the early retiree (Banco Central de Chile 2010; Superintendencia de Pensiones 2010*a*).

Lifetime annuities

Alternatively, a retiree may use the balance in his account to purchase a lifetime payout annuity from a life insurance company. The advantage of annuitizing one's retirement wealth is that the retiree is protected against both mortality risk and capital market risk. Yet, there is a downside: he loses liquidity as he must relinquish the entire capital accumulation to the insurer. In principle, retirees could opt for *both* a PW and annuity payment, but in fact most retirees take either the immediate annuity or the PW, perhaps combined with a deferred annuity.

In all cases, the retiree purchases his annuity benefit from a life insurance company where he relinquishes his pension fund and pays a commission (2 percent of the balance or less) in exchange for a lifelong annuity expressed in UFs (Unidad de Fomento), a standard numeraire for inflation-indexed payments widely used in Chile.[8] The annuity benefit continues until the retiree's death, and if there are dependents, for as long as the latter are eligible. There is, of course, some risk that buyers may suffer from insolvency of the life insurer which sold the life annuity. In such an eventuality, the Chilean Superintendencia de Valores is authorized to conduct a public auction to seek to recapitalize the failed company; all participating life insurers estimate the number of periods during which they will continue paying 100 percent of the promised pension annuity amounts. The life insurer offering the longest contract period wins, and after this, the government guarantees continued benefits up to a cap from general revenue.[9] As of 2010, the average monthly annuity payment benefit for a retiree claiming at the normal retirement age was 11.4 UF (US$458) and for the early retiree, 10.6 UF (US$426).[10]

Table 7.1 provides a descriptive overview of the key features that distinguish the PW form of benefit and the annuity modality. Clearly, the PW approach affords more liquidity but more longevity and capital market risk; the Immediate or Deferred Annuity approach protects against outliving one's assets, but it offers little to no bequest potential.

Figure 7.4 shows the time trend of the fraction of Chilean retirees taking an annuity versus a phased withdrawal. Of particular interest is the time path of annuitization adoption: after only a few years of the system's inception, already one-quarter of pensioners had elected the immediate annuity option, and today close to 60 percent of retirees have taken the immediate life annuity. It is in this sense that the data show quite high levels

TABLE 7.1 Characteristics of alternative payout modes under the Chilean retirement system

	Payout structure		
Attribute	Phased withdrawal (PW)	Immediate annuity (IA)	Temporary withdrawal (TW) and deferred annuity (DA)
Managed by	AFP	Life insurance company	AFP and life insurer
Can payout be changed	Always	No	DA can happen earlier
Who controls funds	Retiree	Life insurer	Retiree (TW) and life insurer (DA)
Benefit amount	Variable	Constant or variable	Variable and constant
Eligible for MPG	Yes	Yes	Yes
Bequest feasible	Yes	No	Only for TW

Source: Authors' calculations; see text.

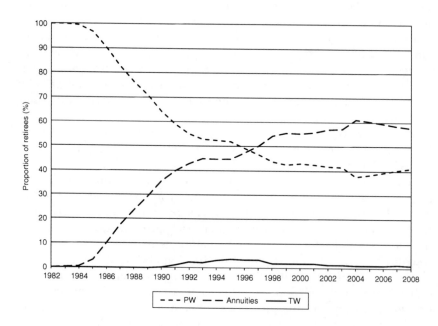

Figure 7.4 Fraction of retirees taking an annuity, phased withdrawal (PW), or temporary withdrawal (TW). *Source*: Superintendencia de Pensiones (2010*a*).

of annuitization in Chile, consistent with others' reports on the time trends (James et al. 2006; Rocha and Thornburn 2006; Thorburn et al. 2007).

Figure 7.5 shows the time path of benefit streams under both the PW and the annuity, respectively, for a single male retiring at age 65 and for a female retiring at age 60 (these figures assume the male retiree has a balance of CP$20 million or approximately US$33,230; the female balance is CP$56 million or approximately US$90,540). We observe that the projected PW amount is initially higher than the annuity payment, but within a decade after retirement, the PW benefit is projected to fall below the annuity payment.

The role of the minimum pension guarantee

Several aspects of the Chilean retirement system are intended to ensure that the system pays 'adequate' benefits. One benchmark against which benefits are valued is the 'minimum pension guarantee' (MPG), set by the federal government as a target minimum monthly nominal income value. This amount is inflation-updated annually and is higher for older retirees. For instance, the MPG value[11] in December 2009 for a retiree younger than age 70 was CP$104,960 per month (~US$209); for those aged 70–74 it was CP$114,776 (US$229); and for people aged 75+ it was CP$122,451 (US$244). A time series of MPGs appears in Figure 7.6, where it can be seen that this is generally higher than the national minimum monthly earnings level, and in fact it is equivalent to about one-fourth of the national average pay of contributors into the pension system.[12]

In terms of the payout choices, the worker retiring at the *normal* age who takes a PW may receive a benefit set by the formula in equation (1), but if this benefit falls below the MPG, he may request a higher payout rate which will naturally reduce his balance more quickly. In the event that he runs out of money, the government will top up his benefit to the MPG amount only if the worker had a minimum of twenty years of contributions into the system and his total old-age income falls below the MPG (SAFP 2010). As Arenas et al. (2008) show, however, this is a relatively stringent criterion. Currently, many retirees who were credited for service under the old PAYGO system may have sufficient years of service, but it has been estimated that no more than half of future retirees will be likely to attain this twenty years of service goal.[13] If the PW is taken at the *early* retirement age, then the benefit would be at least 50 percent of his average salary in the last ten years he paid into the system or 110 percent of the MPG (rising to 70 and 150 percent, respectively, by 2010).

If the worker annuitizes at the *normal* retirement age, he must allocate at least enough of his balance to a fixed real annuity such that his benefit is at

(a)

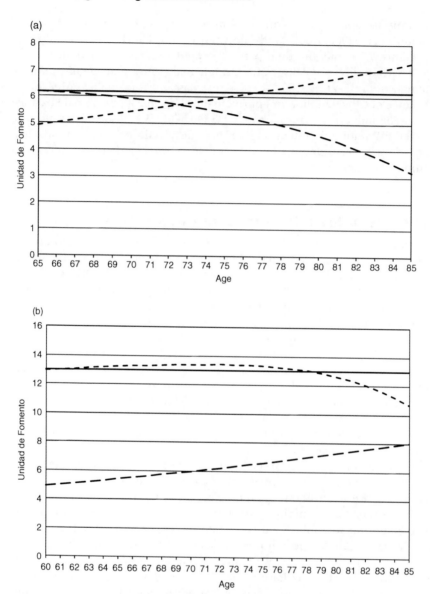

Figure 7.5 Phased withdrawal and annuity payments in Unidad de Formento (UF) units: simulation over the life cycle. Panel (A): single male who retires at age 65 (no dependents); Panel (B): single female who retires at age 60 (no dependents). *Note*: Pension balance of UF962 (~US$33,230 in 2008) for men and UF2632 (~US $109,925 in 2009) for women. *Source*: Superintendencia de Pensiones (2010*a*) and actual SCOMP quotes for life annuity.

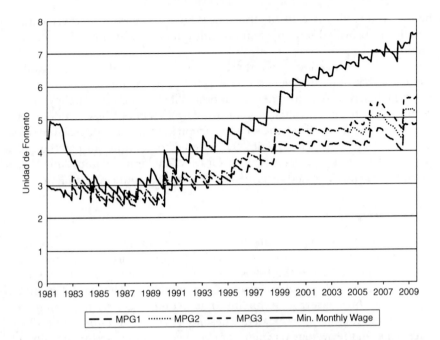

Figure 7.6 Time path of Chilean minimum pension guarantee (MPG) levels and minimum monthly earned income (in Unidad de Fomento). *Notes:* See Figure 7.5. MPG1 applies to those less than age 70; MPG2 to those aged 70–75; MPG3 to those aged 75 and older. The minimum monthly earned income is set by the government as the lowest salary a formal sector worker may earn. *Source:* Authors' calculations based on Superintendencia de Pensiones (2010*a*).

least equal to the MPG. If he retires *early*, he must purchase an annuity that exceeds 50 percent of his average salary in the last ten years he paid into the system or 110 percent of the MPG (rising to 70 and 150 percent, respectively, by 2010). Annuity benefits may be either fixed or variable; in practice, most pay a real fixed payment (expressed in UF) though the variable benefits have some portion devoted to a fixed real benefit with another portion linked to some index (such as a money market or stock index); in the latter case, the fixed part must amount to at least a fraction of the worker's preretirement pay.

It is also worth nothing that the government guarantee covers all of the MPG plus 75 percent of the excess of the annuity value over the MPG, with a maximum payment of 45 UF. The latter means people receiving a pension higher than MPG face some insolvency risk from the life insurance company. The higher the pension amount, the higher is the eventual benefit reduction in case of insolvency. For this reason, at retirement, people are provided not only annuity bids but also company ratings information.

Since the system's inception, there has been only one life insurer bankruptcy; at that time, the regulator undertook provisional intervention until the beneficiaries were assigned to another life insurance company. The regulator then ran an initial auction in March 2006 but it was redone as only one offer was received; the second auction in October 2006 received two bids. In the tender, Euroamerica S.A. offered to continue to pay the full pensions to retirees for 124 months,[14] for US$77 million in equity. After that period, participants would receive the guarantee from the government.

Benefit takeup patterns

It is of interest to explore the time path of retirement benefit takeup patterns. Figure 7.7 shows the time path of people purchasing annuities versus taking the PW: in the 1990s, the number of people who elected the annuity began to rise, and it exceeded the number selecting PW benefits. Figure 7.8 shows average payments that people received according to the payment method they elected. These trends show no important difference between the average payment for people who purchased an annuity at either the normal retirement (NR) or early retirement (ER) age. There is,

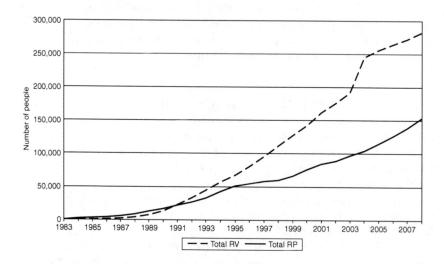

Figure 7.7 Time path of annuities purchased (RV) and phased withdrawal benefits (RP) elected in the Chilean pension system. *Source*: Authors' calculations based on Superintendencia de Pensiones (2010*a*).

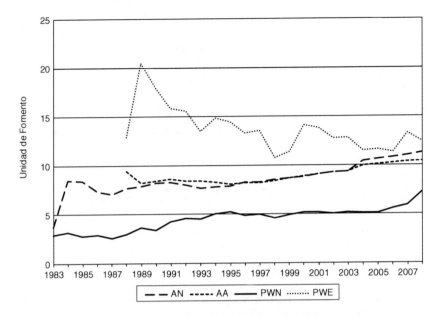

Figure 7.8 Time path of Chilean pension values according to payout method elected. *Notes:* AN corresponds to the value of the annuity purchased at the normal retirement age; AE corresponds to value of the early retirement annuity; PWN refers to the value of a phased withdrawal benefit taken at the normal retirement age; PWE refers to the value of the phased withdrawal taken prior to the normal age. *Source:* Authors' calculations based on Superintendencia de Pensiones (2010*a*).

however, a significant difference between those who elect the PW at the normal age (PWNR) and people who select the PW at the early retirement age (PWER). That is, the average early PW amount actually paid may exceed the normal PW value, inasmuch as those who retire early to start receiving pension benefits must satisfy higher balance requirements. As a result, low-income people who have not accumulated much in their pension funds have little opportunity to take early retirement payments, as a rule. It is for this reason that the normal retirement age PW amount will be expected to be the lowest payout, on average, and likely very close to the MPG.

Understanding the Chilean annuity market

During the early days of the Chilean pension system and throughout the 1990s, a substantial amount of peoples' retirement accounts was charged by

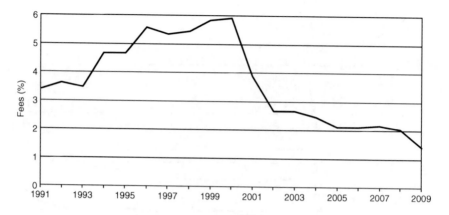

Figure 7.9 Time path of commissions for annuity sales in Chile. *Source*: Authors' calculations based on Superintendencia de Valores (2010*b*).

intermediaries in the form of commissions. Figure 7.9 depicts the time path of front-loaded commissions charged by life insurers over time, which rose to around 6 percent of retiree balances in 2000. In response to the perceived high rate of charges, policymakers began to draft a law that they hoped would hold down commissions. The policy debate took a decade to bear fruit with a draft law emerging in 2001 and the final law passed by the Congress in 2004. Initially, a maximum commission of 2.5 percent of the individual's balance could be charged; this was then lowered to 2 percent in 2008. This regulation is believed to have had an important impact in bringing down commissions, as is clear from Figure 7.9.

In addition to the cap imposed on annuity commissions, this reform also established a system for retirees to obtain anonymous bids via an online offer and quotation system (known as SCOMP, its Spanish acronym). This system was introduced as an electronic competitive market for all those workers who could obtain pension quotes. Specifically, the AFPs and the life insurers receive the same information about each person requesting a quote, including the retiree's age, sex, balance, and any beneficiaries. The main goal of the system was to increase competition and enhance transparency for consumers (Valdes Prieto 2005).

Those who request a price quote via this system and purchase an annuity can elect to do so directly, or they may engage a life insurer, broker, or financial adviser in which case they can pay up to 2.5 percent of their pension balance to such an intermediary. The operation of the SCOMP system may be summarized as follows:

- A member initiates the retirement process by informing his AFP of his intention to claim benefits (this can be either via an agent or over the internet). The AFP issues a certificate reporting the member's balance, and the member then requests premium quotes from his AFP, a life insurer, or any broker licensed to work with SCOMP.
- The affiliate may request up to three quotes for each certificate issued by the AFP.
- After processing and certifying the validity of the request, the system sends information to the pension benefit providers who in turn submit their offers to the system. These are then fed to the member and they are valid for fifteen days.

Worth emphasizing is that the SCOMP system is only informative; that is, each retiree decides his own course of action. He may select any of the offers provided, request additional quotes, negotiate with a provider separately from the SCOMP offers (with the requirement that this external offer cannot be lower than the benefit amount offered by this provider via the SCOMP), or request that SCOMP carry out an auction on his behalf in which case he must take the lowest price offer. To date, the services of the SCOMP platform have been used for approximately 142,000 retirees with an average of 1.3 requests per member since inception in August 2004 (see Tables 7.2 and 7.3). This implies that 81 percent of requests were accepted by the affiliate or pension beneficiary. In practice, it appears that the most popular way to access SCOMP is via the AFPs, who advise 39 percent of the purchasers. Brokers, who represent 32 percent of the market, can also obtain a price quote on the retiree's behalf, and life insurers account for 29 percent of the requests.

TABLE 7.2 Time path of requests for annuity quotes under the Chilean SCOMP system

| | | | | Channel (% of total) | | |
Year	Number requesting	Average number of requests	Accepted requests	Broker	Life insurer	AFP
2004	14,426	1.20	9,849	40.75	27.91	31.35
2005	33,714	1.29	28,294	36.58	25.19	38.23
2006	29,154	1.28	23,146	38.95	26.66	34.40
2007	37,606	1.36	32,524	40.20	27.79	32.01
2008	44,173	1.30	27,260	33.81	26.95	39.24
2009	33,356	1.20	20,955	7.01	41.16	51.83
Total	192,429	1.29	142,028	32.20	29.30	38.50

Source: Authors' calculations of data from Superintendencia de Valores (2010c); see text.

TABLE 7.3 Annuity quotes accepted in Chile based on ranking of benefit offered

Ranking	Year						Total
	2004	2005	2006	2007	2008	2009	
Best quote (%)	66.40	63.42	61.96	63.32	57.56	45.81	62.49
Second-best quote (%)	15.50	15.42	14.15	13.53	14.54	14.10	14.44
Third-best quote (%)	7.52	7.31	7.37	7.36	7.70	9.52	7.34
Other (%)	10.59	13.85	16.53	15.80	20.20	30.56	15.74
Total number	6,640	18,351	16,193	19,711	20,450	17,916	77,300

Source: Authors' calculations of data from Superintendencia de Valores (2010c); see text.

The evidence also indicates that 60 percent of people selected the highest benefit, or best monetary offer, provided by the bidders, and the ratio rises to 80 percent if we consider the highest three monetary offers generated. Though this could be interpreted as savvy purchasing behavior, it must be acknowledged that high benefit levels are not the only consideration. Insurers differ according to their risk classifications, so it is difficult to compare a high benefit payment monetary offer from a lower ranked firm with a lower benefit and a more highly regarded firm.

Further analysis of monetary quotes indicates that takeup rates vary according to the channel used to access the system (Figure 7.10). Specifically, people who referred their decision to brokers elected the highest payout 75 percent of the time; the ratio was 43 percent when the retiree used his AFP for advice, and only 3 percent when the life insurer was consulted. This could indicate that brokers are actually helpful in assisting people's decision-making. A possible explanation for the AFP's poor performance as a channel is related to its lack of incentives during the retirement phase. That is, an AFP participates actively during the worker's accumulation phase, registering contributions, investing, and managing the account; on the other hand, they receive no commission for giving advice about payout products. The fact that so few people obtain the highest payout product when consulting a life insurer may be due to the fact that agents have an incentive to capture customers once they are contacted.

Many have deemed the SCOMP system a success, but buying an annuity is still not a simple task. That is, the SCOMP-generated reports can be ten pages long with multiple numbers and calculations about payments under different payout structures (e.g., simple annuity, annuity with a guaranteed period, etc.). This information seems to be quite daunting for those seeking to shop annuity products at retirement. Furthermore, recent surveys show that people are not well informed about the pension system and may lack the financial literacy to make sensible financial choices

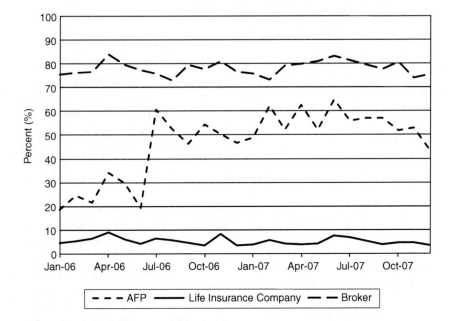

Figure 7.10 Proportion of Chilean AFP member retirees electing the lowest cost annuity quote by access channel utilized. *Source*: Authors' calculations based on Superintendencia de Pensiones (2010*a*).

(Arenas et al. 2008; Mitchell et al. 2009). As a result, retirees are likely to continue requesting the services of intermediaries, which in turn reduces their pension levels due to the commissions charged.

A further consideration is that it is virtually impossible for people to 'learn by doing' as most people undertake this once in a lifetime. The decision requires the purchaser to sign a contract in which he transfers his pension balance to a life insurer in exchange for a cash flow until the purchaser's death. For this reason, the Chilean pension supervisory authority has focused on enhancing information flow and strengthening the platform for annuity bids. Suppliers also benefit from SCOMP. While one-third of retirees do request online quotes directly, thus avoiding paying fees to intermediaries, only 12 percent finalize the process without paying any commissions (Reyes and Stewart 2008). This reinforces the notion that consumers lack financial knowledge for making such a momentous and irreversible decision. For this reason, people seek out and pay advisers, and also for this reason, the regulator continues to seek ways to reduce commissions paid to intermediaries.

Are Chilean annuities attractive?

Earlier studies research has noted that adverse selection is likely when retirees have the option to annuitize (Mitchell et al. 1999; Finkelstein and Poterba 2004), due to an asymmetry of information between the life insurer and the individual seeking to buy the annuity. Specifically, retirees may have better information about their health conditions and thus about life expectancy compared to the information available to the insurer. For instance, people who believe their mortality probability is lower than average will value offered annuities more than people who believe their mortality is higher. Life insurers in Chile are not allowed to discriminate between buyers using health tests, medical records, or familiar history – in fact, they only permit age and sex to be used to classify purchasers. Of course, in fact, mortality patterns do differ across segments of the population for various reasons (McCarthy and Mitchell 2010), and mortality patterns can also change over time as a result of improvements that affect life expectancies of one group more than another (new drugs, new vaccines, etc.). For this reason, it is of interest to ask whether there is adverse selection in the Chilean annuity market, and if so, how important this phenomenon might be.

One way to analyze adverse selection is to simply plot population and annuity mortality patterns, which we do in Figure 7.11.[15] The evidence strongly suggests that, in Chile, the male population does die earlier than those persons who purchase annuities, supporting the notion that people who expect to live longer purchase annuities that allow them to smooth consumption and avoid the longevity risk, and the effect is even stronger for women. Thus, there is some degree of adverse selection in the Chilean annuity market since people who are expected to live longer are more likely to purchase annuities.

We quantify these differences by computing the A/E ratio comparing population and annuitant mortality patterns. Specifically, we compare the number of deaths in the Chilean male population with a given age structure using one table, versus the number of deaths in the annuitant group using the annuity mortality table. The formula for the A/E method is:

$$\frac{A}{E} = \frac{\sum_x w_x q_x^*}{\sum_x w_x q_x} \times 100 \tag{2}$$

where q_x^* is the probability associated with the table in question that an individual of age x dies, and q_x is the corresponding probability for the base table; w_x are the weights which are set with value $w_{65} = 100,000$ and $w_x = w_{x-1}$ $(1-q_{x-1})$. In the Chilean case, we see that for males the ratio is 84.8 and for females, 66.1. By way of comparison, McCarthy and Mitchell (2010) find a

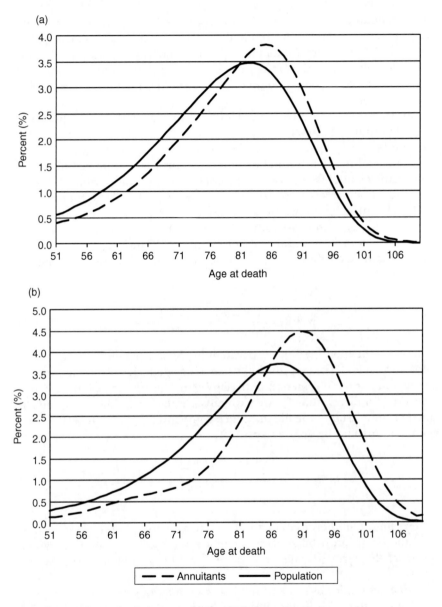

Figure 7.11 Distribution of age at death of Chilean population and annuity purchasers conditional on attaining age 25. Panel (A): males; Panel (B): females. *Source*: Authors' calculations based on INE (2004).

smaller number for US men, 65.3 but a relatively larger ratio for women, 73.6. Thus, we interpret this result as showing that male and female annuitants in Chile live longer than the population, but the women live relatively much longer than in the United States. As a result, it would be reasonable to conjecture that women would find life annuities relatively more appealing than men.

Another way to judge whether Chilean annuity markets are appealing is to compute the so-called money's worth ratio (MWR), or the discounted expected present value of the lifetime payment stream relative to the premium, conditional on survival. This calculation requires that one employs not just a period but a cohortized mortality table and term structure for interest rates (see Mitchell et al. 1999). Also, the formula must take into account whether the person purchased a single annuity or joint annuity (compulsory for married males). In addition, in Chile, life insurers also promise a funeral benefit of 15 UF in case of the purchaser's death. Accordingly, the MWR for a single life annuitant may be defined as:

$$\text{MWR}_i = \frac{\left(A_i \sum_{t=d+1}^{12(w-x)} \frac{{}_tp_x}{(1+i_t)^t}\right) + F}{P} \tag{3}$$

where A is the monthly annuity payment in UF, w is the ultimate age in the mortality table, ${}_tP_x$ is the probability that a life aged x is still alive at time t, d is the number of deferment months chosen in the annuity, i_t is the interest rate used for discounting future payments, F is the funeral benefits, and P is the premium paid to the life insurance company. Similarly, the MWR for a joint annuity may be defined as:

$$\text{MWR}_i = \frac{\left(A_i \sum_{t=d+1}^{12(w-x)} \frac{{}_tp_x + 0.6(1-{}_tp_x){}_tp_y}{(1+i_t)^t}\right) + F}{P} \tag{4}$$

where almost all the variables are the same as before, but now we need to add the death probability of the beneficiary (${}_tP_y$).[16] In case of guarantee periods, the term ${}_tP_x$ takes the value 1 in the periods covered by the guarantee.

Table 7.4 replicates some of the MW computations carried out by prior analysts, at the end of the 1990s and early in the 2000s, and Table 7.5 reports our own updated estimates for the years 2005–8. Overall, and somewhat different from other countries,[17] we find that MWR tends to exceed 1 in Chile and the advantage appears to be rising slightly over time. This suggests that annuity buyers are receiving a relatively generous flow of payments given their premium payments, which explains some of the

TABLE 7.4 Money's worth ratios for Chilean payout annuities derived in prior studies

	James et al. (2006)[a]		Rocha and Thorburn (2006)	
	1999	2003	1999	2003
Male aged 55	0.98	0.98	0.98	1.05
Male aged 65	—	1.01	1.00	1.07
Female aged 55	0.96	0.93	0.99	1.05
Female aged 60	—	0.96	1.02	1.08
Joint life	1.00	1.01	1.00	1.05
Mortality table used	RV-98	RV-98	RV-04	RV-04

[a] Computed for a balance of UF1000.

Source: Authors' calculations from cited sources; all computations use the risk-free rate.

TABLE 7.5 Updated money's worth ratios for Chilean payout annuities

Demographic	Average 2005–8
Male aged 55	1.07
Male aged 65	1.07
Female aged 55	1.09
Female aged 65	1.11
Joint life	1.11

Source: Authors' calculations from Superintendencia de Valores (2010a, 2010b, 2010c); all computations use the risk-free rate.

product's appeal. In results not reported here (but available on request), we examine an OLS regression model relating individual MWRs to participants' age, account balance at purchase, sex and marital status, and other factors. We find that MWRs rise with age, pension balance, and for those who buy deferred rather than immediate products. Single men and women have lower MWRs than do married women, indicating that some of the annuity value derives from what appear to be more than actuarially fair benefits to married women.

The relatively high MWRs we find are also consistent with Rocha and Rudolph (2010), and they are grounds for concern in that insurers selling these products are unlikely to make a positive profit over time as in expectation they will pay out more than they earn. Yet another way to look at the results is that our computations use a risk-free discount rate which enhances the expected present value of the income flow (a long-term government bond rate). If, instead, we used a higher corporate bond rate, annuity payouts would be reduced as would MWRs (note that the PW payout would also decline). Accordingly, while benefits seem relatively generous under conventional assumptions, it is likely that these are risky in the long run.

Conclusion

One of the most interesting features of the Chilean pension system is that approximately two-thirds of all retirees purchase annuities, a very different result than the evidence reported in other countries. In our view, this phenomenon is attributable to several factors specific to Chile:

1. *Generous annuity payments.* As we have shown, MWRs for the Chilean pension system are high in comparison with international experience and appear to be rising.
2. *Information transparency in the annuity bidding process.* The transparency and ease of the SCOMP online mechanism has evidently made it easier for retirees to find better information on annuity premiums than was feasible in the past. In addition, AFPs are now required to issue a list of people nearing retirement age to all the pension providers, as a means to boost competition.
3. *Access to early retirement.* The Chilean law permits people to retire early if their pension accruals are substantial enough. Since workers need not leave the labor force in order to claim their pensions, those who have sufficient wealth in their AFP accounts will value access to the funds. Most of these retirees with decent balances will not expect to see their benefits decline down to the MPG threshold, so they are very likely to annuitize.
4. *Small incentives for the AFPs to promote PW.* In Chile, the AFP managers are mainly paid based on workers' contributions; they are prohibited from paying commissions to brokers. Furthermore, AFPs may not charge a front-end fee to retirees who leave their money with the AFP and take the PW amounts.[18]

The fact that the Chilean life annuity market is continuing to grow bodes well for future retirement security. Nevertheless, some important policy issues remain to be resolved. One is that the system uses sex-specific mortality tables to price retirement benefits, and under the current law, women are able to file as young as age 60. These facts, combined with women's generally lower earnings levels, mean that women's benefits are relatively low compared to men's. By contrast, in many European nations and in the United States, retirement ages are the same for both men and women, and unisex tables apply to the benefit formulas (Bertranou 2001).

If a common mortality table were used for Chilean calculations, men's benefits would fall and women's would rise. Therefore, male retirees taking the PW would deplete their pension balances later and females earlier. Berstein and Tokman (2005) suggest that men's annuity values would fall by 5 percent, while women's would rise by the same percentage. The same authors estimate that raising women's retirement age to 65 would boost their annuities by one-third to 47 percent.

Another issue is that, until recently, poverty benefits under the first pillar were rationed. That is, some poor retirees were unable to qualify for poverty-based old-age income support benefits due to lack of funding for the program. As a result, risk-averse consumers would have been likely to demand an annuity to help smooth old-age consumption, as long as the chance of welfare support was not 100 percent. Also, the MPG benefit level was relatively low, and to receive this benefit, people had to meet strict eligibility requirements (e.g., contributing for twenty years into the system). Both factors would have raised the attractiveness of annuitizing instead of relying on PW payouts.

Nevertheless, the Chilean government has recently enacted several pension system reforms seeking to enhance coverage and boost first-pillar benefits (Godoy 2008; Arenas 2010). Specifically, access to the minimum benefit was made easier and the twenty-year contribution requirement has been dropped. Additionally, the minimum old-age benefit level was increased for those with low or no contribution histories. These reforms are likely to reduce the demand for annuitization in the future, since more people will be able to avail themselves of the social safety net in old age. In addition, the insurance sector is paying what appears to be quite high benefits in exchange for the premiums charged, a pattern that may be challenged as the financial turmoil of 2008–9 takes its toll on insurance company investments.

Acknowledgments

The authors acknowledge research support from the Boettner Center for Pensions and Retirement Security and Pension Research Council at the University of Pennsylvania, and the Centro de Microdatos at the University of Chile for assistance with the Encuesta de Proteccion Social. Ruiz acknowledges date assistance afforded by Osvaldo Macias. Opinions and errors are solely those of the authors and do not reflect views of the institutions supporting the research nor with whom the authors are affiliated.

Notes

[1] This section draws on Arenas et al. (2008) which cites numerous historical references to the development and growth of the Chilean pensions system over the last three decades.

[2] The public defined-benefit entity that administered the old PAYGO defined-benefit program was closed to new entrants by the 1980 reform, but it continues to pay those retirees who remained in the old program at the time of the reform; it also pays 'recognition bonds' at retirement to those who moved to the new system and received credit for prior contributions.

[3] It also provides life insurance and disability benefits as part of the mandatory program.

[4] Mandatory system contributions are capped at an earnings ceiling of approximately US$2,000 a month; fewer than 5 percent of AFP contributors earn over that ceiling.

[5] Strictly speaking, they have other two choices from the combination of these modalities according to recent changes in the regulation, but few people elect these combinations.

[6] The survivorship benefit was made sex-neutral in the most recent 2009 reforms.

[7] This is similar to the $1/E[T]$ rule implemented by the US Internal Revenue Service, when determining how quickly the retiree must spend down his 401(k) plan; see Horneff et al. (2007).

[8] As of 3/10, a UF is equal to CP$20,998, or about US$40.33 (Banco Central de Chile 2010).

[9] The formula for the benefit is

$$\text{Guaranteed pension} = \text{Min}\{45\text{UF}, \text{MPG} + 0.75(\text{Annuity} - \text{MPG})\}$$

[10] Information taken from Superintendencia de Pensiones (2010a) and monetary units were converted into US dollars using data from Banco Central de Chile (2010).

[11] For the reader's convenience, US$1 = CP$501 as of December 2009.

[12] Superintendencia de Pensiones (2010b).

[13] Since the calculation takes into account one's final ten years of contributions, this means that benefits are low for people claiming benefits after a long unemployment period or with many zero-contribution periods. To disincentivize early retirement, the regulator has limited to sixteen the number of zero-contribution months that can be counted in the retiree's final decade of contributions.

[14] From February 2008 to May 2018.

[15] Information collected from The National Institute of Statistics – Chile (INE) where mortality tables are aggregated over five-year periods and disaggregated using the methodology in Ruiz (2010).

[16] Here, we assume that the only potential beneficiary is a spouse; no children are assumed as beneficiaries.

[17] See for instance Doyle et al. (2004), James et al. (2006), Rocha and Rudolph (2010), and Thorburn et al. (2007).

[18] All AFPs charge a fee of 1.25 percent on the pension balance in order to provide pension payouts.

References

Arenas de Mesa, Alberto (2010). *Historia de la Reforma Previsional Chilena: Una Experiencia Exitosa de Política Publica en Democracia.* Santiago, Chile: International Labor Organization.

——David Bravo, Jere R. Behrman, Olivia S. Mitchell, and Petra E. Todd (2008). 'The Chilean Pension Reform Turns 25: Lessons from the Social Protection Survey,' in Stephen Kay and Tapen Sinha, eds., *Lessons from Pension Reform in the Americas.* Oxford, UK: Oxford University Press, pp. 23–58.

Banco Central de Chile (2010). *Series de Indicadores.* Santiago, Chile: Banco Central de Chile. http://www.bcentral.cl/estadisticas-economicas/series-indicadores/index_p.htm

Berstein, Solange and Andrea Tokman (2005). 'Brechas de Ingreso entre Generos: Perpetuadas o Exacerbadas en la Vejez?' Working Paper No. 8. Santiago, Chile: Superintendencia de AFP de Chile.

Bertranou, F.M. (2001). 'Pension Reform and Gender Gaps in Latin America: What are the Policy Options?,' *World Development,* 29(5): 911–23.

Doyle, Suzanne, Olivia S. Mitchell, and John Piggott (2004). 'Annuity Values in Defined Contribution Retirement Systems: Australia and Singapore Compared,' *Australian Economic Review,* 37(4): 402–16.

Finkelstein, Amy and James Poterba (2004). 'Adverse Selection in Insurance Markets: Policyholder Evidence from the U.K. Annuity Market,' *Journal of Political Economy,* 112(1): 183–208.

Godoy Fuentes, Roberto (ed.) (2008). *Manual Informativo: Síntesis de los Conceptos Fundamentales.* Santiago, Chile: Programa de Fortalecimiento del Sistema de Pensiones y Chile Ministerio del Trabajo y Previsión Social.

Horneff, Wolfram, Raimond Maurer, Olivia S. Mitchell, and Ivica Dus (2007). 'Following the Rules: Integrating Asset Allocation and Annuitization in Retirement Portfolios,' *Insurance: Mathematics and Economics,* 42: 396–408.

Instituto Nacional de Estadísticas (INE) (2004). *RV-2004.* Santiago, Chile: Instituto Nacional de Estadísticas. http://www.ine.cl/home.php?lang = eng

James, Estelle, Guillermo Martinez, and Augusto Iglesias (2006). 'The Payout Stage in Chile: Who Annuitizes and Why?' *Journal of Pension Economics and Finance,* 5(2): 121–54.

McCarthy, David and Olivia S. Mitchell (2010). 'International Adverse Selection in Life Insurance and Annuities,' in Shripad Tuljapurkar, Naohiro Ogawa, and Anne Gauthier, eds., *Riding the Age Wave: Responses to Aging in Advanced Industrial States.* Elsevier, NY: Springer, pp. 119–35.

Mitchell, Olivia S., James Poterba, Mark Warshawsky, and Jeffrey Brown (1999). 'New Evidence on the Money's Worth of Individual Annuities,' *American Economic Review*, 89(5): 1299–318.

——Petra Todd, and David Bravo (2009). 'Learning from the Chilean Experience: The Determinants of Pension Switching,' in Annamaria Lusardi, ed., *Overcoming the Saving Slump: Making Financial Education and Saving Programs More Effective*. Chicago, IL: University of Chicago Press, pp. 301–23.

Pino, Francisco (2005). 'Phased Withdrawals and New Mortality Tables.' Technical Notes No. 2. Santiago, Chile: Superintendencia of Pension Funds of Chile.

Reyes, Gonzalo and Fiona Stewart (2008). 'Transparency and Competition in the Choice of Pension Products: The Chilean and UK Experience.' Working Paper No. 7. Paris, France: International Organization of Pension Supervisors (OIPS).

Rocha, Roberto and Heinz P. Rudolph (2010). 'A Summary and Update of Developing Annuities Markets: The Experience of Chile.' World Bank Policy Research Working Paper 5325. Washington, DC: The World Bank.

——Craig Thornburn (2006). *Developing Annuities Markets: The Experience of Chile*. Washington, DC: The World Bank.

Ruiz, Jose Luis (2010). Essays on the Chilean Annuity Market. PhD dissertation. Philadelphia, PA: The Wharton School.

Superintendencia de Administradoras de Fondos de Pensiones (SAFP) 2010. *Beneficios garantizados por el Estado*. Santiago, Chile: Superintendencia de Administradoras de Fondos de Pensiones. http://www.safp.cl/573/printer-3022.html

Superintendencia de Pensiones (2010a). *Centro de Estadísticas*. Santiago, Chile: Superintendencia de Pensiones. http://www.spensiones.cl/safpstats/stats/.sc. php?_cid = 45

——(2010b). *Centro de Estadísticas*. Santiago, Chile: Superintendencia de Pensiones. www.spensiones.cl/safpstats/stats/.sc.php?_cid = 44

——(2010c). *Centro de Estadísticas*. Santiago, Chile: Superintendencia de Pensiones. www.spensiones.cl/safpstats/stats/.sc.php?_cid = 41

Superintendencia de Valores (2010a). *Estadísticas de Mercado*. Santiago, Chile: Superintendencia de Valores. http://www.svs.cl/sitio/estadisticas/seg_mercado. php

——(2010b). *Información Estadística*. Santiago, Chile: Superintendencia de Valores. http://www.svs.cl/sitio/estadisticas/svtas_com_int_rvp.php

——(2010c). *Mercado de Seguros*. Santiago, Chile: Superintendencia de Valores. http://www.svs.cl/sitio/estadisticas/seguros.php

Thorburn, Craig, Roberto Rocha, and Marco Morales (2007). 'An Analysis of the Money's Worth Ratios in Chile,' *Journal of Pension Economics and Finance*, 7(1): 95–119.

Valdes Prieto, Salvador (2005). 'Para Aumentar La Competencia Entre Las AFP,' *Estudios Publicos*, 98: 87–142.

World Bank (1994). *Averting the Old-Age Crisis: Policies to Protect the Old and Promote Growth*. Washington, DC: The World Bank.

Chapter 8

The Private Life Annuity Market in Germany: Products and Money's Worth Ratios

Barbara Kaschützke and Raimond Maurer

Buying a payout annuity is a decision that can shape financial well-being for many decades to come; moreover, it is usually irreversible so it is important to make sure that such a decision is a well-informed one. We focus here on the question of whether annuities deliver an adequate value for money, applying the money's worth methodology to the German voluntary annuity market. After reviewing international research, we examine the German voluntary annuities market. We describe the main product groups, the insurer's crucial statutory obligation to distribute a substantial part of its annual profits to the insured. Then, factors determining the money's worth ratios are represented and scrutinized, and results compared to those of other countries.

Money's worth methodology

Our objective is to verify whether German annuities are delivering an adequate value for money, by applying the money's worth methodology pioneered by Warshawsky (1988) and refined by Mitchell et al. (1999). The main goal is to calculate the value of life annuities to the (prospective) retiree, and make this value comparable across different annuitant ages and product structures. The money's worth ratio (MWR) is based on the calculation of the expected present discounted value of annuity payouts, relative to the purchase price of the annuity. The MWR is calculated according to the following formula:

$$\text{MWR} = \frac{1}{\text{Premium}} \sum_{t=1}^{T} \frac{p_t \times A_t}{(1 + i_t)^t} \tag{1}$$

where i_t denotes an appropriate interest rate for a t-month investment to discount future payouts, p_t stands for the survival probability to period t given the retiree is alive in $t = 0$, A_t represents the monthly payouts to the annuitant as actually quoted by insurance companies in $t = 0$, and *Premium* is the amount charged by the annuity provider in exchange for the benefits promised to the annuitant. T stands for the maximum age as per the respective mortality table.

An MWR of unity means that for every Euro invested in an annuity today, the annuitant can expect to receive 1 Euro back in today's terms, so the insurance company calculates the premium on an actuarially fair basis. More generally, the premium charged by the insurance company exceeds the actuarial present value of future payouts (i.e., MWR < 1) which implies transaction costs. These transaction costs may include administrative and distribution costs incurred by the insurance company, corporate overhead, additions to contingency reserves, costs of equity capital, and costs of adverse selection. Adverse selection may result from the fact that prospective annuitants live longer than the population. An MWR of less than 1 is common, as even in well-functioning markets insurance companies must cover the abovementioned costs at least in the long term. Yet, this does not mean that the retiree does not receive an adequate value for money: Mitchell et al. (1999) report that for an MWR of 0.8, rational individuals (without a bequest motive) would still prefer to buy an annuity, rather than to follow an optimal consumption and investment strategy without having access to the annuity market.

The interpretation of MWRs above unity is not straightforward. Poterba and Warshawsky (2000) argue that MWRs equal or greater than unity are implausible, at least in the long term, because of the administrative costs. James and Song (2001) claim that costs incurred by insurance companies can be covered by the spread between the risk-free rate, on which the MWR calculations are mostly based, and the higher rate they earn on their actual riskier portfolio.[1] Also, in case of immediate annuities, insurance companies receive the whole premium at once but pay out only a fraction over a long period of time. MWRs in excess of 1 may also be a result of optimistic assumptions underlying the calculations of the insurance company in a surveyed period, and for that reason, only short-lived. Indeed, for countries with established life and annuity insurance markets, in absence of regulatory requirements regarding the annuitization rate and for surveyed periods longer than one, the MWRs tend to be below unity.

International empirical evidence on money's worth ratios

Since the introduction of the MWR methodology, it has been used to assess the annuity markets in a number of countries such as Australia, Canada, Chile, Israel, Singapore, Switzerland, the United Kingdom, and the United

States. Table 8.1 is sorted by country surveyed and shows the main studies, time periods, as well as the type of products analyzed. The minimum and maximum MWRs are reported for nominal level annuities, quoted for 65-year-old individuals.

Thus far, the research has mainly focused on two countries – the United Kingdom and the United States. Surprisingly little research has been conducted for countries with well-developed insurance markets such as France, Germany, Italy, and Switzerland. The later countries are similar in that the standard annuity products allow annuitants to participate in insurer profits, and thus the structure of the main products is different from the structure of main products observed for the United Kingdom and the United States. Only two studies (James and Song 2001; Bütler and Rüsch 2007) deal with the annuity markets in Switzerland, only one with the annuity market in Germany (von Gaudecker and Weber 2004), and to our knowledge, so far none deals with annuity markets in France and Italy.

All studies published to date have found that the MWRs for nominal annuities calculated using annuitant mortality tables are relatively high, usually in a range between 0.90 and 1.10. When the money's worth analysis is performed using general population mortality tables, the results are smaller, being approximately 10 percentage points less and lying between 0.80 and unity. Independent of mortality assumptions used, the MWRs differ depending on male and female, being usually somewhat higher for women due to their higher life expectancy. The difference between MWRs resulting from using annuitant versus the population mortality tables is often considered to be a measure of adverse selection in annuity markets. The presence of adverse selection, however, does not indicate that annuity markets are not functioning properly. When a range of annuity products and a freedom of choice are given, such effects can be eliminated by self-selection, meaning that people can buy annuity products which are particularly well suited to their subjectively estimated mortality risk. For example, escalating annuities will be favored by those with low mortality risk and annuities with high initial payments or period-certain guarantees by those with estimated average or high mortality risk.

In what follows, we extend prior literature in several ways. First, the approach introduced by Mitchell et al. (1999) is used to calculate the MWRs for the German voluntary life annuity market during a ten-year period (1997–2006). This is the most comprehensive time span since the deregulation of German insurance markets in 1994, a change that placed the responsibility for and control over the terms and conditions of insurance contracts as well as the design, structure, and pricing of insurance products directly with insurance companies. Second, we comment on the development of observed MWRs over time in connection with the influence of major changes in interest rates, legislative factors, and mortality assumptions.

TABLE 8.1 Main studies on money's worth ratios (MWRs), surveyed countries, and time periods

Country surveyed	Author and publication year	Period	Annuity market	Type of annuity	Min/Max MWRs for nominal level annuity[a], annuitants	Min/Max MWRs for nominal level annuity[a], population
Australia	Knox (2000)	1999	Voluntary	Nominal fixed, indexed, period certain	0.85–0.99	0.85–0.96
Australia, Canada, Chile, Israel, Singapore, Switzerland, the United Kingdom, the United States	James and Song (2001)	1999	Mandatory, voluntary	Nominal fixed, escalating, indexed, period certain, joint	0.91–1.08	0.86–1.08
Australia, Canada, Chile, Israel, Singapore, Switzerland, the United Kingdom, the United States	James and Vittas (1999)	1998–9	Mandatory, voluntary	Nominal fixed, joint, escalating, indexed, period certain	0.9–1.25	0.91–1.02
Australia, Singapore	Doyle et al. (2004)	1999	Voluntary	Nominal fixed, period certain	0.89–0.9 (A) 0.95 (S)	0.83–0.87 (A) 0.95–0.96 (S)
Chile	Thorburn et al. (2007)	1999–2005	Voluntary	Nominal fixed, joint, period certain	0.99–1.12	—
Germany	von Gaudecker and Weber (2004)	2003	Voluntary	Nominal fixed (with profit participation), period certain	0.97–1.01	0.86–0.94
Singapore	Fong (2002)	2000	Voluntary	Nominal fixed	1.01	1.01
Switzerland		2000–5	Mandatory		0.89–1.24	—

Country	Source	Period	Type	Product		
The United Kingdom	Bütler and Rüsch (2007)			Nominal fixed, single/joint		0.95[b]
The United Kingdom	Cannon and Tonks (2004)	1957–2002	Voluntary	Nominal fixed, period certain	0.98	
The United Kingdom	Cannon and Tonks (2008)	1957–2002	Voluntary	Nominal fixed, period certain	0.98 (1957–2002) 0.93 (2001–7)	–
The United Kingdom	Finkelstein and Poterba (2004)	1981–98	Mandatory, voluntary	Nominal/real fixed, escalating	–	0.91–0.99
The United Kingdom	Finkelstein and Poterba (2004)	1998	Mandatory, voluntary	Nominal/real fixed, escalating, period certain	0.94–0.99	0.85–0.9
The United States	Mitchell et al. (1999)	1985–95	Voluntary	Nominal fixed	0.83–0.91	0.75–0.81
The United States	Warshawsky (1988)	1918–84	Voluntary	Nominal fixed	0.88–1.01	–

[a] Money's worth ratio calculations using Treasury yield curve, quotes for 65-year-old males and females, without period-certain guarantees.

[b] Based on products with five-year period-certain payouts over 1972–2002.

Source: Authors' calculations from cited sources; for full citations see references.

Specifics of German annuity markets in money's worth context

Germany is a country with well-developed insurance markets: in 1980, it was second only to the United States in terms of insurance premiums per capita and third after the United States and the United Kingdom in terms of insurance penetration. Since that time, the country has lost its position and currently lies below the G7 average, partly due to the fact that in many other countries, insurance products have shifted from public social security (especially in the pension and health sector) to private contracting, whereas the German social security system still provides generous benefits. The situation is changing, however, as it is becoming difficult to maintain public social security benefits at generous levels, and more incentives are given to provide privately for old age.[2] The economic basis for a sustainable development of German insurance industry and especially the life insurance industry is the availability of adequate fixed income assets, and to a lesser extent, equity capital markets, as well as the long tradition of observing the population's mortality and creating both population and annuitant mortality tables.[3]

The German insurance industry is one of the largest insurance markets in the world, with respect to the premiums written, with life insurance being by far the biggest sector. Assets under management of the life insurance sector amount to more than EUR 681bn. The number of insurance contracts in the life insurance sector surpasses 93 million with insured amounts of more than EUR 2.452bn for a country with a total population of approximately 82 million. Annuity business is an integral but still relatively small part of the life insurance sector (GDV 2007). The main difference between life insurance products and annuity products is their mirror image treatment of mortality risk. Both product categories are subject to the same legislation and are similarly regulated in Germany. In fact, many life insurance contracts contain the option to convert the insured sum into a stream of annuity payments, instead of the lump sum payout, whereas many deferred annuity contracts contain the option for a lump sum payment at the end of the accumulation phase.

Currently, traditional insurance contracts which pay out benefits as an annuity represent approximately 22 percent of the in-service contracts and 13 percent of the paying-out contracts (measured by the number of contracts). This corresponds to approximately 18 percent of the amount insured for in-service contracts, and 15 percent of the paying-out contracts. The abolition of tax privileges in 2005, however, led to the dramatic increase in the popularity of annuity contracts and with time may result in the complete change of patterns. For example, annuity contracts accounted for approximately 50 percent of all new contracts for the year

2007 as measured by the number of contracts, and for 30 percent of all new contracts as measured by amounts insured (GDV 2007).

The standard product in the German market is the single life nominal participating annuity, consisting of a guaranteed portion and a profit participation portion. The guaranteed part is calculated using an interest rate defined by legislation; it must be paid out to the insured independent of actual profits of the insurance company during the whole lifetime of the insurance contract.[4] The profits of the insurance companies stem from the net investment results during the relevant period as well as from cost and mortality experience. Both cost and mortality experience tend to remain quite stable during long time periods, making net investment results the main source of insurer profits (Maurer and Somova 2007). A considerable portion of the surpluses must be distributed to the annuitants, and the supervisory authority ascertains that all insurance companies adequately honor this legislative requirement annually.[5] Such non-guaranteed profit participation can be considered as a quasi-inflation adjustment to the annuity payment, which is otherwise fixed in nominal terms.

There are two main profit participation schemes in the German annuity market: a dynamic participation scheme and a so-called flexible (also termed 'constant') participation scheme. Both offer a guaranteed payout, the minimum amount of which is calculated according to legislative requirements regarding the interest rate. The participation scheme defines the form in which profits are allocated on top of the guaranteed amount, and in this way it determines the total payout the annuitant can receive annually. When the dynamic participation scheme is chosen, the periodic payment starts from a level only insignificantly above the guaranteed payout, and it increases annually depending on the actual profits of the insurance company. Once the annual increase has taken place, the achieved payout level cannot be reduced, even if the insurer were to earn lower profits in subsequent years. On the signing of such an annuity contract, the insurer guarantees the payout during the first year and provides projections regarding expected payouts for up to fifteen years thereafter. Such projections for periods longer than one year are, however, not legally binding and can be revised anytime if the calculation basis of the insurer changes. The major advantage of this payout scheme is that the insured is protected against outright reductions in annuity payments, and benefits will most probably increase with age. The main disadvantage is that payouts from this product start relatively low, thus delivering lower cash flows immediately after retirement when life expectancy is high and financial needs may also be high, compared to more advanced ages. The annual increase of payments in the dynamic profit participation scheme depends mainly on the net interest earned by the insurance company during the period under consideration, and the guaranteed constant interest rate valid at the time of the contract's signing (which by legislation must be applied to its whole lifetime).

The flexible (or constant) profit participation scheme anticipates insurers' future profits from the beginning of the payout period. Thus, benefit payments start at a level considerably above that of the guaranteed payout[6] and remain constant unless the company decides to change the profit participation. The absolute payment amount above the guaranteed payout is not guaranteed on an annual basis in this format;[7] rather, it can be reduced if the insurer's profits fall below a certain level. The advantage of this participation scheme is that it delivers higher payouts at the beginning of the annuity contract's lifetime, offering possibly more financial flexibility for retirees when they are younger. The main disadvantage is that, during periods of low interest rates, payment levels can be reduced.

The partly dynamic participation scheme combines the features of the two schemes described earlier. Herein, payments early in the payout period are higher than with the pure dynamic participation scheme, and annual increases are lower. The payout level, however, cannot be reduced.

In the German market, it is also possible to obtain period-certain guarantees for a range of periods, giving the retiree a surety that the pension would be paid for a set time horizon (e.g., ten years independent of whether the insured person is alive). Another modification of the annuity agreement offers protection for dependants, called the 'premium refund' scheme (*Beitragsrückgewähr*). When this form of guarantee is chosen, the annuitant's heirs are entitled to a payout of the difference between the total contributions paid prior to the start of annuity payments, and the annuity payments so far received.

Independent of the availability of any guarantee, the annuitant can elect a dependent protection option, in which case the insurance company will pay the widow's benefit to the heirs. In case the premium refund option was in place, the heirs can choose either the lump sum payout or a dependent's pension. Both guarantee forms incur costs to the annuitants, making their life annuities more expensive. All abovementioned payout and guarantee options are available for both immediate annuities (which are further analyzed later) and deferred annuities.

Insurance companies are not obliged to offer all annuity products and are free to compile their own product range. Our review of the German market suggests that many companies are more willing to offer quotes for products with guarantees as well as dynamic participation schemes, versus those offering flexible participation schemes. Table 8.2 summarizes the characteristics of typical annuity products in the German market, extending the typology introduced by Poterba (2001).

TABLE 8.2 Structure of the typical annuity product in the German market

Attribute	Structure
Nature of payouts	Nominal fixed
Number of lives covered	Single
Payout guaranteed	Yes, calculation inputs defined by legislation
Profit participation form	Dynamic/flexible/partly dynamic
Waiting period for the start of benefits	Immediate/deferred
Method of premium payment	Single/gradual
Duration of payouts	Lifelong
Period-certain guarantee	Yes, usually 5/10/15 years or premium refund

Source: Authors' calculations; see text.

Setup of the money's worth analysis for German voluntary annuity market

Annuity quotes

We have gathered data for the period 1997–2006 on the monthly payouts for an immediate, single life annuity costing EUR 100,000 in the voluntary market. (Prior to the introduction of the Euro,[8] a purchase price of DM 100,000 was used.) Quotes were obtained from the database 'LV-Win' provided by Morgen and Morgen (2010). This database covers about 90 percent of German annuity product providers, although not every insurance company offers the entire range of annuity products.[9]

Our data on payouts distinguish between annuity payouts for males and females, and then by age; we analyze quotes for 60-, 65-, and 70-year olds.[10] Within the product groups, we first look at those offering no guaranteed payment periods, and then those which offer a period-certain guarantee for the first ten years. For both categories, with and without the period-certain payment, we consider a nominal fixed annuity and then distinguish between the guaranteed payout and two different forms of participation, as described earlier. Table 8.3 summarizes the structure of the sample.

For MWR calculations, it is necessary to model the development of payouts over a period of several decades. Guaranteed payouts remain certain during the lifetime of an annuity contract, but it is necessary to develop a method of determining the applicable annual profit participation rates. For the dynamic profit participation scheme, we follow the conservative approach in Albrecht and Maurer (2002), which uses as a proxy the net investment return of insurance companies. For the years 2001–6, where it was possible to obtain actual data on average profit participation rates for the annuity business (Assekurata 2004, 2005, 2007,

TABLE 8.3 Structure of the data sample for calculation of money's worth ratios in the German voluntary annuity market

Attribute	Time span	
	1997–2001	2002–6
Purchase amount	DM 100,000	EUR 100,000
Annuitant's characteristics	Male/female single life	Male/female single life
Period-certain payments	0 year/10 years	0 year/10 years
Profit participation form	Only guaranteed payment/ flexible/dynamic	Only guaranteed payment/ flexible/dynamic
Purchase age (years)	60/65/75	60/65/75

Source. Authors' calculation using data from Morgen and Morgen (2010); see text.

2009), we calculate the so-called 'dynamization factor' as a difference between the reported market average profit participation rate and the guaranteed interest rate applicable to the year the contract was signed. For years prior to 2001, we estimate the dynamization factor as the difference between 90 percent of the net investment returns reported for the year of contract signing, and the guaranteed interest rate applicable to the corresponding year.[11] For the dynamic profit participation scheme, annual payouts after the first year increase on a yearly basis by the dynamization factor. The annual dynamization rates obtained by both methods are more conservative than those implied by the projected annuity payments as quoted by insurers for the fifth, tenth, and fifteenth year of the annuity contract's lifetime.[12]

For the flexible scheme, we use the amount paid during the first year, since the change in profit participation rate is at the insurer's discretion. German insurance companies have sought to avoid reductions in the profit participation rates, but in 2001–3 some of them actually reduced benefits for products with flexible profit participation. For both dynamic and flexible participation schemes, our procedure for modeling profit participation is similar to that in von Gaudecker and Weber (2004). It is important to note that, outside the framework of the minimum guaranteed payouts and the payouts for the first year, the total annual payouts in each subsequent year are not certain. To account for this, the adjustment either of the cash flows or of the interest rates is required.

Figure 8.1 displays the time series of annuity rates by sex. For example, a monthly quote for a EUR 500 payout for life in exchange for a purchase price of EUR 100,000 gives the (annual) annuity rate of 6 percent (500 × 12/100,000 = 0.06). Panels (A–C) of Figure 8.1 show the time path of

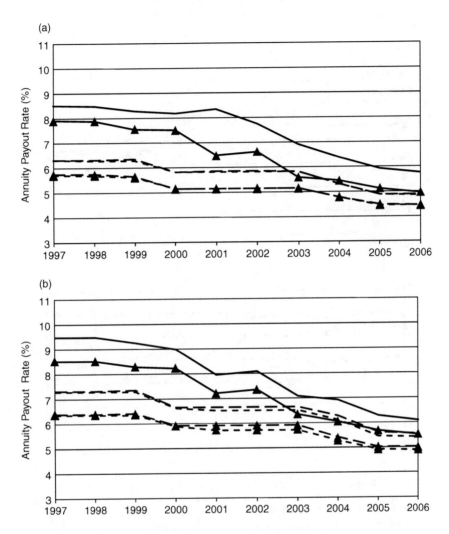

Figure 8.1 Development of average annuity payout rates for German voluntary single immediate life annuities 1997–2006. Panel (A): age 60, without period-certain payout guarantee; Panel (B): age 65, without period-certain guarantee; Panel (C): age 70, without period-certain guarantee; Panel (D): age 70, with period-certain guarantee. *Source*: Authors' calculations; see text.

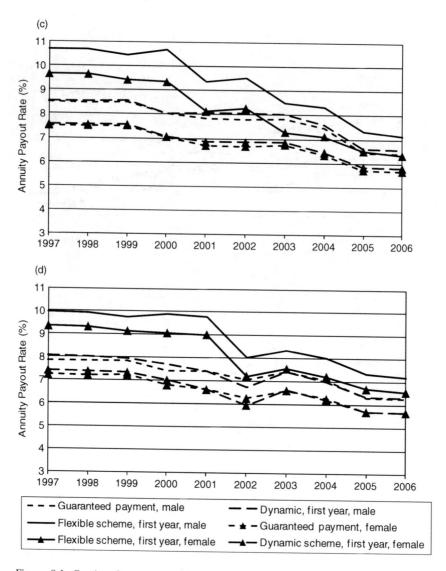

Figure 8.1 *Continued*

average annuity rates for products without a period-certain guarantee, for 1997–2006.

The annuity rates for all age groups and product categories over the period lie between 4 and 11 percent, higher at the beginning of the period and lower toward the end. This pattern is in line with the trend in long-term government bond interest rates, since insurance companies in

Germany predominantly invest in fixed income securities and their guaranteed interest rate is linked to interest rates on government securities. By comparison, the yield for ten-year government bonds moved over the same period from approximately 6 percent in 1997 to under 4 percent in 2006 (German Bundesbank 2007). Looking across the age groups, we see that annuity rates rise for older buyers, consistent with the rising mortality with age; this results from leading mortality credits for surviving annuitants as ages rise. For example, in 1997, the average rate for the guaranteed payment part of the annuity for a 60-year-old male was slightly above 6 percent, while for a 70-year-old male, it was more than 8 percent. By 2006, the rates were about 5 and 6.5 percent, respectively. During the whole surveyed period, annuity rates for males (lines without markers) were higher than annuity rates for females (lines with markers), reflecting females' higher life expectancies.

Figure 8.1 also reports the with-participation rates for the first year of the annuity contract guaranteed by the insurance company at the time the quotes were obtained. Changes over time follow interest rate trends. Rates for the dynamic scheme, shown as first-year quotes, are only slightly higher than the rates for the guaranteed payouts due to the structure of annuity products with dynamic participation schemes (where the latter offer higher payouts as the contract matures). Within a single product category and year, we see considerable differences between insurer quotes. Understandably, those differences are relatively small for the guaranteed payouts, and they become bigger when profit participation is considered. The standard deviation of the offers ranges between 1 and 2 percent of the average for the guaranteed payouts, and from 5 to 9 percent of the average for the schemes having with-profit participation. This translates into potentially huge differences in the payment amounts: the difference between the minimum and maximum quoted monthly payment within a single product category varies in the range of EUR 15–20 for the guaranteed payout, and over EUR 100 for products having with-profit participation. A possible explanation for this dispersion in annuity payouts across firms may be the financial capacity of the company selling the annuities (Mitchell et al. 1999). In addition, insurance product pricing depends on each firm's product strategy and business policy.

The guarantees on the period-certain payments reduce annuity payouts depending on the entry age and sex of the annuitant. In our data, the annuity payments without period-certain payment were 1–5 percent lower, on average, than for the same annuity without a guarantee. The differences between the quotes with and without period-certain payments are bigger for men than for women, due to women's lower mortality. They also increase with entry age, being the highest (up to 8 percent difference) for a 70-year-old male. Across all ages, price differences between the products with and without the period-certain guarantees declined over time. Panel (D) of Figure 8.1 illustrates the developments of the quotes on the example of 70-year-old males. While quotes for products without period-certain guarantees were in the range of 7.5–10.5 percent in the year 1997, they declined to approximately 6–7 percent in the year 2006. The difference between products with and without period-certain guarantees was about 1 percentage point in 1997, and almost nonexistent in 2006.

Relatively small and declining differences in prices of products with and without guarantees may be explained by different mortality assumptions underlying the insurer's price calculation. Figure 8.2 traces survival probabilities for annuitants who purchased at age 60 and 70, based on the DAV 2004R mortality table.[13] For 60-year-old annuitants, the probability of being alive ten years after the start of annuity payments is 95 percent (women) and 91 percent (men) as indicated in Panel (A). This means that, even without a guarantee period, the insurance company almost surely expects to pay benefits during the first decade. Survival probabilities decline by 11 and 17 percent for females and males respectively at age 70 (Panel B). This means that insurers still expect to be paying approximately five (four) out of every six female (male) annuitants at the end of the ten-year guarantee period.

Interest rates

We use as discount rates the yields of government bonds observed in the year the respective annuity was priced, with maturities ranging from one to twenty years.[14] In doing so, we follow the approach in Mitchell et al. (1999), von Gaudecker and Weber (2004), and Cannon and Tonks (2008), among others. After the first twenty years, we assume a flat interest rate structure at the level achieved in year 20. Our procedure is justified because observed differences are small between the yields for maturities over twenty years on German government securities, and also because the estimation error for maturities longer than twenty years is high as there are not many relevant securities in the German bond market. The choice of default-free discount rates in our analysis is justified by the fact that little company risk has been observed in the German life insurance market due to strong regulation. For instance, Maurer and Somova (2007) report that since World War II, there has been only one insurer insolvency. The security of annuity and life insurance payments and the credibility of insurance obligations are also supported by the industry's solvency arrangements.[15] Studies for other countries such as the United States and the United Kingdom also perform the analysis using both government and corporate bond yields, but insurance company insolvency is observed there more often.[16]

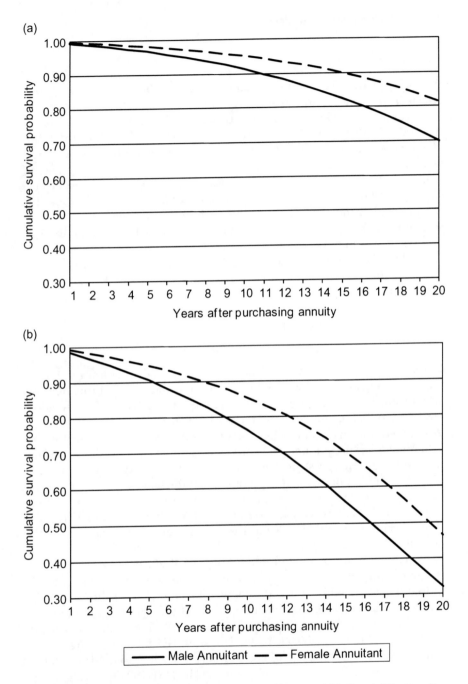

Figure 8.2 Survival probabilities for annuitants aged 60 and 70. Panel (A): annuity is purchased at age 60; Panel (B): annuity is purchased at age 70. *Notes*: In Panel (A), the survival probability ten years after annuity purchase for males is 0.91 and for females is 0.95. In Panel (B), the survival probability ten years after annuity purchase for males is 0.76 and for females is 0.85. *Source*: Authors' calculations based on DAV 2004R German annuitant mortality table.

Mortality assumptions

We use both annuitant and population mortality tables to assess selection effects in the market and to shed light on the thin market for voluntary annuity purchase. The German Society of Actuaries (DAV) recommended the DAV 1994R for 1997–2004, and for the years 2005 onward, the DAV 2004R table. The general population mortality tables are published by the German Statistics Office every three years, the last one currently available being the 2005–7 table (Statistisches Bundesamt 2008). As is expected, survival probabilities in annuity mortality tables are higher than those in the population mortality table, reflecting both insurer loads and adverse selection.[17] Also for both tables, the mortality rates for females are, on average, lower than for males.

To describe the differences between actuarial tables in Germany, we compute the ratio of actual to expected mortality as in McCarthy and Mitchell (2002).

$$\frac{A}{E} = 100 \times \frac{\sum_x^T w_x q_x^*}{\sum_x^T w_x q_x} \tag{2}$$

Here, q_x^* is the probability of an individual of age x dying within the next year according to the mortality table in question, and q_x is the probability of an individual of age x dying according to a benchmark table. The weights w_x are set so that the initial population is 100,000 and $w_x = w_{x-k1}(1 - q_{x-1})$. T is the terminal age of the benchmark table. A/E is a usual metric used by actuaries and demographers to express the number of deaths in a population with a given age structure using one table, and relating it to the expected number of deaths in a population of the same size using a second mortality table. The ratio is multiplied by 100. A value of 100 implies that the number of deaths is equal irrespective of which mortality table is used while a value of less than 100 means that the number of deaths in the benchmark table is bigger.

We compare annuitant mortality tables DAV 2004R and DAV 1994R starting from the age of 65 until the terminal age of the benchmark mortality table, in this case DAV 1994R. The A/E ratio in this case is 96 for both males and females, meaning that on average, the mortality for individuals aged 65 according to the DAV 2004R table is only 4 percent lower than in the DAV 1994R table. This observed relation changes over time, however. Until the age of 90, mortality according to the DAV 2004R table is substantially lower than according to the DAV 1994R. it is bigger up to a factor of 1.5 after the age of 90, the increases being especially pronounced for males. These differences most probably reflect the incorporation of the new statistical observations in DAV 2004R, and the use of different statistical methods to estimate mortalities at the end of the mortality table, where real mortality observations are relatively scarce. The A/E ratio is 69 (67) for males (females) when the annuitants table DAV 2004R is compared to the 2005–7 population table (benchmark table), in line with the results reported by McCarthy and Mitchell (2002) for the United States and the United Kingdom, especially males.[18]

Assessment of mortality improvements in the general population during the surveyed decade also delivers interesting insights. The comparison between population tables 2005–7 and 1995–7 results in an A/E ratio of 70 for males and 65 for females, and the strongest mortality improvements are observed for the time span of 65–75 years. These mortality trends should influence insurers' calculation of annuity rates, and the calculation of MWRs by the prospective retirees.

Main results for the German voluntary annuity market

Results show that over our ten-year period, annuities without a period-certain guarantee deliver a good value for money using annuitant mortality tables (see Table 8.4). Average values for all ages mostly lie slightly below unity when profit participation is accounted for. For the guaranteed payout part, the values are lower due to the conservative assumptions used in the calculation. The values of slightly below 80 percent are also broadly in line with international experience, however (Warshawsky 1988; James and Song 2001). Table 8.4 also shows, for products including profit participation, that the money's worth values are slightly higher for females than males, reflecting female's higher survival probabilities. The difference in MWRs benefiting females stems from the profit participation, since for the guaranteed payouts only, the figures are slightly higher for males. This is due to the fact that insurance companies typically offer lower rates to females because they are expected to benefit longer from the annuity payments, while they distribute profits independently of the sex of the purchaser.

There are few differences by age group for products having with-profit participation. For only the guaranteed part, the ratios slightly increase with age, being the highest for the 70-year-old buyer; this supports the observation that survival credits increase with age. It should be noted that MWRs for products including profit participation are very sensitive to the assumptions about the participation structure and the development of the profit participation over time. The standard deviation of MWRs during the surveyed period across all age groups is very stable for the guaranteed payouts, being approximately 5 percentage points. It is between 8 and 10 percentage points for the flexible participation scheme, and between 10 and 12

TABLE 8.4 German voluntary annuity market money's worth ratios averages from 1997 to 2006 for products with and without period-certain guarantees

	Without guarantee period			With ten-year guarantee period		
	Guaranteed payment	Flexible scheme	Dynamic scheme	Guaranteed payment	Flexible scheme	Dynamic scheme
A. Annuitant mortality table						
Average quotes, age 60						
Male	0.771	1.001	0.989	0.770	0.989	0.988
Female	0.760	1.011	1.004	0.756	0.993	0.998
Average quotes, age 65						
Male	0.789	0.994	0.981	0.791	0.987	0.982
Female	0.779	1.004	0.995	0.778	0.991	0.993
Average quotes, age 70						
Male	0.812	0.992	0.978	0.816	0.992	0.982
Female	0.805	1.001	0.993	0.806	0.994	0.993
B. Population mortality table						
Average quotes, age 60						
Male	0.688	0.894	0.855	0.770	0.989	0.988
Female	0.698	0.928	0.891	0.756	0.993	0.999
Average quotes, age 65						
Male	0.689	0.868	0.829	0.791	0.987	0.981
Female	0.702	0.903	0.864	0.777	0.991	0.993
Average quotes, age 70						
Male	0.694	0.847	0.808	0.816	0.991	0.982
Female	0.704	0.874	0.836	0.806	0.994	0.993

Source: Authors' calculations; see text.

percentage points for the dynamic scheme (see Figure 8.3). When a population mortality table is used, the MWRs become approximately 10 percentage points lower across all product groups and age categories (see Table 8.4). This is consistent with Mitchell et al. (1999), Finkelstein and Poterba (2002), and von Gaudecker and Weber (2004), and it results from the lower life expectancy of the general population compared to that of buyers of voluntary annuities. The other conclusions drawn for the guaranteed payouts, flexible, and dynamic participation schemes are similar, independent of mortality table used.

The mortality advantage of female annuitants becomes more visible when the general population tables are used to calculate MWRs. This can be explained by the fact that survival probabilities have to be assessed using forecast models since data are not available for the very advanced ages typical of annuitant mortality tables. The use of forecast models usually

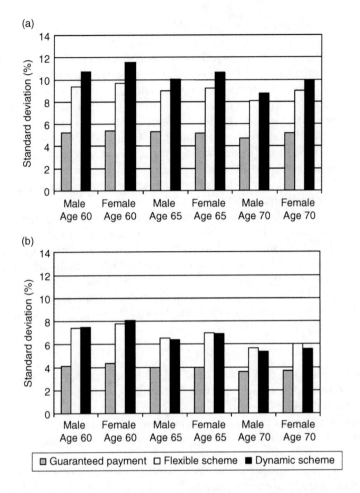

Figure 8.3 Standard deviation of money's worth ratio averages, products without period-certain guarantees, German voluntary annuity market, range of entry ages, 1997–2006. Panel (A): annuitant; Panel (B): population. *Source*: Authors' calculations; see text.

results in a reduction of the male–female differences until a crossover point, when female mortality at advanced ages surpasses male mortality.[19] A slight convergence of mortality rates in advanced ages is also observed for German general population mortality tables. It is pronounced toward the end of the DAV 2004R (annuitant) mortality table, and a complete crossover is observed in the annuitant's mortality table DAV 1994R. The annuitant longer life expectancy may also be driving the higher standard deviation of MWRs calculated with annuitant mortality tables, versus using the population table (compare Panels (A) and (B) of Figure 8.3).

Offering a period-certain payout of ten years makes the annuities more expensive to purchase; thus quotes for period-certain products are lower than for the same products without any period guarantees. Nevertheless, the period-certain annuities may be a useful product for older annuitants and for those with average (or below average) life expectancy. When the annuitant mortality table is used to calculate the money's worth, the effects of the guaranteed payment period are not very pronounced. For instance, for the 60-year olds, the MWRs are slightly reduced, while for the age groups of 65- and 70-year olds a slight increase is observed in comparison to products without guarantee.

The use of a population mortality table highlights the advantages of the guaranteed payment period. Table 8.4 illustrates the described results. Now, the MWRs are similar to those observed using the annuitant tables, coming close to unity for both profit participation schemes. In other words, the differences arising from the use of annuitant versus population tables are eliminated by the payout guarantee. Individuals at advanced entry ages (65 and 70) tend to benefit more from the guaranteed payout period.[20]

Trends during the surveyed period

As noted earlier, the MWRs declined after 2003 for all age groups in the German market. After that year, they were about 90 percent for products with profit participation, and about 75 percent for the guaranteed part only. Figure 8.4 shows the annual results by product category and mortality table used, for an entry age of 65. Results are similar for the other age groups.

Values for males appear in Panels (A) and (B) for products without and with period-certain guarantee, and in Panels (C) and (D) for females. The lines with markers use population tables. As is clear, results depend, to a large extent, on capital market developments experienced during the period. When interest rates declined considerably, this reduced both insurer existing values and new investment opportunities; in turn, this produced a pronounced decline in the net interest earned by insurance companies since German insurance companies predominantly invest in domestic fixed income securities.[21] During 1997–2000, the net interest earned by insurance companies was relatively stable, averaging approximately 7.5 percent. However, in 2001 and 2002, it fell to 6 percent and then to 4.6 percent, after which the net interest remained at the level of approximately 5 percent.

This persistent decline in interest rates affected annuity markets in several ways. First, insurance companies had to reduce the guaranteed

(a)

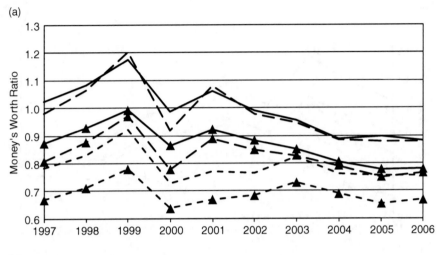

(b)

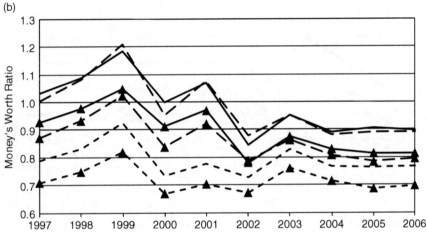

Figure 8.4 Year-by-year development of money's worth ratios for 65-year-old annuitants in the German voluntary annuity market. Panel (A): male aged 65 without
period-certain guarantee; Panel (B): male aged 65 with period-certain guarantee;
Panel (C): female aged 65 without period-certain guarantee; Panel (D): female
aged 65 with period-certain guarantee. *Source*: Authors' calculations; see text.

interest rate for new contracts from 4 percent in 1997–2000, to 3.25 percent
in 2001–3, and 2.75 percent in 2004–6.[22] By legislation, this guaranteed
interest rate cannot exceed 60 percent of the average yield on government
securities during the last ten years.[23] Second, the actual profits of insurance
companies available for distribution to the annuitants and expectations

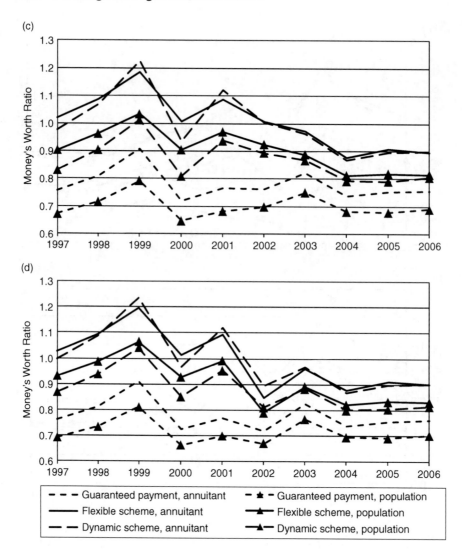

Figure 8.4 *Continued*

about their future profits declined.[24] In 2001, the industry average profit participation rate was about 7 percent; it declined by approximately 40 percent to 4.34 percent by 2006. This reduced offered and projected profit participations rates, which in turn influenced the quotes in our calculated MWRs.

Despite this reduction in MWRs over the surveyed period, recent levels remain relatively high compared to voluntary markets in Australia, the

United Kingdom, and the United States (see Warshawsky 1988; Mitchell et al. 1999; Doyle et al. 2004; Finkelstein and Poterba 2004). In addition, our results in this study for 2003 are close to those by von Gaudecker and Weber (2004: 402) for the same period, the MWRs of this study being on average 2–3 percent lower for males and 6 percent lower for females.[25]

Results obtained using annual market averages differ from those using the sample minimum and maximum quotes; Table 8.5 illustrates this using a 65-year-old retiree for the year 2006. Calculations were performed using annuitant life tables by sex and product type as well as by using the population life expectancy. We show that the with-profit-participation MWRs for annuitants are close to 1 or even slightly above it (0.91–1.01) when the maximum market quotes are used, but they never exceed 0.86 using the minimum market quotes. The use of average rates results in

TABLE 8.5 Money's worth ratios for the year 2006, based on minimum, average, and maximum quotes

	Without guarantee period			With ten-year guarantee period		
	Guaranteed payment	Flexible scheme	Dynamic scheme	Guaranteed payment	Flexible scheme	Dynamic scheme
A. Annuitant mortality table (age 65 in 2006)						
Minimum quotes						
Male	0.739	0.831	0.832	0.749	0.841	0.847
Female	0.742	0.839	0.863	0.748	0.842	0.858
Average quotes						
Male	0.757	0.881	0.880	0.767	0.896	0.890
Female	0.758	0.895	0.899	0.761	0.902	0.900
Maximum quotes						
Male	0.773	0.972	0.908	0.783	0.990	0.947
Female	0.775	1.001	0.934	0.779	1.009	0.961
B. Population mortality table (age 65 in 2006)						
Minimum quotes						
Male	0.653	0.734	0.723	0.681	0.764	0.757
Female	0.677	0.765	0.773	0.690	0.777	0.778
Average quotes						
Male	0.668	0.778	0.765	0.697	0.814	0.795
Female	0.691	0.816	0.806	0.702	0.832	0.815
Maximum quotes						
Male	0.683	0.858	0.789	0.712	0.900	0.846
Female	0.707	0.913	0.837	0.719	0.931	0.871

Source: Authors' calculations; see text.

MWRs between 0.88 and 0.90. For the population life expectancy, the MWRs range between 0.72 and 0.78 for minimum and 0.79 and 0.93 for the maximum market quotes. These differences are relatively small for the guaranteed part of the product due to the binding legal requirements in force. The variation becomes considerable, ranging between 8 and 18 percent of the average figures when the profit participation is accounted for, being understandably more pronounced for products with period-certain guarantees.

Conclusion

This chapter explains products on offer in the German voluntary annuity market, where insurers allow annuitants to participate in the profits of the insurance company, and we show the value for money that prospective retirees can expect, based on the long-term record. We advance the literature by closely examining the long-term developments in such a market, where, besides the guaranteed fixed payment, the distribution of the insurer's annual profits is required by legislation and is thus an important part of the annuity product. We also consider the influence of different profit participation forms, guarantees, and entry ages. Finally, we explain the influence of interest rates and mortality assumptions on the long-term development of MWRs.

Previous studies have found that MWRs for nominal annuities calculated using annuitant mortality tables are relatively high, usually between 0.90 and 1.10. If the calculation is performed using general population mortality tables, the results are typically lower by approximately 10 percentage points, lying between 0.80 and 1.0. Our analysis of the German voluntary annuity market proves that this market is in line with international experience. On average, MWRs for all age categories mostly lie slightly below unity when profit participation is accounted for. Regarding the guaranteed payout part only, the values are lower, at approximately 0.8. Across all age categories for products including profit participation, the money's worth average values are slightly higher for females than males. Interestingly, there are no considerable differences between age groups for products with profit participation. Our analysis indicates that products with period-certain guarantees provide good value for money in Germany, especially for those having average life expectancy. The slight decline of the MWRs in the recent past does not stem from weaker insurance markets but rather it mirrors the development in the capital markets. In sum, payout products for life annuities in Germany deserve a role in the retirement portfolio.

Notes

1. This argument may have only a limited validity for Germany, as German insurers mainly have conservative bond investments in their portfolios.

2. See Maurer and Somova (2007: 309–15) for details on the role of insurance in Germany.

3. In Germany, the first scientific mortality observations date back to the late seventeenth century, while the first official population mortality table covers the years 1871–81 (Statistisches Bundesamt 2008).

4. Under the German Insurance Supervision Law, the interest rate which should be used to calculate the guaranteed part of the product is called the guaranteed interest rate and is limited to 60 percent of the average yield on the government securities during the last ten years. Since 2007, it has been 2.25 percent.

5. §81 VAG (German Insurance Supervision Law).

6. In the available sample, the first payouts with the flexible participation scheme are currently 15–20 percent above the guaranteed payment level. In past periods of high net investment returns, the quoted payouts were even 30–40 percent higher.

7. The monthly payouts remain constant during the year.

8. The Euro was first used in 2002.

9. See Maurer and Somova (2007). The top ten life insurance companies account for approximately 60 percent of the market, as measured by the gross written premium.

10. Our research suggests that it may be difficult to obtain quotes for immediate life annuities for individuals older than age 85.

11. By legislation, German insurance companies are obliged to pay out the lion's share of the profits to the annuitants. Net investment returns of life insurance companies are taken from statistics published by GDV (2007).

12. For products with a dynamic participation scheme, in their quotes insurers guarantee the absolute amount paid during the first year, and give nonbinding projections for the years 5, 10, and 15. These projections can be used as a marketing tool, however, and later revised downward to the extent the guaranteed payout and the rules of the participation scheme allow.

13. DAV 2004 is recommended for use in the calculation of annuity products since the year 2005 by the German Society of Actuaries.

14. The data was provided by German Bundesbank (2007).

15. The life insurance company *Protector* was created in 2002 by the insurers, members of the German Insurance Association, representing more than 97 percent of gross insurance premiums in the German life insurance market. This company is financed from the members' contributions and has the purpose of taking over the existing insurance contracts of an insolvent insurer, leaving the benefits unchanged. So far, the services of *Protector* were used only once in 2003 (for Mannheimer Lebensversicherung). See Maurer and Somova (2007: 338–9) for more details.

[16]   For example, BarNiv and Herschbarger (1990) report that during 1975–86 more than seventy life insurance companies failed in the American insurance market.

[17]   See Mitchell et al. (1999) and McCarthy and Mitchell (2002) for discussion on the subject.

[18]   McCarthy and Mitchell (2002) report that the A/E ratio for UK males is 67.5, for US males, 65.3; for females they are 73.5 (the United Kingdom) and 73.6 (the United States).

[19]   Statistisches Bundesamt (2008).

[20]   Similar results have been obtained in other studies such as James and Song (2001), Finkelstein and Poterba (2002), and von Gaudecker and Weber (2004), while the results in Knox (2000) depend on the underlying mortality tables.

[21]   Almost 70 percent of life insurance companies' investment portfolio consists of fixed income securities (Maurer and Somova 2007).

[22]   The reduction continued in 2007: the guaranteed interest rate was further reduced to 2.25 percent for new contracts (Assekurata 2009).

[23]   The reduction of the guaranteed interest rate is suggested by the nongovernmental body German Society of Actuaries (Deutsche Aktuarvereinigung, DAV). The decision, however, is made by the Ministry of Finance in cooperation with Ministry of Justice, which are responsible for drafting the necessary legislation. The legislation is implemented by the BaFin (Federal Financial Supervisory Authority).

[24]   The so-called non-guaranteed surplus depends on the performance of the investment portfolio and on the insurance company experience with mortality and expenses. §81 VAG ensures that a considerable portion of surplus is distributed to the insured. Both mortality and expenses remained quite stable during the surveyed period (Maurer and Somova 2007).

[25]   Given the similarity of procedure, the differences can be explained by the fact that the annuity quotes for the year 2003 used in this study are lower for all product categories, and especially for females, as compared to the averages reported by von Gaudecker and Weber (2004).

References

Albrecht, Peter and Raimond Maurer (2002). 'Self-Annuitization, Consumption Shortfall in Retirement, and Asset Allocation: The Annuity Benchmark,' *Journal of Pension Economics and Finance*, 1: 269–88.

Assekurata (2004). *Marktstudie 2004: Die Überschussbeteiligung in der Lebensversicherung, Köln 2004.* Koln, Germany: Assekurata. www.assekurata.de/

——(2005). *Marktstudie 2005: Die Überschussbeteiligung in der Lebensversicherung, Köln 2005.* Koln, Germany: Assekurata. www.assekurata.de/

——(2007). *Marktstudie 2007: Die Überschussbeteiligung in der Lebensversicherung, Köln 2007.* Koln, Germany: Assekurata. www.assekurata.de/

——(2009). *Marktstudie 2009: Die Überschusbeteiligung in der Lebensversicherung, Köln 2009.* Koln, Germany: Assekurata. www.assekurata.de/

BarNiv, Ran and Robert A. Herschbarger (1990). 'Classifying Financial Distress in the Life Insurance Industry,' *Journal of Risk and Insurance*, 57(1): 110–36.

Bütler, Monika and Martin Rüsch (2007). 'Annuities in Switzerland.' World Bank Research Paper 4438. Washington, DC: The World Bank.

Cannon, Edmund and Ian Tonks (2004). 'U.K. Annuity Rates, Money's Worth and Pension Replacement Ratios 1957–2002,' *Geneva Papers on Risk and Insurance*, 29: 371–93.

——(2008): *Annuity Markets.* Oxford, UK: Oxford University Press.

Doyle, Suzanne, Olivia S. Mitchell, and John Piggott (2004). 'Annuity Values in Defined Contribution Retirement Systems: Australia and Singapore Compared,' *Australian Economic Review*, 37(4): 402–16.

Finkelstein, Amy and James Poterba (2002). 'Adverse Selection in the Annuity Markets: Policyholder Evidence from the UK Annuity Market,' *Economic Journal*, 112: 28–50.

——(2004). 'Adverse Selection in Insurance Markets: Policyholder Evidence from the UK Annuity Market,' *Journal of Political Economy*, 112: 183–208.

Fong, Wai Mun (2002). 'On the Cost of Adverse Selection in Individual Annuity Markets: Evidence from Singapore,' *Journal of Risk and Insurance*, 69: 193–207.

von Gaudecker, Hans-Martin and Carsten Weber (2004). 'Surprises in a Growing Market Niche: An Evaluation of the German Private Life Annuities Market,' *Geneva Papers on Risk and Insurance*, 29: 394–416.

German Bundesbank (2007). *Data on the Government Bond Yield Curves for the Time Span 1997–2006.* Personal communication to authors on 8/1/2007 sent to EWU-zinsstatistik@bundesbank.de

Gesamtverband der Deutschen Versicherungswirtschaft (GDV) (2007). *Die deutsche Lebensversicherung in Zahlen.* Berlin, Germany: Geschäftsentwicklung.

James, Estelle and Xue Song (2001). 'Annuities Markets Around the World: Money's Worth and Risk Intermediation.' SSRN Working Paper. Chicago, IL: Social Science Research Network.

——Dimitri Vittas (1999). 'Annuities Markets in Comparative Perspective: Do Consurmers Get Their Money's Worth?' World Bank Research Paper 2493. Washington, DC: The World Bank.

Knox, David (2000): 'The Australian Annuity Market.' World Bank Research Paper 2495. Washington, DC: The World Bank.

Maurer, Raimond and Barbara Somova (2007). 'The German Insurance Industry: Market Overview and Trends,' in David Cummins and Bertrand Venard, eds., *Handbook of International Insurance.* New York, NY: Springer, pp. 305–46.

McCarthy, David and Olivia S. Mitchell (2002). 'Estimating International Adverse Selection in Annuities,' *North American Actuarial Journal*, 6(4): 38–54.

Mitchell Olivia S., James Poterba, Mark Warshawsky, and Jeffrey R. Brown (1999). 'New Evidence on the Money's Worth of Individual Annuities,' *American Economic Review*, 89(5): 1299–318.

Morgen and Morgen (2010). *LV-Win Database.* Hofheim am Taunus, Germany: Morgen and Morgen.

Poterba, James (2001). 'A Brief History of Annuities in the United States,' in Jeffrey Brown, Olivia S. Mitchell, James Poterba, and Mark Warshawsky, eds., *The Role of Annuity Markets in Financing Retirement.* Cambridge, MA: MIT Press, pp. 23–56.

——Mark Warshawsky (2000). 'The Costs of Annuitizing Retirement Payouts from Individual Accounts,' in John B. Shoven, ed., *Administrative Aspects of Investment-Based Social Security Reform.* Chicago, IL: University of Chicago Press, pp. 173–206.

Statistisches Bundesamt (2008). *Berechnung von Periodensterbetafeln.* Methodische Erläuterungen zur Berechnung von Periodensterbetafeln für Deutschland 1871/81 bis 2005/2007. Wiesbaden, Germany.

Thorburn, Craig, Roberto Rocha, and Marco Morales (2007). 'An Analysis of Money's Worth Ratios in Chile,' *Journal of Pension Economics and Finance,* 6: 287–312.

Warshawsky, Mark (1988). 'Private Annuity Markets in the United States: 1919–1984,' *Journal of Risk and Insurance,* 55: 518–28.

Chapter 9

Annuity Markets in Japan

Junichi Sakamoto

In Japan, some retirees are fortunate enough to receive generous occupational pensions from their former employers, but the number of such people is relatively small and most must save to pay for life in retirement.[1] Financial institutions provide vehicles to facilitate them to do so, including bank saving deposits, life annuities, life insurance, equities, bonds, and others. Nevertheless, the Japanese Survey on Life Insurance conducted by the Life Insurance Culture Centre (2009) shows that more than 40 percent of people surveyed consider bank deposits as the most reliable saving vehicle, while 16 percent considered annuities as a reliable vehicle; also 30 percent of respondents believed there was no reliable vehicle. In short, annuity products are not especially popular among Japanese as a way to provide retirement income.

In this chapter, we first describe the framework for income security in retirement in Japan, including financial vehicles available to individuals. Next, we discuss attitudes toward these financial products and show that annuities are not especially popular in Japan. Finally, we explore possible causes for the unpopularity of annuity products, including tax policy that seems inequitable to those who work for enterprises without corporate pensions or with those receiving low benefit levels.

The Japanese retirement income security system

To understand the roles played by annuity products offered by life insurance companies or cooperatives in Japan, it is useful to understand the Japanese retirement income security system (see Figure 9.1). A basic level of benefit is provided by social insurance schemes. For instance, all residents are compulsorily covered by the Japanese National Pension (NP) scheme that provides flat-rate benefits called 'basic pensions'. Those covered by the NP scheme are classified into three categories, including (*a*) workers aged 20–59 who are self-employed, farmers, fishermen, unemployed, or students, as well as their spouses who work with them or do not

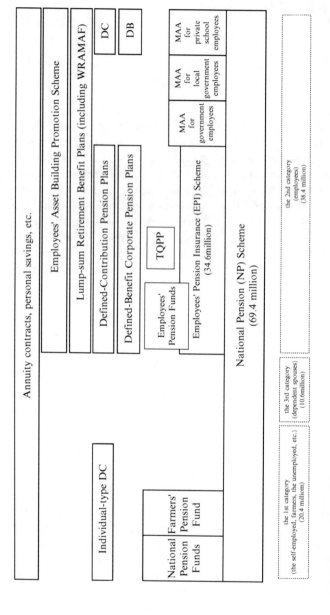

Figure 9.1 Framework of the retirement income security system in Japan *Notes*: The figures indicate the number of active participants as of the end of March 2008. MAA, Mutual Aid Association; TQPP, Tax-Qualified Pension Plans, to be abolished at the end of March 2012; WRAMAF, Workers' Retirement Allowance Mutual Aid Fund; DC, Defined Contribution Pension Plans; and DB, Defined Benefit Corporate Pension Plans. *Source*: Author's calculation; see text.

work for pay; (*b*) a second category consisting of both private and public employees; and (*c*) a third category which includes the dependent spouses aged 20–59 of employees in the second category. This last group is mainly dependent housewives who can receive the flat-rate basic pension without paying contributions into the NP scheme.[2] All employees are also compulsorily covered by one of the employee pension schemes[3] that provide earnings-related benefits.[4] So, a married retiree couple can receive two basic pensions and one or two earnings-related pensions if they have careers as employees. If they have been self-employed throughout their career, they have two basic pensions. The monthly basic pension amount in the case of forty years of coverage is about JPY 66,000 (US $730, Euro 530)[5] in FY 2010.[6] On the other hand, the earnings-related pensions will, roughly speaking, eventually be about 20 percent[7] of the career average of indexed (or 'revalued')[8] annual pensionable remunerations in the case of forty-year coverage.

On top of this base are complementary pension plans, of two types: employment-based plans and other plans for individuals. There are four employment-based plans including the Employees' Pension Funds (EPF), the Defined Benefit Corporate Pension Plans (DB), the Corporate-type Defined Contribution Pension Plans (DC), and the Lump-Sum Retirement Benefit (LSRB) Plans.[9] The EPF plans are defined benefit plans but substitute a portion of the old-age EPI (Employees' Pension Insurance) benefits; they normally cover employees satisfying a certain set of conditions prescribed in the plan statute, and there is no room for individual employees to decide whether to opt in or out. There are three types of complementary pension plans for individuals, where the first category includes four schemes established by law: the National Pension Funds (NPFs), the Farmers' Pension Fund (FPF), the Individual-type DC, and the Employees' Asset Building Promotion Scheme (Government of Japan 2009; we say more on these below). A second group includes annuity products offered by life insurance companies, agricultural cooperatives, and mutual cooperatives. The third group includes bank deposits and similar vehicles by securities companies.

One may argue that bank deposits are not annuities and hence not a form of complementary pension plan. Yet, it is very difficult to tell the difference from the perspective of retired persons' economic life between drawing money regularly out of a bank account versus receiving annuities from an annuity-certain contract. Both of them make complementary income for the retired people to enrich their retirement life. Consequently, this chapter focuses on complementary pension plans offered to individuals.

Complementary pension plans for individuals

Delving into more detail into the four statutory schemes mentioned above, the NPF system is for the people in the first category of the NP scheme. Introduced in 1991, the system is not compulsory and people may join the fund on a voluntary basis. Two kinds of NPF funds are available, the regional type and the occupational type. Each one of the forty-seven Japanese prefectures has one regional-type NPF fund. Other than these, there are also twenty-five occupational-type NPF funds such as the fund for medical practitioners, for lawyers, etc. The NPF funds offer life annuities and annuities-certain, where participants can choose one of them or combine them. It is generally argued that the first layer should be a life annuity; if a participant chooses several of them, the sum of the annuity amount from the life annuities should exceed the sum of the annuity amount of an annuity-certain payout. The upper ceiling of the total amount of premiums is JPY 68,000 per month (approximately US $756 or EUR 548). This ceiling only applies to an individual; if a couple participates in the NPF fund, each of them can pay premiums up to JPY 68,000. However, if the participant also participates in the FPF or in the Individual-type DC, then contributions to these plans are also counted and the ceiling of the premiums for the NPF fund is lowered accordingly (Farmers' Pension Fund 2009a). The premiums are tax-deductible.

Although the NPF funds provide a fairly generous premium ceiling, the number of participants in these funds is limited. As of end-March 2009, the number of participants was only 610,000, or 3 percent of the people in the first NP category. The number of pensioners was about 244,000. The size of the reserve fund was about JPY 2.2 trillion, that is, about US $24 billion or EUR 17.5 billion. The FPF is a defined contribution pension for farmers where the reserve fund is collectively invested and managed. Each participant pays contributions of no less than JPY 20,000 and no more than JPY 67,000, per month. The number of participants is also small, at end-March 2009 being only 57,000 in total, and the reserve fund stood at JPY 110 billion (Farmers' Pension Fund 2009b). The FPF was introduced in 1971 and started as a defined benefit plan. Yet, as the number of farmers decreased rapidly, its financial conditions worsened and eventually it changed into a defined contribution plan in 2003. It began registering its first defined-contribution participants in April 2004.

The Individual-type DC was implemented in 2002 and its implementation is delegated to the National Pension Fund Association (2009). Anyone in the first category of the NP scheme or any employee except for those covered by either an EPF plan, or a DB, a Corporate-type DC, or a Tax-Qualified Pension Plans (TQPP), can join the Individual-type DC on a voluntary basis. The participants in the first category of the NP scheme can contribute up to JPY 68,000 per month, while employee participants can contribute up to JPY 23,000 per month.[10] If a participant in the Individual-type DC is also a participant in the NPF fund or in the FPF fund, the contribution ceiling is lowered by the contribution amount to these schemes. As of end-March 2009, there were 101,000 participants in the Individual-type DC, out of which 39,000 participants were in the first category of the NP scheme and 62,000 were employees. The number is still very small. The share of the participants in the first category of the NP scheme is about 0.2 percent and that of the employee participants in the EPI scheme is about 0.2 percent.

The Employees' Asset Building Promotion Scheme is a saving promotion program operated in cooperation with employers and the government. It tends to be introduced in enterprises at the initiative of the employer, and employees join it on a voluntary basis. There are three options in the scheme: the first is an ordinary saving course wherein employees contract with banking corporations and accumulate a fixed amount of money in the account every month. There is no tax advantage for this, but since employers deduct the fixed amount from the salary and hand it over to the bank directly, it seems a more certain way to build up. The second option involves a contract with life insurance companies or banks; the employer then deducts a fixed amount of salary and hands it over to the life insurance firm or bank. This option provides some tax advantages on the interest, but if one terminates the contract before the retirement age, one must pay some penalty (the tax advantage is explained below with the third option). If the provider is a life insurer, the worker may have a life annuity contract, but if the provider is a bank, only an annuity-certain contract is feasible. The third option is a dedicated saving account for housing, and if one terminates the contract for the purpose other than obtaining a house to live in, a penalty is then incurred. The tax advantage for the second and the third options is that interest is not taxed as long as the sum of the principal and interest does not exceed JPY 5.5 million (about US $61,000 or EUR 44,000) when the contract is with a financial institution other than an insurer, or as long as the principal is no more than JPY 3,850,000 (about US $42,800 or EUR 31,000) if the contract is with an insurance company.

The Employees' Asset Building Promotion Scheme was introduced in 1971, and as of March 2009, there were 6.7 million contracts for the first option, 2.2 million contracts for the second option, and 1.1 million contracts for the third option (corresponding assets were JPY 10.4 trillion, JPY 3.9 trillion, and JPY 2.7 trillion, respectively). Since annuity contracts are part of the second option,[11] there are not so many annuity contracts in this program, either.

A second group of complementary pension plans for individuals involves annuity products offered by life insurance companies,[12] agricultural coop-

eratives, and mutual cooperatives. Unfortunately, there are no statistics on
how many people have annuity contracts with those financial institutions or
what average benefit levels are. Nevertheless, the Life Insurance Culture
Centre (2009) conducted a survey on household relationships with life
insurers in Spring 2009 and obtained 4,054 responses from households
with at least two members. To summarize survey results related to annuity
contracts, we first see that 23 percent of the households had annuity
contracts with life insurance companies, agricultural cooperatives, or
mutual cooperatives; there, the average annual amount of the annuities
was JPY 1,119,000 (US \$12,400, EUR 9,000). These annuity contracts partly
duplicate the tallies for annuity contracts under the Employees' Asset
Building Promotion Scheme. But here, the majority are annuities-certain
and life annuities make up only 17 percent of the whole. The distribution
of how long the annuity payments last is provided in Table 9.1. Table 9.2
shows the distribution of the ages when the annuity begins to be paid.

The survey also looked into the types of financial vehicles on which
people rely for retirement life, and the results appear in Table 9.3. The
most popular vehicle is bank deposits and similar products, in that over 40
percent of the households surveyed relied on them. The next most popular
was life insurance, with 23 percent of the households holding these. The
third was annuity products, held by 16.3 percent, much less than bank
deposits. Also, about 30 percent of the households stated that there is no
reliable financial vehicle for retirement living.

Other statistics also show that annuity products are not popular among
the Japanese. For instance, the Life Insurance Association of Japan pub-
lishes annual statistics on the number of contracts by type of insurance, and
in March 2009, the forty-five life insurance companies[13] that were members
of the Association had about 17.4 million annuity contracts[14] worth a total

TABLE 9.1 Duration of annuity payments in Japan

Duration of annuity payment	Household heads having such contracts as percentage of households surveyed (%)
5 years	9.6
10 years	38.6
15 years	7.6
Lifetime	16.5
Other	2.1
Unclear	29.2

Note: If a household head has two or more annuity contracts, each of his/her contracts is
counted.

Source: Author's calculations based on Life Insurance Association of Japan (2009); see text.

TABLE 9.2 Age at which annuity payments start in Japan

Age when annuity payments start	Household head having such contracts as percentage of households surveyed (%)
Younger than 60	5.6
60	30.5
61–64	5.3
65	25.8
66–69	3.0
70 or older	7.6
Unclear	26.7

Note: If a household head has two or more annuity contracts, each of his/her contracts is counted.

Source: Author's calculations based on Life Insurance Association of Japan (2009); see text.

TABLE 9.3 Reliable financial vehicles to save for retirement

Financial vehicles	Households that answered 'yes' to this financial vehicle as percentage of households surveyed (%)
Deposits in banks or trusts	41.7
Life insurance	23.1
Annuity	16.3
Real estate	15.9
Securities	9.4
Employees' Asset Building Promotion Scheme	5.2
Casualty insurance	3.1
Others	1.4
No reliable vehicle	30.3
Unclear	6.5

Note: If a household head has two or more annuity contracts, each of his/her contracts is counted.

Source: Author's calculations based on Life Insurance Association of Japan (2009); see text.

of JPY 89.3 trillion (US $1.0 trillion, EUR 720 billion). Here the amount of the contract refers to the present value of the annuity from its payment start date (if not yet in payment status), and the present value of remaining payments in payout. In Japan, many households have multiple annuity contracts, so the number of households with annuity contracts is much smaller than 17.4 million (Life Insurance Association of Japan 2009). The National Institute of Population and Social Security Research (2009) estimated that the total number of households was about 50 million, confirming that annuity contracts are not widespread in Japan.

The third group of complementary pensions for individuals consists principally of bank deposits and financial vehicles offered by securities companies. On average, people surveyed by the National Survey of Family Income and Expenditure of 2004[15] had bank deposits and other financial vehicles worth JPY 13,591,000 (US $151,000 or EUR 110,000), and securities averaging JPY 2,980,000 (US $33,000 or EUR 24,000). This shows that bank deposits are very popular among Japanese. Relatively few rely entirely on own saving for retirement income, since only about 6 percent relied entirely on private pensions in 2005 (Government of Japan 2005).[16] Instead, most people rely mainly on social security benefits; their annual income is JPY 4,139,000 (US $46,000 or EUR 33,000) and the average social security benefit is JPY 3,120,000 (US $35,000 or EUR 25,000) or about three-quarters. The share of the benefits from private pensions was about 6 percent.

Why annuity products are unpopular in Japan

The private annuity market is very small in most countries, with few exceptions (Mackenzie 2006), and Japan is not one of them. Nevertheless, it is difficult to identify the exact causes for their unpopularity. One reason might be that people perceive that commissions on the annuity products are expensive. While people may not know insurance mathematics, they can add up the premiums they pay and the sum of the annuity benefits they expect to receive. They may also believe that bank deposits are free of commissions, despite the fact that the interest paid is very low.

Another reason is that Japanese people tend to be disinterested in life annuities, a trait observed in pension plan designs and member behaviors in occupational pension plans as well. Many DB plans only offer term-certain annuities, and even when a plan does offer a life annuity, there is always a provision that allows members to convert it into a lump-sum benefit. In the latter case, most members choose the lump-sum. We also observe that life insurance companies and cooperatives do not seem active in promoting the sales of life annuities, perhaps seeking to avoid longevity risk.

An additional explanation for the peoples' reluctance to purchase annuities is that some may want to keep money on hand to deal with catastrophically expensive events such as hospitalization or unemployment, or home repairs. Bank deposits are more liquid for this purpose than annuity contracts. Also, banks in Japan are seen as more reliable than life insurance companies or cooperatives, particularly since in some instances, life insurance companies have declared bankruptcy and annuitants suffered large losses. People might also believe that the government would give bailouts to banks if they got into difficulty.

A final reason people do not favor lifetime annuities is that the tax system does not encourage them. Although individual tax advantages exist for some retirement income programs, there is no comprehensive tax treatment for such financial vehicles. For example, if a person took out an annuity contract with a life insurance company or cooperative, the annual premiums paid are only tax-deductible up to the low ceiling of JPY 50,000 (US $556 or EUR 400), and benefits received are taxed. Another example is that there is no tax advantage for bank deposits even if one put money in them for retirement purposes. Thus, the current tax system is indifferent to individual efforts to accumulate assets for retirement security.

While these factors surely contribute to the unpopularity of annuity products in Japan, it might be the case that some defined contribution plan participants may seek to convert these assets into annuity contracts at retirement in the future. But currently, few people do so, suggesting that it is unlikely that the number of annuity contracts will grow rapidly in the future.

Taxation issues

Whether the market for annuities grows in Japan will depend on the tax system. While occupational pension plans enjoy tax advantages, these plans are prevalent. But there are no or small tax advantages for individual efforts for income security, outside the NPF, the FPF, the Individual-type DC, and the Employees' Asset Building Promotion Scheme. There is no tax incentive to encourage those people whose firms offer no occupational pension plans or have occupational pension plans which pay low benefit levels, to accumulate retirement assets for themselves. One reason this may be true is that there is no way to verify that the tax advantages are used properly. Of course, this is a big disadvantage for employees without employment-based complementary pension plans or with low levels of employment-based complementary pension plans. Accordingly, the current inequitable tax treatment deserves another look.

A more equitable opportunity to save for retirement would allow a uniform ceiling for tax-deductible contributions, including contributions by employers to the employment-based complementary pension plans, and statutory complementary pension contributions for individuals. Interest on these contributions could also be tax-deductible. In this sense, the reform would follow the logic of an Individual Retirement Account (IRA) and would include a comprehensive and consistent tax treatment for complementary pensions as a whole.

Some technical difficulties might result including the need to gather information on pension contributions and earnings; perhaps it would be necessary to introduce a tax-filing number to track these. Another issue would be how to treat lump-sum contributions to the complementary pension plans for individuals. Many people save most of their lump-sum retirement payments for retirement when they retire from their companies. It would be sensible to impose a similar tax treatment for such lump-sum payments as for monthly contributions.

Finally, it would be useful to review existing tax treatments for the variety of old-age schemes already in place in Japan. For example, employee contributions to the EPF and NPF are tax-deductible,[17] while employee contributions to DB are not.[18] This sort of irregularity can be corrected and made consistent with other tax-favored retirement programs, to make it easier to meet income needs in retirement.

Conclusion

Annuities have not been popular in Japan as a means to finance retirement. And when annuities are found, they tend not to be life payouts but rather term-certain products. Possible reasons for the unpopularity of annuity products include costs and inequitable taxation that hinders people from buying them. To date, the tax authority has not discussed reforming the tax system comprehensively and consistently to enhance people's efforts to save for retirement. Doing so would expand the annuity market as by-product.

Notes

[1] The Comprehensive Survey on Working Conditions (Government of Japan 2009) reports that retirement benefit plans are offered by 84 percent of enterprises with more than thirty employees, but benefit levels vary from one enterprise to another.

[2] To finance the benefit expenditures of the basic pensions, every social security pension scheme transfers the designated amount of money to the Basic Pension Sub-account that manages the revenue and expenditures for the basic pension payments. The designated amount of money is determined in the following way. The total amount of basic pension expenditures is divided among the social security pension schemes in proportion to the number of active participants aged 20–59 of the schemes plus, in the case of schemes for employees, the number of dependent spouses aged 20–59. The share is the designated amount of money for each scheme. Thus, the dependent spouses in the third category of the NP scheme are deemed to have paid contributions to the NP scheme.

[3] The social security pension schemes in Japan include the Employees' Pension Insurance (EPI) scheme that covers private sector employees, the Mutual Aid Association (MAA) scheme for government employees, the MAA scheme for local government employees, and the MAA scheme for private school employees.

[4] Enterprises that are not legal entities with fewer than five employees are not covered by the EPI scheme. The employees therefore only have the flat-rate NP benefits. Part-time employees of any enterprises who work for fewer than three-quarters of the working hours of regular employees are not covered by the EPI scheme, either.

[5] We assume that US $1 = JPY 90, Euro 1 = JPY 124.

[6] FY means fiscal year. In Japan, the fiscal year starts on 1 April and ends on 31 March.

[7] Currently, it is about 26 percent of the career average of revalued annual disposable income. It is projected that it will eventually reduce to about 23 percent, after modified indexation reforms are applied.

[8] 'Revalued pensionable remunerations' mean pensionable remunerations indexed to the increase of gross wages minus the accumulated difference between the increase of gross wages and the increase of disposable income since 1988. Furthermore, the 2009 actuarial valuation shows that the benefit level is projected to be reduced by about 8.6 percent through modified indexation; the ultimate benefit level would be 20 percent of the career average of revalued annual pensionable remunerations in the case of forty years of coverage.

[9] There is another group of corporate pension plans called Tax-Qualified Pension Plans (TQPP), but they are to be abolished by the end of March 2012. LSRB plans of individual companies are managed on a book reserve basis, but, for small companies that cannot manage such LSRB plans for themselves, there is a fund called the Workers' Retirement Allowance Mutual Aid Fund (WRAMAF) for small companies established on a statute. Small companies can join the WRAMAF on a voluntary basis.

[10] The fairly large difference in the contribution ceilings between the participants in the first category of the NP scheme and the employees is mainly attributable to the fact that there are no earnings-related social security pensions for the people in the first category of the NP scheme.

[11] They are the contracts with life insurance companies in the second option.

[12] Life insurance companies include the Japan Post Insurance Co. Ltd. that was privatized in 2007.

[13] The number of the member companies was forty-six at the end of March 2009, but the Yamato Life went bankrupt in 2008, so the statistics exclude data for Yamato Life.

[14] The statistics exclude contracts with agricultural cooperatives and mutual cooperatives, but these are few in number. According to Life Insurance Association of Japan (2009), the number of annuity contracts with agricultural cooperatives was about 3.2 million and that of annuity contracts with mutual cooperatives was 0.2 million in March 2009.

[15] The National Survey of Family Income and Expenditure is conducted every five years and the latest survey was carried out in 2009. Results are yet to be published as of summer 2010, so we can only refer to the 2004 survey.

[16] They may mainly be medical practitioners or lawyers.

[17] The bill to introduce employee contributions to DC also stipulates that employee contributions are tax-deductible; the bill is slated for discussion in the Diet in 2010.

[18] Strictly speaking, employee contributions to DB are treated in the same way as the premiums for life insurance contracts. A tax deduction is permitted up to JPY 50,000 (US $556 or EUR 400) per year, which is very little. The ceiling is applied to the sum of the employee contributions and other premiums for life insurance contracts. In many cases, premiums for life insurance contracts already exceed the ceiling leaving no room for employee tax-deductible contributions.

References

Government of Japan (2005). *Heisei 16 nendo Zenkou Shouhi Jittai Chousa (National Survey of Family Income and Expenditure in 2004)*. Tokyo, Japan: Ministry of Internal Affairs and Communications.

——(2009). *Kokumin Nenkin oyobi Kouseinenkin ni kakaru Zaisei no Genkyou oyobi Mitooshi (Gaiyou) – Heisei 21 Nen Zaiseikennshou Kekka – (Abridged Report of the 2009 Actuarial Valuation of the Employees' Pension Insurance Scheme and the National Pension Scheme)*. Tokyo, Japan: Ministry of Health, Labor, and Welfare.

Kigyounenkin Rengoukai (National Pension Fund Association) (2009). *Kigyounenkin ni kansuru Kisoshiryou (Fact Book on Corporate Pension Plans)*. Tokyo, Japan: National Pension Fund Association.

Kokuritsu Shakaihoshou Jinkou Mondai Kenkyusho (National Institute of Population and Social Security Research) (2009). *Nihon no Setaisu no Shouraisuikei (Todouhukenbetsu Suikei) no Youshi (Summary of Projections of Japan's Future Number of Households by Prefecture)*. Tokyo, Japan: National Institute of Population and Social Security Research.

Mackenzie, George A. (2006). *Annuity Markets and Pension Reform*. Cambridge, UK: Cambridge University Press.

Nougyousha Nenkin Kikin (Farmers' Pension Fund) (2009a). *Heisei 20 Nendo Nougyousha Nenkin Kikin Seido no Jisshi Joukyou (FY 2008 Annual Report)*. Tokyo, Japan: Farmers' Pension Fund.

——(2009b). *Heisei 20 Nendo ni okeru Unyoujoukyou tou (FY 2008 Investment Report)*. Tokyo, Japan: Farmers' Pension Fund.

Seimei Hoken Bunka Senta (Life Insurance Culture Centre) (2009). *Heisei 21 Nendo Seimei Hoken ni kansuru Zennkoku Jittai Chousa (2009 Survey on Life Insurance)*. Tokyo, Japan: Life Insurance Culture Centre.

Seimei Hoken Kyoukai (Life Insurance Association of Japan) (2009). *Heisei 20 Nendo Jigyou Houkokusho (FY 2008 Annual Report)*. Tokyo, Japan: Life Insurance Association of Japan.

Chapter 10

Compulsory and Voluntary Annuity Markets in the United Kingdom

Edmund Cannon and Ian Tonks

This chapter discusses the UK annuity market, which is the largest in the world. The reason for its size is mainly because anyone who has saved in a tax-privileged private pension in the United Kingdom must annuitize 75 percent of their pension wealth, which they do by buying a Compulsory Purchase Annuity. It is also possible to buy an annuity voluntarily, referred to as a Purchased Life Annuity. Mortality experiences are different in the two markets and the price of annuities is consequently different too. We report and discuss voluntary annuity rates over the period 1957–2009 and compulsory annuity rates for 1994–2009. Annuity rates have fallen in both markets since 1994 and we assess whether this decline is larger than could be justified by changes in longevity and bond yields. Our analysis centers on calculations of the money's worth ratio (MWR) which is the conventional measure to determine whether annuities are fairly priced. The money's worth measure suggests that falls in annuity rates can only be explained by lower interest rates and increased life expectancy up to about 2004.

In the remainder of the chapter, we start with a description of the institutional framework of the annuity market and the determinants of supply and demand. We then report time series of average annuity rates. We use these to calculate the money's worth and conclude by discussing possible reasons for the fall in the money's worth after 2004.

The structure of UK annuity markets

Pension provision and demand for annuities

Where annuities are purchased voluntarily, the annuity market tends to be small (Brown et al. 2001). Figure 10.1 illustrates that in this respect, the United Kingdom is similar to other countries: the voluntary annuity market is small, with total premiums in 2006 of only £40 million. There are a variety

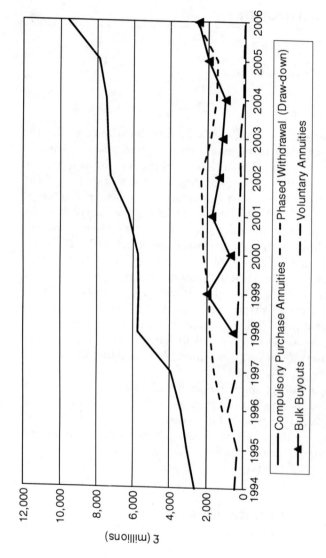

Figure 10.1 Growth in annuity sales 1994–2006. *Source:* Association of British Insurers (2010).

of reasons why annuity demand is low which we consider in detail in Cannon and Tonks (2008). But it is worth noting that most elderly people in the United Kingdom already have an annuity in the form of a state pension and this makes up a high proportion of their wealth (Pensions Commission 2004: 182).

What makes the UK annuity market so large is the compulsory market where total premiums amounted to £9.58 billion in 2006 (see Figure 10.1). Compulsory-purchase annuities are those purchased by individuals who have saved in a personal pension fund which has received tax privileges: contributions into the scheme are made before income tax is deducted from income and all investment returns are also tax free. Typically, the pension fund is managed by a life insurance company: the value of the fund at retirement is then used by the pensioner to buy an annuity, either from the life insurer with whom they accumulated the fund or from another life insurer (the 'open market option').

Pemberton (2006) documents the frequent changes to rules governing pensions since the original introduction of individual accounts in 1956 (when they were called 'retirement annuity contracts'). The result was a complicated set of regulations which even professional pension advisors found difficult to understand: it was quite possible for an individual to have a variety of pension funds all with different requirements on how they be annuitized at retirement. The 2004 Finance Act cut through this Gordian knot by allowing all pension wealth[1] to be amalgamated into one fund of which 75 percent had to be used to purchase an authorized annuity: the legislation became effective from 'A-day' on April 6, 2006. There is a cap on the total amount that can be paid into the fund (£1.5 million on A-day, rising annually thereafter) and also limits on how much can be paid into the fund in any given year. These constraints are sufficiently generous that they affect only a very small proportion of the population.

The compulsory purchase rule still leaves considerable flexibility to the annuitant, in three ways. First, the definition of an annuity includes products where some of the wealth is not in annuity form. A 'guaranteed' annuity is one where the first few years' payments are paid regardless of whether or not the annuitant is alive (if the annuitant dies, then the payments are made to the heirs). Annuities with guarantees of up to ten years are permitted, although five years is more common. A similar idea is the 'value-protected' annuity which pays a given sum to the estate on the death of the annuitant. Neither of these products is a pure annuity.

Second, it is not necessary to annuitize until age 75: up to that age, one can access pension wealth through phased withdrawal (referred to as 'drawdown' or 'unsecured' income).[2] The maximum amount of pension wealth that can be taken as income through drawdown is 120 percent of the best single-life annuity payment for the relevant age and sex. Figure

10.1 shows that drawdown is large relative to annuity purchase. Even at age 75, it is possible to avoid annuitization through a process known as 'alternatively secured income', originally designed to meet the objections of a small Christian sect to pooling mortality risk. It quickly became clear that some rich individuals were using this as a means to avoid paying tax and the regulations were changed in 2007, so that it became compulsory to take an income of between 65 and 90 percent of the best annuity rate aged 75, and any remaining assets in the pension fund are taxed at a penal rate on the death of the annuitant.[3] Finally, there is a bulk annuity market where an annuity provider acquires a package of individual pension liabilities, typically from the closure of a defined-benefit occupational scheme.

The main determinant of purchases of annuities in the compulsory market is the number of individuals reaching retirement age and their pension wealth. Given the information available on individual personal pensions, the Pensions Commission (2005) made predictions about demand for annuities up to 2012, illustrated in Table 10.1. The demand for bulk annuities is very difficult to predict since it will be determined almost entirely by the ongoing choices of firms to close their defined-benefit schemes. The collapse of the stock market in 2007 has almost certainly made it harder to predict the bulk market: firms would probably be even keener to shed their pension liabilities but, since their pension obligations are in deficit, the transfer to the bulk market is a costly option.

Following the recommendations of the Pensions Commission (2006), the 2008 Pensions Act introduced a new workplace pension scheme to become effective in 2012. This makes it compulsory for all employers to offer a defined-contribution pension scheme with a minimum pension saving for most workers of 8 percent of income, of which a minimum of 3 percent must come from the employer (the rest from the employee and tax relief). The Pensions Commission (2005) suggested that, were such a

TABLE 10.1 Scenarios for the size of the annuity market (estimated annual flows, £ billion)

Annuity type	2002	2012 (projected)		
		Low	Medium	High
Individual annuities	7.2	16.6	18.1	19.7
Drawdown	2.3	5.3	5.8	6.3
Bulk buyout	1.4	1.5	35.4	128.1

Source: Pension Commission (2005).

scheme to target successfully the population without provision, then there would be an increase in the annual demand for annuities of £13 billion by the year 2040 at current earnings levels (this demand would represent an additional increase on the numbers in Table 10.1). However, the saving rate of 8 percent is relatively low by existing standards: if this saving rate were to become a focal point for all pension saving, then the result could be lower saving by existing savers.

Supply of annuities and regulation

Annuities in the United Kingdom are typically sold by life insurance companies. Some of these companies are also involved in other forms of insurance and some are owned by other financial institutions such as banks. A series of scandals in the nineteenth century resulted in life insurers being regulated from 1870 onward: the current regulatory body is the Financial Services Authority (the FSA). Every year, life insurers are required to produce 'FSA Returns' which summarize their balance sheet. Standard and Poor's compiles these returns for commercial use in the *SynThesys* database, and most companies make their own returns available for free on the Internet.

The total number of life insurance companies has fallen since the Second World War due to mergers and acquisitions (Cannon and Tonks 2004*b*), and many of these companies no longer actively market these products. Important sources of annuity rates enabling comparison of different companies' prices are the FSA website and the private provider *Money Facts*. These sources suggest that only about ten companies are actively marketing annuity products in the compulsory market. Further confirmation that the industry is heavily concentrated is provided by Figure 10.2.

Typically, annuity prices depend on age and gender, but from 2007 some life insurers also started to price annuities based on the annuitant's address (postcode) since this is a good predictor of life expectancy, and the variations by location are large (up to ten years). Four of the largest companies now price annuities on this basis.

It is also possible to buy 'enhanced' annuities or annuities on 'impaired lives'. These offer better rates to smokers or to individuals with health problems such as diabetes. Since the annuity rate offered depends upon the circumstances of the individual, these are often sold through specialist brokers. These annuities form an increasingly large part of the market. A consequence of this is that the remaining annuities sold are increasingly only sold to relatively healthy individuals.

From Form 49 of the FSA returns, we are able to see how annuity providers manage their annuity liabilities, illustrated in Figure 10.3. The

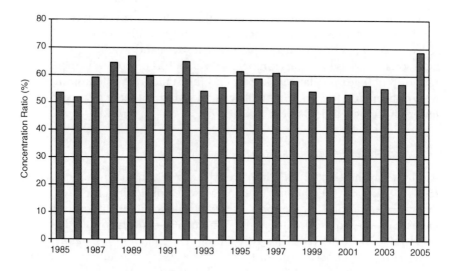

Figure 10.2 Six-firm concentration ratio in the compulsory purchase market. *Source:* Authors' calculations based on data provided by Standard and Poor's (2005).

most important asset class is long-dated government bonds. This makes sense since it is a good hedge; when the yield curve slopes up (as it usually does), then providers can take advantage of the higher yields on longer dated debt. Other important asset classes are commercial bonds and commercial mortgages. When valuing these assets, companies are required to make explicit risk adjustments in the FSA returns, and it is clear that the UK regulator effectively prevents life insurers from investing in risky assets. Figure 10.3 shows that the mixture of government and corporate bonds has shifted over time. In 1985, life insurance companies held five times as many government bonds as corporate bonds; by 2005, this ratio was almost 1, though over most of the sample, 1989–2004, the percentage of debt instruments that were government bonds was between 60 and 70 percent.

Life insurers predict life expectancy using mortality tables produced by the Central Mortality Investigation Bureau (CMI). This collects data from life insurers, anonymizes it, and then produces periodical reports as well as other research papers, published either on the website of the Institute of Actuaries or the *British Actuarial Journal*. Each individual life insurer makes adjustments to the CMI projections to take account of the different consumers of each company and they report the details in the FSA Returns. Aggregate mortality risk is borne predominantly by the life insurers themselves, although a small amount is reinsured.

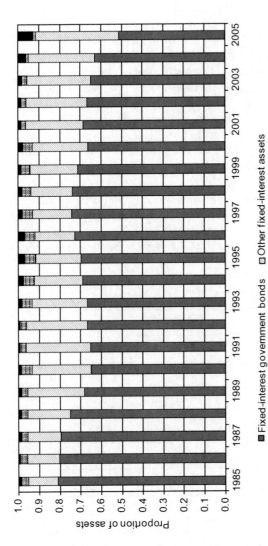

Figure 10.3 Composition of life insurers' assets. *Source*: Authors' calculations based on data provided by Standard and Poor's (2005).

Data on UK annuity rates

Compulsory purchase life annuities

Although legislation for individual pension accounts was passed in 1956, the market for compulsory annuities was small for a long time because it took time for pension funds to accumulate sufficiently to create much demand. The earliest data we can find on annuity rates in this market are those provided by *Money Facts* from 1994 onward. Between twenty and twenty-five companies were quoting at the beginning of the period: by the end, this had reduced to nine. The FSA's price comparison website in January 2010 reported annuity rates for only six companies (with a seventh company providing annuities only for construction workers) with an additional three companies refraining from providing any indicative annuity rate since they price annuities entirely on the postcode of the annuitant. Figure 10.4 illustrates the evolution of the simple average annuity rate for nominal and real annuities.

From the FSA Returns, we know that sixty-two companies were selling compulsory annuities in 2005. But the five-firm concentration ratio is 72 percent and the largest firm, the Prudential, supplies over 23 percent of new business. The annuity rates in the *Money Facts* database represent all of the major providers.

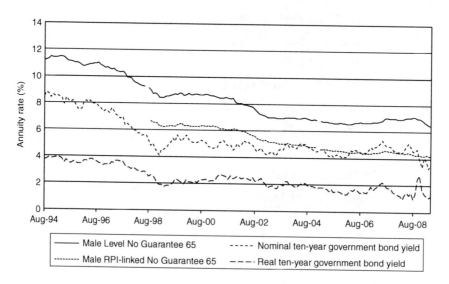

Figure 10.4 Annuity rates in the compulsory market (65-year-old male). *Source*: Authors' calculations based on annuity data from Moneyfacts Group (2010) and interest rates from Bank of England (2010); see text.

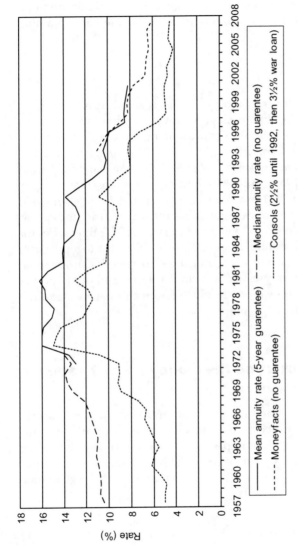

Figure 10.5 Annuity rates in the voluntary market (65-year-old male). *Source.* Cannon and Tonks (2004*b*) and authors' calculations based on annuity data from Moneyfacts Group (2010) and interest rates from Bank of England (2010); see text.

Figure 10.4 also provides a comparison of annuity rates in the compulsory market with long-term interest rates. It compares the nominal annuity rate for 65-year-old males with the UK government ten-year bond yield. It can be seen that the two series clearly move very closely together, although the annuity rate is slightly smoother. The figure also plots the inflation-adjusted annuity rate in the real annuity market and the corresponding real government bond yield.

Voluntary annuities

Although the voluntary (purchase life) market is small, it is interesting because it has existed in the United Kingdom for a long time, allowing us to see the long-run effect of mortality improvement on annuity rates. For Cannon and Tonks (2004b), we collected data for 1957–2002 from a variety of sources: here we update the series to 2009 using data purchased from *Money Facts*. During the 1950s and 1960s, it was common for about seventy companies to be quoting in the voluntary market, but in 2009 this had reduced to four, since many of the remaining life insurers do not appear to quote in the voluntary market. In Figure 10.5, we plot the time series for the simple average of all annuity rates of 65-year-old males together with the interest rate payable on consols (government perpetuities). It can be seen that long-term interest rates are very similar at the end of the period to the beginning, but annuity rates are much lower: this narrowing of the gap is due to increased life expectancy.

Measuring annuities using the money's worth ratio

Definition of the money's worth ratio

A conventional measure of the value of an annuity is the money's worth, which is the ratio of the expected present value of the flow of payments made by an annuity to the premium paid for it.[4] More formally, define the annuity rate A_t as the annuity payment received by an individual made per year per £1 purchase price in year t. For a level annuity with no guarantee period, this can be calculated using:

$$\text{Money's worth} \equiv A_t \sum_{i=1}^{i=T} \pi_{t,t+i}(1 + R_{t,i})^{-i} \tag{1}$$

where $\pi_{t,t+i}$ is the probability of someone living i more periods, believed in period t. Notice that the survival probabilities depend upon the age, gender, and type (compulsory or voluntary) of annuitant. T is chosen so that $\pi_{t,t+T} \approx 0$ and $R_{t,i}$ is the appropriate discount rate in period t for payments received in period $t + i$, expressed at an annual rate: typically, this is the rate on government bonds.[5]

To calculate the money's worth in year t, it is necessary to know the yield curve for that year (sometimes this must be estimated) and the most up-to-date actuarial table for the relevant annuitant type that was available in that year. Using such data, the money's worth also is based on the information available when the annuity was sold and is not affected by the benefit of hindsight. All of our calculations use the best historical data that we can find and are thus true *ex ante* estimates of the value of an annuity.

The mortality tables used by actuaries are projections of future survival (or death) probabilities. It has not proved practicable to produce projections based on causal models of death, and most projections consist of extrapolations in trends in existing data.[6]

The last ten years have seen large theoretical advances in projection methods based on time series econometrics and finance theory (for a survey, see Pitacco et al. 2009). In our analysis, however, we use the projections in the actuarial tables published by the UK Institute of Actuaries. Our justification for this is that there is still considerable debate about the newer methods and they are unlikely to have been taken up by practitioners immediately after publication in academic journals. In addition, the notes to the FSA returns say explicitly that liabilities were valued using the official actuarial tables.

Even using the official actuarial tables leaves two important problems to be confronted. First, it is necessary to choose the correct mortality data for projection. For the voluntary market, this is not problematic because there is only one table available. For the compulsory purchase market, there are several potential mortality tables, which we discuss. Second, although life expectancy has steadily increased with each birth cohort, there is some evidence of a structural break in the trend of life expectancy (Willets 1999). This 'cohort effect' occurs for cohorts born in around 1930, suggesting that simple extrapolation of life expectancy would be unreliable for individuals retiring aged 65 from about 1995 onward. For most of the period we are analyzing, data did not (and could not) exist for the mortality experience of individuals born after 1930 when they were older than 65: the cohort effect had been observed in the mortality of individuals aged less than 65 who had purchased life insurance. This meant that there was considerable uncertainty about how to model the cohort effect. In our calculations, we use the 'long cohort' projection, which is the least optimistic about increases in life expectancy and thus gives the highest money's worth figures.

With 'actuarially fair' pricing, the money's worth would be exactly equal to unity. However, this ignores the fact that annuity providers have additional costs: administrative and marketing costs; costs of managing the assets; the need to reserve against investment; and mortality risk. Quantifying these costs is difficult since the information needed is commercially sensitive.

Money's worth ratios for compulsory annuities

We now turn to MWRs of pension annuities in the larger compulsory purchase market. The biggest problem in this analysis is the absence of a long time series of mortality data for personal pensioners. The Institute of Actuaries' data on personal pensioners is small until about 1995, because most personal pensions were in accrual up until that point. This is because personal pensions in a form similar to what we have today were only introduced in 1987, when the term 'personal pension' was originally coined. Before 1987, pensions for individuals, originally called 'retirement annuity contracts', were primarily designed for the self-employed (who would not have had access to an occupational pension) and employees would either have an occupational pension or be members of the State Earnings-Related Pension scheme (currently called the State Second Pension or S2P).

This means that we have to choose between three mortality tables when calculating the money's worth of compulsory purchase annuities:

1. Data on personal pensioners, from tables PPM and PPF for males and females, respectively. But the dataset is too small for reliable projection, since there were as few as 50,000 male annuitants of all ages as recently as 1991–4 (CMI 2004).
2. Data from individuals who had retirement annuity contracts and have now retired, tables RMV and RFV. The dataset is large enough for reliable projection (more than 600,000 male annuitants in payment), but these individuals appear to have different life expectancies from other personal pensioners buying in the compulsory market.
3. Data for members of pensions which are administered by life insurance companies, called the 'life office pensioners', tables PML and PFL. Where a firm wants to have an occupational pension but is too small to administer this itself it runs the scheme through a life insurance company. Although members of such occupational pension schemes may top up their pensions with defined contribution 'additional voluntary contributions' and form a small part of the compulsory annuity market as a result, these members of defined benefit schemes are likely to have different characteristics to those people who are buying a pension annuity (Cocco and Lopes 2004; Brander and Finucane 2007).

Given the problems with interpreting RAC and PP life expectancy, Finkelstein and Poterba (2002) use the Life Office Pensioners, of whom there were over 1 million in 1999–2002 and for whom data are available for a longer period of time. Using these data has the advantage that life expectancy information is available on both a lives and an amounts basis (tables PML and PMA, etc.). The former shows the life expectancy of each life (possibly more accurately of each policy – if a pensioner has more than one policy, then he or she may be counted twice). The latter basis reweighs the life expectancy by the size of the pension so that richer pensioners have a higher weight – unsurprisingly, life expectancy of amounts is longer than life expectancy of lives since richer people tend to live longer. From the point of view of a life insurer, the amounts measure is more relevant, since that determines the profitability of the company; from the point of view of a typical pensioner, the lives basis may be more relevant since the amounts measure is affected by a small number of rich individuals. Furthermore, the most recent life office pensioner data allow us to exclude individuals who retired early and concentrate on those who retired at a 'normal' age (tables PNML and PNFL).

In addition to the choice of actuarial table, we need to estimate the projection methods that were used to forecast future mortality. The '80' and '92' tables (published in CMI (1990) and CMI (1999), respectively) contained projections of future mortality. Within a few years, it became clear that mortality was improving faster than projected in the '92' tables, and CMI (2002) provided 'interim adjustments' which came in three versions: short, medium, and long cohort projections. The long cohort projection has the highest forecast increase in life expectancy and hence using it gives the highest money's worth. The most recent set of tables was the '00' series published in CMI (2006), but this did not attempt to make any projections. Where we have used this series to calculate the MWRs, we spliced the interim projection improvements in mortality on to the '00' mortality levels.

To give some idea of the magnitude of the changes due to revisions to projected mortality, the remaining life expectancy of a 65-year-old man was forecast to be just over fifteen years in 1994 using the PML80 Table; by 1999 using the PML92 Table, a 65-year old's life expectancy was seventeen years and two months; by 2002, it was nineteen years using the short cohort adjustment and twenty-one years using the long cohort adjustment. In addition, the data from the personal pensioner table (PPM00) suggests that these annuitants had an additional two years of life expectancy compared to the life office pensioners.

To account for the problems in deciding which actuarial table to use, we report MWRs based on a variety of actuarial tables: where there is uncertainty about the precise point at which a given table was used, we allow overlap years. In all cases, the annuity rates are taken from the *Money Facts* data described earlier and interest rates are taken from the Bank of England's contemporary estimates of the yield curve (available from the Bank's website). Our results are summarized in Table 10.2; Figure 10.6 graphs the money's worth based on 'lives' for 65-year-old males using the life office pensioner mortalities.

The money's worth for the base case of a 65-year-old man has averaged 0.90 over the period, which represents a fair value after allowing for load factors (see Table 10.2). The results for women are similar, with the money's worth for 65-year-old females averaging 0.91. But it is apparent that regardless of mortality table used, the MWRs appear to be falling in the period 2000–4. And when a new mortality table is introduced, the MWR jumps up. This is consistent with information on increased life expectancy gradually becoming apparent to life insurers, resulting in annuity prices gradually falling: because we only update our mortality improvements discretely, there are discrete jumps up in the MWRs that we calculate. The only exception to this is when we switch to using the '00' tables: these followed on very quickly from the 'interim adjustments' and were almost exactly in line with their projections.

If the long cohort adjustment is appropriate, then, except for the hiatus when new data on life expectancy arrived in 2000–4, the MWRs remain roughly constant in the range 0.86–0.92 for the whole period. If the short cohort adjustment is more appropriate, then the MWRs appear to have fallen to the range 0.80–0.85. The fall became apparent in about 2006 and was a major concern to the government, since some commentators using out-of-date mortality data, incorrectly suggested that the money's worth had fallen dramatically.

The finding that the MWRs did not fall over the period relies upon using not just the long cohort adjustment but also concentrating on male annuitants buying level annuities. We summarize the money's worth calculations in Columns 1–6 of Table 10.2 in the tenth column, which just splices the different series together. In Columns 11–13, we report the analogous spliced series for males based on amounts data, for women and for men buying real annuities.[7] In all of the spliced series, we use the long cohort adjustment which gives the highest MWRs for 2002 onward. Despite this, the money's worth measures fall in all three cases. Based on 'amounts', the money's worth appears to fall from the range 0.91–0.99 to 0.88–0.91 and for women it falls from 0.89–0.92 to 0.85–0.89. The most remarkable fall, however, is in real annuities, whose MWRs fall from 0.89 in 1999 to 0.76 in 2009 (real annuity rate data are not available before 1999).

The difference between nominal annuities and real annuities is partly in the level of the money's worth, always lower for real annuities: compare the MWR of 0.94 for a nominal and 0.90 for an RPI-linked annuity for a 65-year-

TABLE 10.2 Money's worth ratios (MWRs) in the UK compulsory market for 65-year olds

Year	PML80	PML92	PML92 short cohort	PML92 long cohort	PNML00 short cohort	PNML00 long cohort	RMV92	RMV92 long cohort	PPM00 long cohort	MWRs for 'lives' – spliced series based on Columns (1)–(6)	MWRs calculated using 'amounts'	MWRs for women calculated using 'lives'	MWRs for men, real annuities
1994	0.875									0.88	0.914	0.891	
1995	0.910									0.91	0.951	0.931	
1996	0.884									0.88	0.922	0.897	
1997	0.899									0.90	0.941	0.924	
1998	0.886									0.89	0.931	0.918	
1999	0.863	0.931					1.001			0.86	0.989	0.92	0.891
2000	0.876	0.951					1.026			0.95	1.011	0.954	0.876
2001		0.912					0.978			0.91	0.966	0.921	0.831
2002		0.860	0.920	0.975			0.922	1.031		0.86	0.991	0.947	0.902
2003		0.822	0.880	0.936			0.883	0.992		0.94	0.95	0.911	0.856
2004			0.824	0.876				0.926		0.88	0.888	0.868	0.813
2005			0.836	0.891	0.832	0.888		0.943	0.946	0.89	0.892	0.86	0.779
2006			0.827	0.883	0.824	0.880		0.935	0.94	0.88	0.884	0.851	0.768
2007			0.800	0.851	0.797	0.848		0.898	0.904	0.85	0.852	0.825	0.754
2008			0.831	0.884	0.828	0.882		0.933	0.941	0.88	0.885	0.862	0.816
2009			0.857	0.908	0.854	0.905		0.955	0.964	0.91	0.91	0.887	0.759

Source: Authors' calculations; see text.

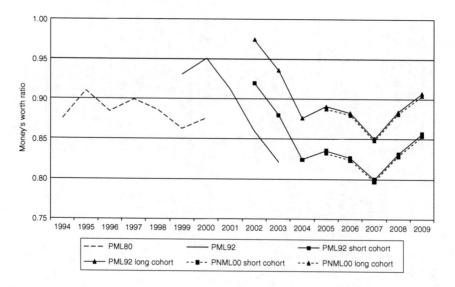

Figure 10.6 Money's worth for compulsory annuities for a 65-year-old male. *Note*: The figures are the same as in Columns 1–6 of Table 10.2. *Source*: Authors' calculations; see text.

old man in 1999. Finkelstein and Poterba (2002) suggest this is due to selection effects, as longer lived people would be more likely to choose real than nominal annuities. But, the discrepancy has more than doubled since 1999 and it is implausible to suggest that this is entirely due to selection effects. This raises the question of whether other issues, such as the higher costs of inflation-proofing annuities, are the major cause of the difference in the MWRs.

Until this point, we have continued to follow Finkelstein and Poterba (2002) in using Life Office Pensioner mortality to calculate the MWRs. In Columns 7–9 of Table 10.2, we consider the effect of using the mortality of people with retirement annuitant contracts, and for the few years that they are available, the data based on personal pensioners. With these mortality tables, the MWRs are much higher and suggest that annuities would have been very good value for the typical annuitant.

The money's worth for voluntary annuities

Murthi et al. (1999), Finkelstein and Poterba (2002), and Cannon and Tonks (2004a) all report that UK voluntary annuities are approximately fairly priced, calculating the money's worth measures for 65-year-old men as 0.99, 0.93, and 0.98, respectively. However, the choice of survival prob-

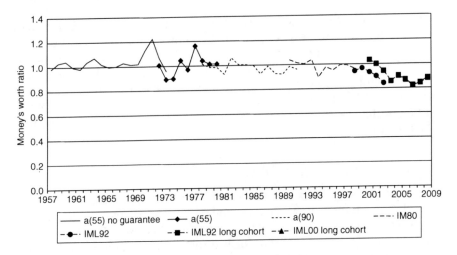

Figure 10.7 Money's worth for voluntary annuities for a 65-year-old male. *Source*: Cannon and Tonks (2004*a*) and authors' calculations; see text.

abilities is crucial: our result of 0.98 for 1990 was based upon the MWR calculated using the actuaries' a(90) table; yet using the IM80 table (which was only published in that year), the figure would have been 1.03. Over the entire period 1957–2002, we calculated an average money's worth of 0.97.

Figure 10.7 updates the analysis to 2009. Annuity rates for 1957–73 are for an annuity without a guarantee: thereafter they are guaranteed for five years. Where there is uncertainty over the date of introduction of a new actuarial table, we calculate the MWR using both sets of survival probabilities for comparison. To obtain a single statistic on the money's worth over the sample 1957–2009, we splice together the guaranteed and non-guaranteed annuity series to obtain an overall average of 0.98, which is not significantly different from unity (statistically or economically). Since these MWRs are based upon the average annuity rate in each year, it would have been possible to obtain even better value for money by buying an annuity from the life insurer with the highest rate. However, just as in the compulsory market, there is a decline in the MWR toward the end of the period.

Evaluating and explaining the money's worth

Our calculations in the previous section suggest that the money's worth for nominal annuities has been about 0.90 for the compulsory market and around unity for the voluntary market. Even after a decline at the end of the period, the money's worth was 0.80 or higher. But we need to know whether this is a satisfactory level for the money's worth. Given the presence of unavoidable transaction costs, we should certainly expect a money's worth less than one, but it is difficult to know how much less than one as the magnitude of transaction costs is commercially sensitive information and not revealed by life insurers. Real annuities have a lower money's worth, although this may be because insuring against inflation is more costly for the life insurers.

Is the money's worth good value?

One possible benchmark for the MWR for annuities is the analogous figure for other forms of insurance, namely the ratio of the value of claims paid by insurance companies to the value of premiums received. Using information provided by the Association of British Insurers for the period 1994–2006, we calculate average figures of 0.79 for motor insurance, 0.60 for domestic property insurance, and 0.57 for commercial property insurance. These figures are much lower than for the money's worth of nominal annuities and comparable to that for real annuities: except for motor insurance in 1997 and 1998, the insurance products we consider were always less good value than nominal annuities.

An alternative benchmark would be other long-term investment products. James (2000) examines the cost of investing in a variety of retail investment products in the United Kingdom, and she finds that to get the market rate of return on £1, a consumer would have to invest £1.50 in a managed fund, and between £1.10 and £1.25 in an index tracker. These figures imply a money's worth of 0.66 for a managed fund and less than 0.91 for a tracker. Again these figures are comparable or lower than the money's worth on annuities. They also suggest that it is during the accumulation phase that charges from the insurance companies have a significant reduction on the effective rate of return and not in the decumulation phase.

Why did the money's worth fall after 2004?

Despite the money's worth appearing good compared with other insurance or investment products, recent experience seems less satisfactory. In particular, the period from 2004 onward has seen a fall in the MWRs for all sorts of annuity products, reaching a minimum of about 0.80 in both voluntary and compulsory nominal annuities in 2007. Although there has been a small recovery since then, the fall in the money's worth value is clearly a cause for concern to policymakers: in particular, we need to have some idea why these measures fell so dramatically. In the compulsory market, the fall in the money's worth based upon life office pensioner mortality may be because life insurers were moving to using the personal pensioner mortality tables. But this still would not explain the contemporaneous fall in the MWRs in the voluntary market.

Because we do not know exactly when different actuarial assumptions were made, it is impossible to gauge the precise point at which the money's worth measures fell. This is one reason why we calculate the values annually rather than monthly: timing actuarial changes to the nearest month is impossible. A consequence of this is that we cannot use the timing of changes in the money's worth to identify causes. Nevertheless, we can still evaluate several possible drivers of the money's worth and see whether they have changed at some point over this period.

INSURANCE REGULATION

Life insurers in the United Kingdom are regulated by the FSA, which incorporates the European Union Life Directives for the insurance industry. The EU's proposed changes to regulation are described by 'Solvency II', which will take a more risk-sensitive approach than hitherto. In anticipation of these changes, the FSA has proceeded with its own risk-based solvency requirements (FSA 2003, 2005). This new regime may have increased the regulatory cost associated with providing annuities, by imposing higher levels of regulatory capital on annuity providers.

INCREASED LACK OF COMPETITION IN THE INSURANCE INDUSTRY

Although there are relatively few large providers, there is a significant number of potential entrants, as there are so many firms who still sell small numbers of annuities and could presumably expand their operations fairly quickly if they thought it profitable to do so. The FSA comparative tables provide information on annuity rates in the compulsory market, which enables consumers to find the best prices. So, although the small number of annuity providers is a potential cause for concern, there is no evidence that it is a cause of the low money's worth. In any case, it is difficult to see how the fall in the money's worth could be due to changes in the degree of competition, since there has been no discernable change in measures of competition such as the six-firm concentration ratio (illustrated in Figure 10.2).

THE INSURANCE CYCLE

After periods when negative shocks have resulted in *ex post* losses, insurers tend to increase their premia, a phenomenon called the 'insurance cycle' (Harrington 2004). Since life insurers may have been making *ex post* losses on annuities over some of this period, due to unanticipated reductions in mortality (i.e., when the money's worth was close to or above unity), the observed reductions in annuity rates may be an example of the insurance cycle.

In a perfectly competitive market with perfect information, insurers would be unable to recoup their losses in this fashion. Absent perfect information, however, there are two reasons why prices would rise: first, the negative shock would result in rational updating of probabilities which might cause life insurers to reduce their projections of mortality by more than suggested in the CMI reports; and second, the negative shock would have resulted in a reduction in life insurers' capital on annuities in payment which could not be replaced in the short term, or which could only be replaced at relatively high cost.

PRICING OF MORTALITY UNCERTAINTY

The money's worth methodology assumes that life insurers price annuities in an actuarially fair fashion. In practice, both prudence and regulation mean that they must build in prudential capital for downside risk. Alternatively, they could reinsure their risks, but this would also be costly and we know that reinsurance markets for mortality risk are small.

During the period we consider, it is probable that life insurers have been paying more explicit attention to cohort mortality risk. Cannon (2009) shows that increased uncertainty in mortality projections need not reduce the money's worth if life insurers aim to price on the expected value of the annuity. But if life insurers increase their prudential reserves when risk appears to rise, then this would result in the money's worth falling.

An additional incentive came directly from the regulator. In April 2007, the FSA sent a 'Dear CEO' letter to chief executives of annuity providers, reflecting on the debate over future annuitant longevity improvements. The letter recognized that companies would usually make assumptions based on their own mortality experiences; however, if this was not possible, firms might consider the different industry views in this area and err on the side of caution (FSA 2007). In other words, annuity providers, according to the regulator, should price annuities conservatively to reflect the risk of mortality improvements.

IMPAIRED LIVES

According to Quinton (2003), there was an increase in the impaired life market of 23 percent between 2001 and 2002. In 2005, the *Synthesis* database reports that of £8.5 billion sales of CPA annuities, only £386 million (4.5 percent) were impaired life. This growth in the impaired life market would have resulted in the remaining annuitants in the conventional market having higher average life expectancy, which would mean that life insurers would have to lower annuity rates to remain profitable. Our estimates of MWRs make no allowance for any growth in the impaired life market, since the life tables that we use are unable to distinguish between impaired and non-impaired lives. This means that our money's worth calculations would be based on annuitants systematically different from those buying in the non-impaired market, biasing our results downward.

Conclusion

In this chapter, we have examined a time series of UK voluntary annuity rates for 1957–2009 and compulsory annuity rates for 1994–2009. In the larger compulsory pension annuity market over a shorter sample period, we estimate that the UK MWRs for 65-year-old males and females have been approximately 0.90. In the smaller voluntary market, the money's worth is close to one for much of the period. Taking into account transactions costs, and compared to other financial and insurance products, this implies that annuities are fairly priced.

Toward the end of the period, the compulsory market is difficult to evaluate because the money's worth calculations are sensitive to the assumptions made about life expectancy and there is some uncertainty over which actuarial table we should use. Despite this, however, the MWRs have fallen in both markets since 2004, reaching a nadir in 2007.

We have discussed a number of factors that could have contributed to this result. Changes in industrial concentration do not look to have been important but more promising explanations include changes in insurance regulation; life expectancy shocks and the insurance cycle; pricing of mortality uncertainty; and the growth in the impaired lives market.

Acknowledgments

During the course of this research, Tonks was a Houblon-Norman fellow at the Bank of England and Cannon was a visiting professor at the University of Verona; the authors thank these institutions for their hospitality and support. The authors are also involved in a project for the UK Department of Work and Pensions, and they thank Tatiana Goussarova, Alexa Hime, and David Burnett for data entry. The chapter has benefited from comments made at seminars held at the Bank of England, the Department of Work and Pensions, the Association of British Insurers, and the Royal Economics Society Conference in April 2009.

Notes

[1] This includes wealth in defined-benefit occupational pension schemes, although the terms on which an individual can access this wealth are partly determined by the scheme.

[2] The stated aim of simplifying the pension system has been attenuated by the authorities' frequent changes of terminology.

[3] The precise details are complicated. The maximum income is to reduce the possibility that the pension fund is exhausted before death. The minimum income is to ensure that an income is taken and the authorities can collect the resulting income tax. A penal tax rate of 70 percent on the fund at death is to discourage *inter vivos* transfers.

[4] For a general discussion of the calculation of the money's worth, see the introduction to the collection of papers in Brown et al. (2001).

[5] Finkelstein and Poterba (2004) use the return on UK corporate bonds instead of government bonds. From the data in Figure 10.4, the difference between yields on UK commercial banks' bonds and ten-year government bonds has averaged 0.44 percentage points over the period 1994–2009.

[6] The Board of Actuarial Standards (2008) emphasizes that there is no consensus on the best type of model to use for projecting future changes in mortality.

[7] The interest rates used for real annuities are taken from the yield curve based on government bonds whose payments are RPI-linked. Note that although the current official inflation rate in the United Kingdom is based on the CPI, both government bonds and annuities are indexed to the older RPI measure.

References

Association of British Insurers (2010). *Statistical Database*. London, UK: Association of British Insurers.

Bank of England (2010). *Statistical Database*. London, UK: Bank of England.

Board for Actuarial Standards (2008). 'Discussion Paper on Mortality.' London, UK: Financial Reporting Council.

Brander, James A. and Seán Finucane (2007). 'Pensions and Corporate Performance: Effect of the Shift from Defined Benefit to Defined Contribution Pension Plans.' Xfi Centre for Finance & Investment Discussion Paper No. 07/06. Exeter, UK: University of Exeter.

Brown, Jeffrey R., Olivia S. Mitchell, James M. Poterba, and Mark J. Warshawsky (2001). *The Role of Annuity Markets in Financing Retirement*. Cambridge, MA: MIT Press.

Cannon, Edmund (2009). 'Estimation and Pricing with the Cairns-Blake-Dowd Model of Mortality,' Department of Economics Working Paper No. 65. Verona, Italy: University of Verona.

——Ian Tonks (2004a). 'UK Annuity Rates, Money's Worth and Pension Replacement Ratios 1957–2002,' *The Geneva Papers on Risk and Insurance*, 29(3): 394–416.

Cannon, Edmund and Ian Tonks (2004b). 'UK Annuity Price Series 1957 to 2002,' *Financial History Review*, 11(2): 165–96.

—— —— (2008). *Annuity Markets*. Oxford, UK: Oxford University Press.

CMI (1990). *Continuous Mortality Investigation Report*, Number 10. London, UK: Institute of Actuaries and Faculty of Actuaries.

—— (1999). *Continuous Mortality Investigation Report*, Number 17. London, UK: Institute of Actuaries and Faculty of Actuaries.

—— (2002). 'An Interim Basis for Adjusting the "92" Series Mortality Projections for Cohort Effects.' Continuous Mortality Investigation Working Paper 1. London, UK: Institute of Actuaries and Faculty of Actuaries.

—— (2004). *Continuous Mortality Investigation Report*, Number 21. London, UK: Institute of Actuaries and Faculty of Actuaries.

—— (2006). 'The Graduation of the CMI 1999–2002 Mortality Experience: Final "00" Series Mortality Tables – Annuitants and Pensioners.' Continuous Mortality Investigation Working Paper 21. London, UK: Institute of Actuaries and Faculty of Actuaries.

Cocco, João F. and Paula Lopes (2004). 'Defined Benefit or Defined Contribution? An Empirical Study of Pension Choices,' Discussion Paper No. 505. London, UK: FMG/UBS London School of Economics.

Financial Services Authority (FSA) (2003). 'Enhanced Capital Requirements and Individual Capital Assessments for Life Insurers.' Consultation Paper No. 195. London, UK: Financial Services Authority.

—— (2005). *Insurance Sector Briefing: Delivering the Tiner Insurance Reforms*. London, UK: Financial Services Authority. http://www.fsa.gov.uk/pubs/other/tiner_insurance_report.pdf

—— (2007). *Annuitant Longevity Improvements: FSA Dear CEO Letter*. London, UK: Financial Services Authority. http://www.fsa.gov.uk/pubs/ceo/Annuitant_longevity.pdf

Finkelstein, Amy and James M. Poterba (2002). 'Selection Effects in the United Kingdom Individual Annuities Market,' *Economic Journal*, 112(476): 28–50.

—— —— (2004). 'Adverse Selection in Insurance Markets: Policyholder Evidence from the UK Annuity Market,' *Journal of Political Economy*, 112(1): 183–208.

Harrington, Scott E. (2004). 'Tort Liability, Insurance Rates, and the Insurance Cycle,' *Brookings-Wharton Papers on Financial Services*, 2004: 97–138.

James, Kevin (2000). 'The Price of Retail Investing in the UK.' Occasional Paper 6. London, UK: Financial Services Authority.

Moneyfacts Group (2010). *Statistical Database*. Norwich, UK: Moneyfacts Group PLC.

Murthi, Mamta, Orszag, J. Michael, and Orszag, Peter R. (1999). 'The Value for Money of Annuities in the UK: Theory, Experience and Policy.' Birkbeck College Working Paper No. 99-19. London, UK: University of London.

Pemberton, Hugh (2006). 'Politics and Pensions in Post-war Britain,' in H. Pemberton, P. Thane and N. Whiteside, eds., *Britain's Pension Crisis: History and Policy*. Oxford, UK: Oxford University Press.

Pensions Commission (2004). *Pensions: Challenges and Choices: The First Report of the Pensions Commission*. London, UK: HMSO.

——— (2005). *A New Pension Settlement for the Twenty-First Century: The Second Report of the Pensions Commission.* London, UK: HMSO.

——— (2006). *Implementing an Integrated Package of Pension Reforms: The Final Report of the Pensions Commission.* London, UK: HMSO.

Pitacco, Ermanno, Michel Denuit, Steven Haberman, and Annamaria Olivieri (2009). *Modelling Longevity Dynamics for Pensions and Annuity Business.* Oxford, UK: Oxford University Press.

Quinton, Peter (2003). 'Enhancing Retirement Income,' *Pensions Management,* June.

Standard and Poor's (2005). *SynThesys Database.* London, UK: Standard and Poor's.

Willets, Richard (1999). *Mortality in the Next Millennium.* London, UK: Staple Inn Actuarial Society. http://www.sias.org.uk/view_paper?id = MortalityMillennium

Chapter 11

Payouts in Switzerland: Explaining Developments in Annuitization

Monika Bütler and Stefan Staubli

Overview

Occupational pensions in Switzerland were widespread long before the first pillar of old-age security was introduced in 1948. Even before the second pillar was mandated in 1985 (based on a change in the constitution approved by the Swiss electorate in 1972), more than half of the Swiss workforce participated in occupational pension funds. For these employees, participation in a fund was mandated; employees had to participate if they were employed by a company that offered a fully funded pension scheme. Although payouts were traditionally in the form of annuities, lump-sum payments were not uncommon.

Together with the Netherlands, the Swiss pension system is rather unique in an international context, since in both countries, a large fraction of retirement income stems from the mandatory fully funded second pillar. There are generous income guarantees, and there is no choice as to pension provider. In contrast to the Dutch system, however, Swiss retirees are given more withdrawal options and there is more diversity in pension plan providers. Swiss annuitization rates are high, but they also vary greatly over time and between pension providers. Despite the mandate, there are very few legal restrictions regarding the size of the lump sum payout. Full annuitization is always possible (subject to the minimum requirements specified in pension law), but many providers also allow the total pension capital to be paid out as a lump sum. Since first-pillar benefits are below the level of subsistence, full cash-outs of occupational pension capital jeopardize the adequacy of retirement income and may in turn be costly for the government.

This chapter sheds light on two interconnected aspects of the choice between the annuity and the lump sum within the Swiss pension system. First, we explore the annuitization decision from an individual perspective: what are the most important factors in the individual decision to cash out, and how do changes in policy effect individual payout decisions? Second, we describe the policymaker perspective: what intentions and goals define pension policies? What are the most significant problems to be addressed: regulation, or interdependence with other social insurance schemes, notably guaranteed income in old age? This chapter highlights the impact of recent changes in second-pillar legislation such as conversion rate reductions, and we also examine additional factors that are important in the annuitization decision in Switzerland.

The idiosyncrasies of the Swiss pension system have attracted considerable interest, and this study is not the first to focus on the Swiss second pillar. Queisser and Vittas (2000) provide a detailed analysis of the strengths and weaknesses of the Swiss pension system, but they do not include a discussion of second-pillar retirement payouts. Queisser and Whitehouse (2003) focus on participant withdrawal options in Swiss occupational pension schemes, but that analysis is based on aggregate data from the Pension Funds Statistics, which cannot be used to shed light on the determinants of individual retirement payouts. The World Bank report on annuity markets in Switzerland by Bütler and Ruesch (2007) is most closely related to this chapter, in that it examines the role of the second pillar in the provision of old-age benefits and calculates money's worth ratios for different subgroups of the population. Yet, we go farther in the present chapter by exploring individual retirement decisions.

The structure of the chapter is as follows. In the next section, we present a brief history of the Swiss pension system, provide an overview of the institutional structure with a focus on the occupational pension pillar, and discuss the current demographic and economic situation in Switzerland. Next, we analyze key determinants defining the high annuitization rates among middle- and high-income earners and the relatively low annuitization rates for low-income earners in Switzerland. Finally, we discuss the future of the Swiss pension system and identify important areas calling for reform, and provide concluding remarks.

Institutional frame

Historical perspective

The first pension funds in Switzerland were established over a century ago, initially in the engineering industry. Unlike today, insurance then was optional and depended on employer goodwill. Persons not gainfully employed had no insurance and no institutionalized means of making provision for their old age, as the first-pillar welfare scheme (AVS) was established only much later (1948). In 1972, occupational pension plans were incorporated into the Constitution, where they represent the second pillar in the three-pillar system. They are designed to complement the first pillar. Based on this provision in the Constitution, the Federal Law on Occupational Retirement, Survivors and Disability Pension Plans (LPP) was elaborated and enacted in 1985. The system design was largely based on the structure of existing pension funds. It kept the previous benefit schemes based on a single earner, but introduced the principle of a minimum provision guaranteed by law. With the introduction of mandatory participation, coverage rates jumped from around 50 percent in the 1970s to almost 90 percent. Currently, around 96 percent of working men and 83 percent of working women are covered by an occupational pension plan.

Due to the evolution of pension funds and the LPP allowance for different organizational structures within occupational pension plans, the second pillar has always been highly fragmented. Even though the number of pension funds was roughly cut in half over the period 1994–2007, there were still 2,543 pension funds active in 2007. This consolidation is mainly the result of small firms outsourcing the organization of the second pillar to insurance companies, instead of operating a completely autonomous pension fund.

The scheme's long history is also reflected in the size of the accumulated capital stock. In 2007, assets of occupational pension funds amounted to approximately 120 percent of GDP. Initially, all schemes were set up as defined benefit (DB) plans. Over the last twenty years, a majority of pension funds changed to a more flexible defined contribution (DC) structure. But practically speaking, the difference between DB and DC schemes is negligible because the occupational pension scheme is strongly regulated with respect to minimum accrual and interest rates, as well as the conversion factor.

Pension plans have always been considered an important device in attracting skilled workers. For a long time, they were a disadvantage for mobile workers, given that the accumulated capital was not transferable across pension funds until 1995. The predominant payout option was, and still is, a lifetime annuity. Since 2005, Swiss pension funds are required by law to offer a partial lump sum option as well. While the LPP defines minimum requirements for various pension factors, the system was characterized by a lack of transparency: in many cases, individuals had no idea of how much accumulated capital they had. The fragmentation of the system added to this problem. Only recently, new transparency standards have been enacted, which are legally binding for all pension plan providers.

Structure of the Swiss pension system

Switzerland's pension system is based on two pillars which are more or less of equal importance. The first pillar AHV/AVS is a pay-as-you-go (PAYG) system that seeks to provide a basic subsistence level of income to all retired residents. The second pillar is an employer-based, fully funded occupational pension scheme and is mandatory for all employees whose annual income exceeds a certain threshold. When total income does not cover basic needs in old age, means-tested supplemental benefits may be claimed as part of the first pillar. The first and second pillars are complemented by a voluntary third pillar, which is an individual tax-deductible savings account for retirement.

Adding the first and second pillar together, an individual with an uninterrupted working career has a replacement rate of approximately 50–60 percent of insured income. The net replacement rate after taxes often amounts to 70–80 percent, even for higher levels of income, and can reach 100 percent for beneficiaries with dependent children. In contrast to other countries, the structure of the second pillar leads to replacement rates that are similar for both lower and higher incomes. In addition to retirement income, the first and the second pillars also provide disability insurance.

First-pillar benefits in Switzerland vary depending on average earned income and the number of contribution years, including those granted for child care. Conditional on having contributed at least forty-five years to the system, a minimum pension of 13,680 CHF per year is guaranteed, which is equivalent to an annual 12,670 US$ (exchange rate as of February 12, 2010). A majority of retirees qualify for a pension close to the maximum benefit level, which is equal to twice the minimum pension (i.e., 27,360 CHF). The statutory retirement age is 64 for women and 65 for men. The earliest age at which first pillar benefits can be claimed is 62 for women and 63 for men, subject to an actuarially fair reduction in benefits of 6.8 percent per year. Working beyond age 64/65 is possible, but most work contracts specify a retirement age that coincides with the statutory age of retirement. If a spouse dies, first-pillar benefits of the surviving spouse are increased by 20 percent up to the maximum benefit level. In addition, retirees can claim child benefits equivalent to 40 percent of the base first-pillar pension for each dependent child. First-pillar contributions are proportional to earned income (without a cap), and they account for approximately 70 percent of AVS/AHV revenue. The remaining revenue comes from earmarked value-added taxes and additional funds paid from general government revenues.

Participation in the second pillar is mandatory for all employees with annual earnings of approximately 20,000 CHF or more. The insured income above this threshold and below an upper threshold (at present 82,080 CHF) is called the mandatory part. The income above the upper threshold is called the super-mandatory part of the second pillar. The mandatory part is subject to stringent regulation with respect to minimum contribution rates, minimum interest rates, and the conversion rate at which the accumulated pension wealth is translated into an annuity. By contrast, there are few restrictions on the contract conditions offered by the insurance companies in the super-mandatory part. By law, pension plan providers are required to insure the mandatory share. They are free to provide insurance for the super-mandatory part, and most do because the second pillar is important in attracting a well-educated workforce and both mandatory and super-mandatory pension components are treated favorably under tax law.

Contributions to the occupational pension plans correspond to a certain fraction of an employee's salary, of which the employer has to pay at least half. When an employee moves to another company, all of the accumulated contributions (including the employer's part) are transferred to the new fund. The total amount of assets at retirement has thus been accumulated over the entire working life and is a good proxy for lifetime income. The occupational pension wealth can be withdrawn either as a monthly lifelong annuity, a lump sum, or a combination of the two options. In some plans, the cash-out limit is equal to 50 or 25 percent (the legal minimum) of accumulated capital. To mitigate adverse selection effects, individuals must declare their choice between three months and three years prior to the effective withdrawal date, depending on the insurer's regulations. Many pension insurers define a default option if the beneficiary does not make an active choice.

Occupational pension annuities are strictly proportional to the accumulated retirement assets (contributions made during the working lifetime plus accrued interest). The capital K is translated into a yearly nominal annuity B using the conversion rate γ: $B = \gamma \times K$. The conversion rate is independent of marital status, income, or gender (at least in the mandatory part), but it depends on the retirement age. By law, the annuity option includes dependent children's benefits of up to 20 percent of the main claimant's benefit for each child younger than 18 (or below the age of 25 if still dependent). The annuity option's regulation also specifies that survivor benefits must be equivalent to 60 percent of the deceased's pension. As will be illustrated later, these additional benefits combined with the uniform conversion rate create a sizeable redistribution between married and non-married annuitants.

Until 2004, the minimum conversion rate in the mandatory part was fixed at 7.2 percent. With the aim of improving the stability of the second pillar, the Swiss government implemented a series of changes in 2004, 2005, and 2006. An integral part of these changes is that the minimum conversion rate in the mandatory part will be successively lowered to 6.8 percent by 2015. Pension funds are free to set the conversion rate for the less-regulated super-mandatory part of the second pillar, but until 2003, conversion rates in the mandatory and super-mandatory part were virtually identical. In 2004, several large pension funds started to reduce the conversion rate in the super-mandatory part to 5.4 percent for women and 5.8 percent for men. Since then, many other pension funds have followed.

By law, pension providers are not allowed to differentiate payout rates according to gender or marital status. The difference in gender conversion rates in some super-mandatory plans stems from women's younger retirement age and is not related to differences in life expectancy. Female longer life expectancy is compensated with survivor benefits. Many pension funds offer an early retirement option at an actuarially fair adjustment of the conversion rate. This option is very popular and in many pension plans, the observed retirement age is substantially lower than the statutory age of retirement. Pension funds are requested to index annuities to inflation, if the fund's financial situation allows it to do so. At present, only a few funds are actually able to index pensions to inflation, mainly due to the great liabilities created by a very high conversion factor in the mandatory part.

The annuity is subject to normal income tax rates. Additional income from other sources, for example from the first pillar, increases the effective marginal tax rate under the annuity option. The lump sum, on the other hand, is taxed only once (at retirement). The tax rate applied to the capital option varies greatly across Swiss cantons. The present value of the tax bill is almost always smaller under the lump sum option compared to the annuity option, particularly for average and higher levels of second-pillar pension wealth. Therefore, the differential tax treatment is expected to reduce the demand for an annuity.

Introduced in 1966, means-tested supplemental benefits may be claimed as part of the first pillar when the retiree's total income does not cover basic needs in old age. Eligibility for benefits is limited to individuals who receive an old-age or disability pension, live in Switzerland, and have Swiss or EU citizenship or have been living in Switzerland for at least ten years. These additional benefits usually result in an income that is above the poverty threshold. The guaranteed total income is approximately 36,000 CHF for singles and 51,000 CHF for legal couples (without children).

A voluntary third pillar of individual saving complements the first and second pillars for retirement. Given the already high replacement rate provided by the first and second pillar, the third pillar is primarily important for the self-employed (who are not covered by the second pillar) and individuals with contribution gaps. Since contributions are fully tax-deductible up to a certain amount, the third pillar has also become a popular instrument for middle- and high-income earners to save on taxes. Due to the high degree of annuitization in the first and second pillars, the accumulated capital in the third pillar is usually paid out as a lump sum. Reliable data on the volume of the third pillar is very difficult to get, as third-pillar contracts are provided not only by insurance companies but also by most banks and other financial intermediaries.

There exists a very small market for annuities outside the second pillar, but the offered contract conditions are far less generous compared to the second-pillar annuities mainly for two reasons. First, occupational pension plans are less plagued by adverse selection problems. Second and far more important, since the introduction of mandatory participation in 1985, the regulated high conversion factors in the second pillar have dominated market conversion rates by far for most individuals.

The Swiss demographic and economic situation

As in other industrialized countries, the demographic situation in Switzerland is characterized by a substantial increase in life expectancy together with a low fertility rate. As shown in Table 11.1, the total fertility rate declined from 2.1 children per woman in 1970 to 1.5 children per woman in 2000. Over the same period, the remaining life expectancy at age 65 increased for men from 13.3 to 17.3 years and for women from 16.2 to 21.1 years. This trend in life expectancy is projected to continue at the same rate until 2030, if not beyond. This demographic transition will result in a substantial increase in the old-age dependency ratio. The ratio of individuals aged 65 and older to individuals aged 21–64 has grown from approximately 18 percent in 1970 to 25 percent in 2000 and will increase further to 43 percent in 2030. Due to the high rate of immigration, the Swiss population is aging at a slower rate compared to other industrialized nations. Nonetheless, the strong increase in the old-age dependency ratio has a direct impact on the financial stability of the first pillar. If the current levels of contributions and benefits are left unchanged, the scheme will start running a sustained deficit in 2012.

Despite these gloomy forecasts, and contrary to other European countries, the main structure of the first pillar as well as the contribution levels has remained essentially unchanged. Swiss policymakers face strong

TABLE 11.1 Demographic trends in Switzerland

Demographic statistic	1970	2000	2030	Change (1970–2030)
Total fertility rate	2.1	1.5	1.4	−0.7
Life expectancy at age 65				
Men	13.3	17.3	20.9	+7.6
Women	16.2	21.1	24.1	+7.9
Old-age dependency ratio[a]	17.7	25	42.6	+24.9

[a] Ratio of individuals aged 65 and over to number of individuals aged 20–64.

Source: Bundesamt für Statistik (2009a, 2009b).

political constraints for potential reforms as the public possesses a veto power (Bütler 2009). Any change in the law can be (and usually is) challenged by a national referendum. The last reform to the first pillar dates back to 1997. The most important element of the reform was an increase in the female retirement age in two steps from 62 to 64.

There have also been no fundamental changes in the second pillar of the pension system. Given the increase since 1985 in life expectancy at age 65 of about three years and the fall in capital market returns, the conversion factor should have been reduced by approximately 15–20 percent. Yet, the regulation of nominal interest rates and the conversion factor have remained constant for almost twenty years. The illusion of perpetual stability was only squashed after the stock market downturn at the beginning of 2000. As a consequence, market returns fell below the 4 percent minimum return requirement and many pension funds reported an underfunding. After an intense political debate, the Swiss Federal Council agreed to reduce the minimum return requirement to 3.25 percent as of January 2003. Since then, the interest rate has been adjusted several times to its current rate of 2 percent.

At the same time, the Swiss government enacted the first revision to the second pillar, which was implemented in three steps. In 2004, new regulations concerning transparency became effective. The changes implemented in 2005 include an extension of the coverage of the second pillar to low-income and part-time workers and a stepwise reduction of the conversion rate in the mandatory part to 6.8 percent by 2015. Finally, in 2006, new tax law regulations concerning occupational pensions became effective. However, the adjustments in the second pillar proved far too weak and further reductions in the conversion factor are planned.

The necessity for additional reforms in the second pillar was brought to light by the strong impact of the global financial crisis of 2008–10, which reduced the value of assets and uncovered structural deficiencies in the second pillar with respect to the funding ratio, regulation, and supervision. In 2008, private pension plan providers suffered from an average performance of −13 percent. In contrast, under the current regulatory framework, a return of roughly 5 percent is required to secure the liabilities in autonomous pension funds. As a consequence, the average funding ratio fell from 110 percent in 2007 to 96 percent in 2008. Insurance companies that mainly provide pension plans for small and medium companies were affected less due to their more stringent asset allocation rules. Retirees and individuals close to retirement were not directly affected by the crisis due to the many built-in guaranteed income benefits. However, most funds will be forced to undergo restructuring, and a reduction in benefits for present retirees is no longer off limits (though still difficult to implement by law).

Determinants of annuitization

Figure 11.1 presents the fraction of capital cashed out at retirement based on administrative records from several pension funds and large insurance companies. Compared to other industrialized countries, the Swiss annuitization rate is very high: only between 10 and 30 percent of all individuals covered by an autonomous pension plan cash out their pension wealth. Annuitization rates in collective funds, that is, large insurance companies that provide occupational pension plans for small and medium-sized firms, are lower but still rather high compared to other countries.

There are at least two reasons for the difference in cash-out behavior between autonomous pension plans and insurance companies. The first is a composition effect. Individuals covered by collective funds tend to earn less and be poorer as measured by their accumulated pension wealth. The second reason relates to differences in the standard cash-out option. In most autonomous pension plans, the default option is the annuity. In most insurance companies, individuals do not face a default option. They are thus forced to make an active choice which might work to the disadvantage of the annuity option.

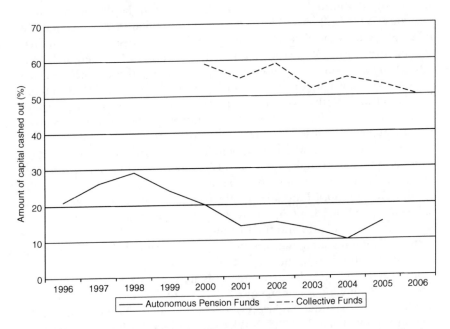

Figure 11.1 Annual cash-out rates in autonomous pension funds and collective funds. *Source:* Authors' calculations; see text.

We now discuss three factors that might explain the cash-out pattern in Switzerland: high money's worth ratios, framing effects, and other behavioral factors, as well as generous means-tested supplemental benefits, which act as a supplementary longevity insurance. Each of these determinants will be analyzed in turn using individual retirement decisions from Swiss occupational pension plans.

Money's worth ratio: the value of the annuity

A commonly used measure for the value of an annuity is the money's worth ratio (MWR), which relates the expected present discounted value of future payouts to the premium cost of the annuity. An MWR above 1 indicates that an individual will, on average, expect to get back more in annuity payments than what he or she paid in. On the other hand, when the MWR is less than 1, annuitants will expect to receive less in annuity payouts than they paid in premiums. Both administrative costs and adverse selection with respect to private health information about expected longevity may give rise to actuarially unfair MWRs. Annuities in the mandatory fully funded second pillar in Switzerland, which account for more than 99 percent of all (funded) pension payments in Switzerland, are extremely generous. Table 11.2 shows MWRs for the second pillar in 2009 using three different strategies to discount future annuity payments: (*a*) the nominal yield curve in 2009, (*b*) the return on a five-year bond (1.5 percent in 2009), and (*c*) the discount factor used by most pension providers, which is 3.5 percent. As shown in the first three rows of Table 11.2, MWRs in the mandatory part of the system are greater than 1 for single women and married men in 2009, even when future annuity payments are discounted with a (rather high) discount factor of 3.5 percent.

Only for single men, who do not benefit from survivor benefits and have a higher average mortality rate, are MWRs less than 1 (when a discount factor of 3.5 percent is applied). Thus, it is not surprising that many pension funds report difficulties in meeting their financial obligations. As is illustrated in Rows 4 and 5, the stepwise reduction in the conversion rate to 6.8 percent until 2014 and the further reduction to 6.4 percent, which is currently being debated, may not be sufficient to restore financial stability in the mandatory part of the second pillar.

Since 2004, many Swiss pension funds have reduced their conversion rates to 5.8 percent for men and 5.4 percent for women, in the less-regulated super-mandatory part of the second pillar. Therefore, as can be seen in Rows 6–8 of Table 11.2, MWRs are considerably lower in the super-mandatory part compared to the mandatory part of the scheme. Because the reduction was more pronounced for women relative to men, the adjustment in conversion rates also reduced the redistribution in the super-mandatory part of the scheme, at least between single women and single men. Due to survivor benefits and lower average mortality, MWRs in the super-mandatory part are still substantially higher for married men.

One reason for the high MWRs in the fully funded pillar is the generous income guarantees. Another reason is that since the introduction of the second pillar in 1985, the minimum conversion rate has hardly been adjusted to changes in life expectancy. To highlight the impact of the demographic transition on the financial well-being of the second pillar, Figure 11.2 shows trends in MWRs for different subpopulations over the last twenty years. The calculations are based on a fixed interest rate of 3.5 percent, but they do account for greater survival rates over time. For single men, the MWR increased from 0.85 in 1989 to 0.92 in 2004. It has remained relatively constant since 2005, due to the stepwise reduction in the minimum conversion rate. Similarly, the MWR for married men grew from 0.99 in 1989 to 1.07 in 2009. These numbers suggest that in order to hold the MWR constant, the annuitization factor should have been reduced by approximately 10 percent over the last twenty years. Until 2001, the MWR for women increased at roughly the same rate as the MWRs for single and married men. In 2002, the women's MWR declined by 2 percent, which is explained by the increase in the female retirement age from 62 to 63. A similar dip can be observed in 2005 when the female retirement age was increased further to 64. Together with the reduction in the conversion rate, these changes narrowed the gap between the MWRs for men and women.

Bütler et al. (2010) exploit a recent large and sudden cutback in the conversion rate in the super-mandatory part to examine how changes in

TABLE 11.2 Money's worth ratios for the Swiss second pillar in 2009

	Female single	Male single	Male married
Mandatory part			
Five-year bond (1.5%)	1.311	1.117	1.324
Yield curve	1.153	1.007	1.161
Fixed: 3.5%	1.051	0.920	1.059
Projections			
CR 6.8% (five-year bond)	1.274	1.077	1.277
CR 6.4% (five-year bond)	1.218	1.030	1.220
Super-mandatory part			
Five-year bond (1.5%)	1.022	0.924	1.096
Yield curve	0.898	0.833	0.961
Fixed: 3.5%	0.819	0.762	0.876

Source: Authors' calculations; see text.

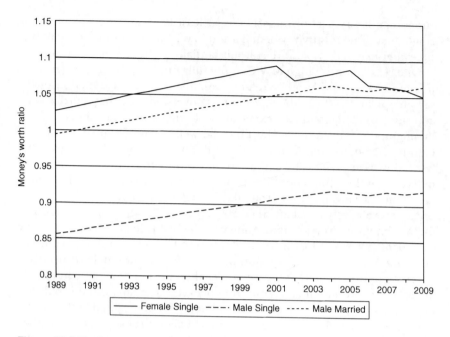

Figure 11.2 Evolution of money's worth ratios over time. *Source:* Authors' calculations; see text.

the annuity's value impact the annuitization decision. The authors compare the annuitization behavior of individuals who were affected by the reduction in the conversion rate with observably similar individuals who were covered by an insurance company that did not reduce the conversion rate. They show that the 20 percent reduction in the annuity value led to an approximately 14 percentage point drop in the annuitization rate. Interestingly, the policy change also triggered substantial anticipatory behavior: individuals who had planned to retire after the policy change shifted their retirement date to take advantage of the favorable conditions prior to the change. In particular, there is a large spike in the number of retirees in the month before the lower conversion rates became effective. This pattern suggests that individuals were well aware of the large losses in the annuity value.

Calculation of MWRs implicitly assumes risk-neutrality. However, given that the annuity provides an insurance against the longevity risk, the utility value of an annuity may well exceed its money's worth for a risk-averse individual. Consistent with this view, Mitchell et al. (1999) show that, as risk aversion increases, individuals are willing to forgo more wealth for actuarially fair annuities. Annuity equivalent wealth (AEW) is a utility-based measure that takes into account this insurance aspect. Using data from several autonomous pension funds in Switzerland, Bütler and Teppa (2007) show that the AEW is indeed the most important determinant of the annuitization decision. Actually, a 1 percentage point increase in the AEW increases the annuitization rate by 1.5 percentage points for women and by 0.5 percentage points for men. This estimate of the responsiveness of the annuitization decision with respect to changes in the value of an annuity is thus close to the value in Bütler et al. (2010). Brown (2001) finds similar results using survey data from the United States.

Behavioral factors

Behavioral economics has been able to explain many aspects of retirement planning such as participation in employer-provided pension plans (Duflo and Saez 2003), saving rates (Beshears et al. 2008), and portfolio allocation decisions (Choi et al. 2009). Recent literature on the determinants of individual cash-out behavior suggests that behavioral biases play an important role in the annuitization decision as well. Brown et al. (2008), for example, show that framing matters for the annuitization decision. Under an 'investment frame' that focuses on risk and return, only 21 percent of individuals prefer a life annuity over a saving account. On the other hand, under the 'consumption frame' that highlights the consequences for life-long consumption, 72 percent choose the life annuity.

Research by Bütler and Teppa (2007) suggests that observed annuitization behavior in Swiss occupational pension plans is partially related to behavioral factors. For instance, the authors observe that individuals largely stick with the sponsor's default option rather than making active decisions. In particular, the likelihood of cashing out pension wealth is significantly higher in companies that provide the (partial) lump sum as a default option. This finding is highly relevant for policymakers: the annuitization default is likely to decrease the propensity to cash out and increase longevity insurance. Since the annuity is the default option in most pension plans, this finding also helps to explain the high overall annuitization rate in Switzerland. Interestingly, several small pension funds displayed almost no variation with respect to the annuitization decision: all retirees chose either the lump sum or the annuity. Pension fund managers usually explain the phenomenon with peer effects and an implicit standard option ('it has always been done this way').

The impact of the reduction in the super-mandatory conversion rate, analyzed by Bütler et al. (2010), provides further (informal) evidence that behavioral aspects might be important. They show that almost all beneficiaries chose a polar option and did not distinguish between the mandatory and super-mandatory part, although implicit annuity prices were dramatically different after the reduction in the conversion rate in 2004. This result is consistent with the proposition that many retirees do not make properly informed choices.

The high degree of annuitization in Switzerland may also be attributed to the framing of the scheme. That is, Swiss occupational pension benefits were traditionally framed as annuities. Until very recently, many contributors to the system were not even aware of the sum of money they had accumulated, but merely knew the approximate amount of the monthly payments. To improve transparency, starting in 2005, all pension funds are required to provide all insured participants with a yearly statement (many funds offered such statements already before the mandatory introduction). The statement declares the accumulated capital to date and contains information on the expected approximate annuity stream (based on an extrapolation of current earnings and interest rates). However, with respect to framing, the space given to annuity streams, which also includes survivor benefits and benefits in case of disability, is much larger compared to the space given to the accumulated capital. The statement on an individual's occupational pension benefits thus comes close to what Brown et al. (2008) call a consumption frame, which is much more likely to induce beneficiaries to choose the annuity.

Means-tested benefits and annuitization

Approximately 12 percent of all retirees receive means-tested benefits as part of the first pillar, because their total income does not cover basic needs in old age. These very generous supplemental benefits have contributed to a low poverty rate among the elderly in Switzerland, but they may also have unintended consequences on the annuitization decision. In particular, because means-tested benefits provide an implicit insurance against the financial consequences of longevity, individuals have a strong incentive to cash out accumulated pension wealth even if full annuitization were optimal in the absence of a consumption floor.

The yearly amount of means-tested benefits is obtained by summing up all applicable expenditures and subtracting all pension income, investment income, and earnings, plus one-tenth of the wealth exceeding a threshold level of 25,000 CHF for singles and 40,000 CHF for married claimants. The applicable expenditures include a cost-of-living allowance, health insurance expenditures, and rent payments. Given that pension income is fully taken into account in the calculation of means-tested benefits, an annuity reduces the means-tested benefits proportionally. On the other hand, a lump sum payment has no effect on supplemental benefits as long as the total wealth (including the lump sum) is below the threshold level.

Even if the total wealth exceeds the threshold level, only one-tenth of the lump sum is credited against means-tested benefits. Moreover, since the eligibility age for benefits in pension plans is typically less than the statutory retirement age, the lump sum can be used to finance early retirement. Once the statutory age of retirement is reached, means-tested benefits can be claimed.

The incentive to cash out the accumulated wealth in order to apply for means-tested benefits later is particularly strong for individuals with less pension wealth. Middle-income individuals have to weigh the benefit of taking a lump sum and later receiving generous supplemental benefits, against the disadvantage of not receiving the wealth-enhancing mortality credit and not being able to smooth consumption optimally. Maximal first-pillar benefits amount to roughly 2,000 CHF per month; the means-tested benefits increase the total income to approximately 3,000 CHF a month. Thus, an individual with a monthly second-pillar benefit of less than 1,000 CHF a month (which corresponds to accumulated occupational pension wealth of approximately 170,000 CHF) and little non-pension wealth is always better off withdrawing the accumulated capital upon retirement, spending it quickly, and then applying for means-tested benefits.

Informal evidence for this conjecture is provided in Figure 11.3, which plots the fraction of capital cashed out at retirement as a function of the accumulated old-age capital. Clearly, the probability of cashing out is very high for those with a capital stock and it decreases continuously for higher levels of second-pillar wealth. This pattern is in line with Bütler and Teppa (2007) who show that the probability of annuitizing increases with the accumulated wealth. Bütler et al. (2009) analyze optimal annuity demand and consumption decisions in a realistic life-cycle model under a social security scheme in which means-tested benefits can be claimed if income falls below a certain subsistence level. A comparison of model results and real-world data from several Swiss pension funds suggests that means-tested benefits substantially decrease the annuity demand for individuals with low or medium levels of pension wealth. Moreover, the observed cash-out pattern is consistent with the predictions of the model.

Our findings do not preclude other explanations for the increase in annuitization rates with accumulated capital. Less wealthy individuals may prefer the lump sum because they tend to have a higher mortality risk. However, the likelihood of cashing out continues to decline even for relatively high levels of pension wealth where health is not an important factor. It is well known that financial literacy is positively correlated with income and wealth (see Lusardi and Mitchell 2007). Therefore, annuitization rates may increase with accumulated capital because wealthier individuals make more informed choices.

Financial instability and future reforms

While the basic structure of Swiss old-age insurance based on the three pillars is generally undisputed, both the first and the second pillar will primarily have to tackle the problem of too generous benefits combined with insufficient contributions. For both systems, there are political constraints to reforming the system because the political system in Switzerland leaves the population with a strong veto power. And indeed, the future of occupational pension plans continues to spark debate. Increasing life expectancy and lessening market returns jeopardize the financial sustainability of second-pillar pensions. In spite of this, attempts to stabilize the occupational pension system, as a whole, have failed thus far. Instead, individual parameters such as the conversion rate are being tweaked. Two directions of reform are outlined, both of which are likely to affect individuals' choice between a lump sum and an annuity.

The generous nominal income guarantees implicit in the high conversion rate limit the ability of pension funds to adjust pensions to the rate of inflation. Without any significant inflation in many years, the Swiss may have forgotten just how important indexing annuities is. Just as an example of its importance, an annual inflation rate of 2 percent (which the Swiss National Bank still considers price stability) results in a real loss of one-third of benefits after twenty years of retirement. A change from nominal to real annuities would protect individuals against erosion of annuity value by inflation. But, it would also entail sizeable reductions in initial benefits, which are difficult to communicate. It might also lead to lower annuitization rates and thus to higher government expenditures in the form of means-tested benefits. Moreover, real annuities penalize individuals with a short life expectancy as a larger fraction of annuity income is paid out later in life. This might further reduce annuitization rates unless payout choices are restricted.

A second aspect that should be addressed is how risk is shared between different generations with respect to systemic risks (e.g., financial crises, life expectancy). Due to this intergenerational risk-sharing, in international comparisons, those insured by Swiss pension funds have done relatively well in the current financial crisis. But, now there is a threat that risk-sharing between generations leads to a redistribution at the expense of those currently working. Reforming the occupational pension plan should put more emphasis on the risk-sharing agreements between generations. This would entail, for example, a clear definition of the ownership of pension fund surpluses and reserves. These definitions would have to be taken into consideration when either a job is changed or a lump sum is paid. Another important issue to conceptualize and regulate is the situation in which a deficit emerges. The nature of (predefined) deficit recovery

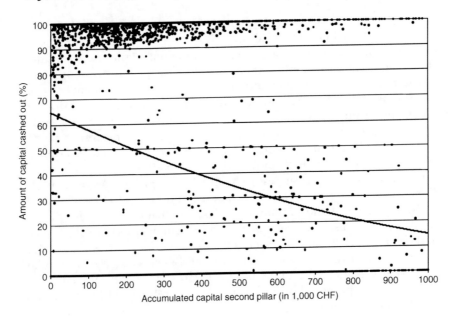

Figure 11.3 Cash-out rates and accumulated pension wealth in the second pillar.
Source: Authors' calculations; see text.

plans – in particular, to what degree retirees participate – will most likely also influence annuitization decisions.

Conclusion

Switzerland has a very comprehensive mandatory occupational pension scheme with accumulated capital exceeding one year's GDP. Consequently, a large part of retirement income comes from the second pillar. In international comparisons, Switzerland has markedly higher annuitization rates, in part due to the history of Swiss occupational pension schemes. Occupational plans, introduced well before the Swiss PAYG system, were traditionally set up as DB schemes. Even today, the political discussion focuses on the annuity stream and not on the size of capital stock at retirement. Furthermore, the high degree of regulation in the Swiss pension scheme introduces yet another bias in favor of the annuity. The strong historical dimension and stringent regulation make it difficult to extract lessons for other countries regarding the level of annuitization.

This is not true, however, where the gradient of annuitization demand is concerned. A number of exogenous variations in annuities values as well as

pension plan details allow conclusions to be drawn that seem more generally applicable. While individuals in Swiss occupational pension plans do
not have much choice during the accumulation phase, they have considerable freedom in choosing how their capital will be paid out at retirement.
By law, retirees can withdraw a certain fraction of their retirement balances
in cash, and in most cases, there is no upper limit to cash withdrawals.
While this feature is fortunate for the empirical researcher, it has the
potential to undermine the adequacy of retirement income, especially for
low- and middle-income earners, and it may lead to additional governmen-
tal expenditures in the form of means-tested benefits.

Based on our empirical research with Swiss data, we argue that the
demand for annuities entails both rational and behavioral factors. Obviously, the value of the annuity is a good predictor for the decision to
annuitize. The responsiveness of the annuitization decision with respect
to the change in the annuity value is 0.7, as found in previous studies. It is
also shown that reinsurance in the form of a means-tested consumption
floor lowers the demand for an annuity for low- and middle-income earners. Moreover, payout choices are significantly influenced by default options and peer effects.

The Swiss three-pillar retirement system provides policymakers with a
rich context to explore policy revisions. Our analysis shows that reducing
overly optimistic income guarantees might reduce annuitization rates.
Lower annuities in turn might decrease the desirability of an annuity,
favoring instead an outside option of means-tested benefits. To prevent
individuals from taking advantage of means-tested benefits, limits on cash-
outs at retirement could be discussed. Last but not least, well-designed
default options may indeed be central in achieving the goal of providing
adequate retirement income, without putting too many restrictions on
individual choice.

References

Beshears, John, James J. Choi, David Laibson, and Brigitte Madrian (2008). 'The
Importance of Default Options for Retirement Saving Outcomes: Evidence from
the United States,' in Stephen J. Kay and Tapen Sinha, eds., *Lessons from Pension
Reform in the Americas*. Oxford, UK: Oxford University Press, pp. 59–87.

Brown, Jeffrey (2001). 'Private Pensions, Mortality Risk, and the Decision to Annuitize,' *Journal of Public Economics*, 82: 29–62.

——Jeffrey R. Kling, Sendhil Mullainathan, and Marian V. Wrobel (2008). 'Why
Don't People Insure Late Life Consumption? A Framing Explanation of the
Under-Annuitization Puzzle,' *The American Economic Review: Papers and Proceedings*,
98: 304–9.

Bundesamt für Statistik (2009a). 'Demographisches Porträt der Schweiz.' Sektion Demographie und Migration, BFS. Neuenburg: Bundesamt für Statistik.

—— (2009b). 'Die Zukunft der Langlebigkeit in der Schweiz.' Sektion Demographie und Migration, BFS. Neuenburg: Bundesamt für Statistik.

Bütler, Monika (2009). 'Switzerland: High Replacement Rates and Generous Subsistence as a Barrier to Work in Old Age,' *The Geneva Papers*, 34: 561–77.

—— Martin Ruesch (2007). 'Annuities in Switzerland.' Policy Research Working Paper No. 4438. Washington, DC: The World Bank.

—— Federica Teppa (2007). 'The Choice Between an Annuity and a Lump Sum: Results from Swiss Pension Funds,' *Journal of Public Economics*, 91: 1944–66.

—— Kim Peijnenburg, and Stefan Staubli (2009). 'Do Means-Tested Benefits Reduce the Demand for Annuities? – Evidence from Switzerland.' Department of Economics Discussion Paper. St.Gallen, Switzerland: University of St. Gallen.

—— Stefan Staubli, and Maria Grazia Zito (2010). 'The Role of the Annuity's Value on the Decision (Not) to Annuitize: Evidence from a Large Policy Change.' Department of Economics Discussion Paper No. 2010-05. St.Gallen, Switzerland: University of St. Gallen.

Choi, James J., David Laibson, and Brigitte C. Madrian (2009). 'Mental Accounting in Portfolio Choice: Evidence from a Flypaper Effect,' *American Economic Review*, 99(5): 2085–95.

Duflo, Esther and Emmanuel Saez (2003). 'The Role of Information and Social Interactions in Retirement Plan Decisions: Evidence From a Randomized Experiment,' *Quarterly Journal of Economics*, 118: 815–42.

Lusardi, Annamaria and Olivia S. Mitchell (2007). 'Baby Boomer Retirement Security: The Role of Planning, Financial Literacy, and Housing Wealth,' *Journal of Monetary Economics*, 54: 205–24.

Mitchell, Olivia S., James M. Poterba, Mark J. Warshawsky, and Jeffrey R. Brown (1999). 'New Evidence on the Money's Worth of Individual Annuities,' *American Economic Review*, 89(5): 1299–318.

Queisser, Monika and Dimitri Vittas (2000). 'The Swiss Multi-Pillar Pension System: Triumph of Common Sense?' World Bank Policy Reserach Working Paper No. 2416. Washington, DC: The World Bank.

—— Edward R. Whitehouse (2003). 'Individual Choice in Social Protection: The Case of Swiss Pensions.' OECD Social, Employment and Migration Working Papers No. 11. Paris, France: OECD.

End Pages

The Pension Research Council

The Pension Research Council of the Wharton School at the University of Pennsylvania is committed to generating debate on key policy issues affecting pensions and other employee benefits. The Council sponsors interdisciplinary research on private and social retirement security and related benefit plans in the United States and around the world. It seeks to broaden understanding of these complex arrangements through basic research into their economic, social, legal, actuarial, and financial foundations. Members of the Advisory Board of the Council, appointed by the Dean of the Wharton School, are leaders in the employee benefits field, and they recognize the essential role of social security and other public sector income maintenance programs while sharing a desire to strengthen private sector approaches to economic security. For more information, see http://www.pensionresearchcouncil.org.

The Boettner Center for Pensions and Retirement Security

Founded at the Wharton School to support scholarly research, teaching, and outreach on global aging, retirement, and public and private pensions, the Center is named after Joseph E. Boettner. Funding to the University of Pennsylvania was provided through the generosity of the Boettner family whose intent was to spur financial well-being at older ages through work on how aging influences financial security and life satisfaction. The Center disseminates research and evaluation on challenges and opportunities associated with global aging and retirement, how to strengthen retirement income systems, saving and investment behavior of the young and the old, interactions between physical and mental health, and successful retirement. For more information, see http://www.pensionresearchcouncil.org/boettner/.

Executive Director

Olivia S. Mitchell, *International Foundation of Employee Benefit Plans Professor,* Department of Insurance and Risk Management, The Wharton School, University of Pennsylvania.

Advisory Board:
Gary W. Anderson, Austin, TX
David S. Blitzstein, United Food & Commercial Workers, Washington, DC
Robert L. Clark, College of Management, North Carolina State University,
    Raleigh, NC
Julia Coronado, BNP Paribas, New York, NY
Peter Fisher, Pyramis Global Advisors, Smithfield, RI
P. Brett Hammond, TIAA-CREF, New York, NY
Beth Hirschhorn, MetLife, New York, NY
Emily Kessler, Society of Actuaries, Retirement Systems Solutions,
    Schaumburg, IL
David I. Laibson, Department of Economics, Harvard University,
    Cambridge, MA
Annamaria Lusardi, National Bureau of Economic Research,
    Cambridge, MA
Jeannine Markoe Raymond, National Association of State Retirement
    Administrators, Washington, DC
Raimond Maurer, Finance Department, Goethe University, Frankfurt,
    Germany
Judith F. Mazo, The Segal Company, Washington, DC
Alicia H. Munnell, School of Management, Boston College,
    Chestnut Hill, MA
Richard Prosten, Amalgamated Resources, Washington, DC
Anna M. Rappaport, Anna Rappaport Consulting, Chicago, IL
Kent Smetters, The Wharton School, University of Pennsylvania,
    Philadelphia, PA
Nicholas S. Souleles, The Wharton School, University of Pennsylvania,
    Philadelphia, PA
Stephen P. Utkus, The Vanguard Group, Malvern, PA
Jack L. VanDerhei, Employee Benefit Research Institute, Washington, DC
Mark Warshawsky, Towers Watson, Arlington, VA
Stephen P. Zeldes, Graduate School of Business, Columbia University,
    New York, NY

Senior Partners:
Allianz SE
AXA Equitable
BlackRock
Callan Associates
William A. Frey
Invesco Ltd
Investment Company Institute
John Hancock Life Insurance Company

Lincoln Financial Group
MetLife
Mutual of America Life Insurance Company
Pacific Investment Mgmt. Co. LLC
Prudential Financial
Pyramis Global Advisors
Social Security Administration
TIAA-CREF Institute
The Vanguard Group
Towers Watson

Institutional Members:
AARP Public Policy Institute
Financial Engines, Inc.
International Foundation of Employee Benefit Plans
Loomis, Sayles and Company, LP
Mercer Human Resource Consulting
Ontario Pension Board
Society of Actuaries
Symetra Financial
Texas Municipal Retirement System

Recent Pension Research Council Publications

Reorienting Retirement Risk Management. Robert L. Clark and Olivia S. Mitchell, eds. 2010 (ISBN 0-19-959260-9).

Fundamentals of Private Pensions. Dan M. McGill, Kyle N. Brown, John J. Haley, Sylvester Schieber, and Mark J. Warshawsky. 9th Ed. 2010 (ISBN 0-19-954451-6).

The Future of Public Employees Retirement Systems. Olivia S. Mitchell and Gary Anderson, eds. 2009 (ISBN 0-19-957334-9).

Recalibrating Retirement Spending and Saving. John Ameriks and Olivia S. Mitchell, eds. 2008 (ISBN 0-19-954910-8).

Lessons from Pension Reform in the Americas. Stephen J. Kay and Tapen Sinha, eds. 2008 (ISBN 0-19-922680-6).

Redefining Retirement: How Will Boomers Fare? Brigitte Madrian, Olivia S. Mitchell, and Beth J. Soldo, eds. 2007 (ISBN 0-19-923077-3).

Restructuring Retirement Risks. David Blitzstein, Olivia S. Mitchell, and Steven P. Utkus, eds. 2006 (ISBN 0-19-920465-9).

Reinventing the Retirement Paradigm. Robert L. Clark and Olivia S. Mitchell, eds. 2005 (ISBN 0-19-928460-1).

Pension Design and Structure: New Lessons from Behavioral Finance. Olivia S. Mitchell and Steven P. Utkus, eds. 2004 (ISBN 0-19-927339-1).

The Pension Challenge: Risk Transfers and Retirement Income Security. Olivia S. Mitchell and Kent Smetters, eds. 2003 (ISBN 0-19-926691-3).

A History of Public Sector Pensions in the United States. Robert L. Clark, Lee A. Craig, and Jack W. Wilson, eds. 2003 (ISBN 0-8122-3714-5).

Benefits for the Workplace of the Future. Olivia S. Mitchell, David Blitzstein, Michael Gordon, and Judith Mazo, eds. 2003 (ISBN 0-8122-3708-0).

Innovations in Retirement Financing. Olivia S. Mitchell, Zvi Bodie, P. Brett Hammond, and Stephen Zeldes, eds. 2002 (ISBN 0-8122-3641-6).

To Retire or Not: Retirement Policy and Practice in Higher Education. Robert L. Clark and P. Brett Hammond, eds. 2001 (ISBN 0-8122-3572-X).

Pensions in the Public Sector. Olivia S. Mitchell and Edwin Hustead, eds. 2001 (ISBN 0-8122-3578-9).

The Role of Annuity Markets in Financing Retirement. Jeffrey Brown, Olivia S. Mitchell, James Poterba, and Mark Warshawsky, eds. 2001 (ISBN 0-262-02509-4).

Forecasting Retirement Needs and Retirement Wealth. Olivia S. Mitchell, P. Brett Hammond, and Anna Rappaport, eds. 2000 (ISBN 0-8122-3529-0).

Prospects for Social Security Reform. Olivia S. Mitchell, Robert J. Myers, and Howard Young, eds. 1999 (ISBN 0-8122-3479-0).

Living with Defined Contribution Pensions: Remaking Responsibility for Retirement. Olivia S. Mitchell and Sylvester J. Schieber, eds. 1998 (ISBN 0-8122-3439-1).

Positioning Pensions for the Twenty-First Century. Michael S. Gordon, Olivia S. Mitchell, and Marc M. Twinney, eds. 1997 (ISBN 0-8122-3391-3).

Securing Employer-Based Pensions: An International Perspective. Zvi Bodie, Olivia S. Mitchell, and John A. Turner, eds. 1996 (ISBN 0-8122-3334-4).

Available from the Pension Research Council web site: http://www.pensionresearchcouncil.org/

Index